WOMEN, CLASS AND EDUCATION

This is a book about some women of the working class. It is about particular and personal journeys; complicated lives lived within the shifting landscape of class, education and gendered identity over the last forty years.

Making use of theory, reflection, narrativity, biographical and autobiographical writing, Jane Thompson provides an accessible understanding of what learning means and what education can contribute to the struggles of working class women intent on changing the circumstances of their lives. The book is organised into three parts. In Part 1, Thompson draws on autobiographical experience to root theoretical understanding in the authority of personal knowledge. In Part 2, she illustrates how theoretical analysis can inform arguments about women's changing relationships to class, community, consciousness and education. In Part 3, she provides detailed examples of educational work she has been involved in with working class women.

Women, Class and Education explores compelling personal narratives that underline the importance of feminism as a source of political inspiration, social analysis and change.

Jane Thompson is Research and Development Officer at The National Institute of Adult Continuing Education, and Research Associate at the University of Warwick.

WOMEN & SOCIAL CLASS

Series editors: Pat Mahony and Christine Zmroczek
Roehampton Institute, UK

This series aims to address a rather neglected area of feminist theory, women and social class. The series is intended to analyse social class in relation to women's lives, to theorise it by highlighting personal experience and to understand it in ways which move beyond the macro analysis provided by male, 'left' oriented accounts. In developing feminist understandings and analyses of how class continues to operate across and within diverse contexts, the series is committed to evaluating the ways in which social class combines with other social forces to produce inequalities for women in the present and in the future.

Already published:

CLASS MATTERS: 'WORKING-CLASS' WOMEN'S PERSPECTIVES ON SOCIAL CLASS
Edited by Pat Mahony and Christine Zmroczek

CLASS WORK: MOTHERS' INVOLVEMENT IN THEIR CHILDREN'S PRIMARY SCHOOLING
Diane Reay

WOMEN AND SOCIAL CLASS: INTERNATIONAL FEMINIST PERSPECTIVES
Edited by Christine Zmroczek and Pat Mahony

WOMEN, CLASS AND EDUCATION

Jane Thompson

London and New York

First published 2000
by Routledge
11 New Fetter Lane, London EC4P 4EE

Simultaneously published in the USA and Canada
by Routledge
29 West 35th Street, New York, NY 10001

Routledge is an imprint of the Taylor & Francis Group

Typeset in Goudy by M Rules
Printed and bound in Great Britain by
Clays Ltd, St Ives plc

British Library Cataloguing in Publication Data
A catalogue record for this book is available from the British Library

Library of Congress Cataloging in Publication Data

Thompson Jane
Women, class and education/Jane Thompson.
p. cm. – (Women and social class)
Includes bibliographical references and index.
1. Working class women – Education – Great Britain – History – 20th century – Biography. 2. Adult education of women – Social aspects – Great Britain – History – 20th century. 3. Feminism and education – Great Britain – History – 20th century. 4. Thompson, Jane. I. Title. II. Women and social class (G. Routledge & Co.)

LC5056.A3 T56 2000
374'.0082 – dc21
00-036993

ISBN 1–857–28942–0 (hbk)
ISBN 1–857–28943–9 (pbk)

DEDICATION

This book is dedicated to the students of Women's Studies at Ruskin College, Oxford; to the Women's Group at the Rosemount Resources Centre in Derry; and to women involved in trade union education courses with the General Federation of Trade Unions. Some of their words are included here amidst my own. They speak for themselves and for each other, in ways that confirm the importance of education in the struggle to defeat social and economic adversity and political inequalities.

CONTENTS

ACKNOWLEDGEMENTS

My thanks to the many women who wrote personal accounts for this book and to Marie Devine, Trisha Harris and Gloria Isham who helped to record some of the contributions from women at work included in Chapter 12.

1

RESOURCES FOR A JOURNEY

Once the inevitabilities are challenged, we begin gathering our resources for a journey of hope.

(Williams 1989)

This book is about some women of the working class, about particular and personal journeys, about complicated lives lived within the shifting landscape of class and gendered identity in Britain since the 1950s; and about the importance of feminism as a source of political inspiration, social analysis and change. Most specifically it is about the ways in which, as working class women, we have learned things from life, through our experiences and from the struggle to change unsatisfactory circumstances. It is about informal learning and formal education and about how both have helped to shape our lives; about the knowledge that has been useful in the struggle for our liberation; and about the interpretations that can be made to throw some theoretical light upon the particularities and commonalities of our various, related and different journeys.

I use the idea of journeys quite deliberately. They provide a familiar metaphor for life, and for episodes within the passage of a lifetime that have particular significance. Journeys capture the qualities of agency, movement and change. Journeys cover territory, in time, as well as distance, and can create the conditions for intellectual and emotional changes, including the negotiation of identity. Applied to the meanings and the experiences we associate with class and gender, the imaginative possibilities of journeys can serve to avoid some of the more arbitrary, closed and rigid definitions of social divisions that were common in malestream social science before the intervention of feminist and post-structuralist analysis, without losing the significance of continuity, connection and relationship which is frequently absent from some versions of postmodernism.

The landscapes we inhabit can be regarded as physical and symbolic places, as intersecting and overlapping spaces, with multiple and changing boundaries, that are constituted and maintained by relationships of power, connections and exclusion. The places we inhabit are rarely neutral, but are defined, maintained and altered through the impact of unequal power relations, especially those of class and gender. In retrospect, my early childhood prepared me well for the shifting boundaries of class and gender relations. The daily bus route from the working class council estate on the east side of Hull where I grew up, into and out of town, towards the leafy suburbs of the west, involved an actual and symbolic journey between different physical and material landscapes, different social class relations and different representations of class/gender identity. I have spent a lifetime recovering similar territory. Moving further away in miles, material well being and emotional distance from my roots in working class community, but never quite letting go of the loyalties and structure of feelings (Williams 1979) which I associate with those beginnings. Still needing something of the distance and the duration of the journey back to renegotiate the landscape and to review the territory. In transit between different, complicated and contradictory versions of myself.

Academia has rarely provided complex understandings of working class life. Even celebrated studies like that of Willis (1977) can be read as an indictment of the working class: they are so stupid that they invest time and energy into ensuring their own oppression (Reay 1977). In all the classic studies of working class life and working class communities, women remain largely invisible, or confined to domestic settings that are noted but not explained or understood. Men's association with paid work and women's association with the home are largely taken for granted. Richard Hoggart's classic account of northern working class life in the 1950s (Hoggart 1959) at least displays an insight born of knowledge and empathy but the 'only young women in his analysis are the undifferentiated, briefly flowering girls in flimsy frocks and bright lipstick, the scholarship boy's flighty factory working sisters, giggling together on the way to the cinema or the dance hall' (Kuhn 1995: 102). Cultural and sociological studies are redolent of literary studies of an earlier period, in which the romantic attachment to the working class (in the writing of Orwell, for example) is with constructions of masculinity as agents of socialist history, in which more complex relationships with the world are not allowed and women scarcely appear at all. Whether it is sociological or literary, much of the writing produced by white male writers in the enlightenment tradition fought to maintain the 'form' of masculinity deemed appropriate: 'a form that marginalised relationships with women, was deeply involved in, yet denied, emotional relationships with men and gave an absolute priority to objective, rather than subjective, reality and experience' (Evans 1997).

Feminist commentators such as Beatrix Campbell (Campbell 1984) and Carolyn Steedman (Steedman 1986) have done much to challenge all this, and to examine the lives of working class people in communities in a way that recognises, but does not romanticise, working class masculinity; which identifies class and gender politics; and which pays attention to working class women's lived experience as something very different from that of working class men's, in ways that can no longer be subsumed conceptually within masculinist generalisations. A recognition, which given the now widespread publication of feminism, you would think would make it quite impossible for male writers on social class to continue to treat women's position as the same, or of less interest, than men's. But you would be wrong. Perhaps the most significant publication of 1998 on the matter, which sparked considerable attention and complimentary reviews in the press, was David Cannadine's *Class in Britain*. In the preface he felt able to say, without much recognition of its gravity,

> there is one shortcoming of which I am especially aware: . . . these pages do not specifically address the question of what British women have thought about class. If Jilly Cooper's book is any guide, they think about it very much as men do, which is hardly surprising, since, for most of recorded history, the social position and social identities of women have been determined first by their fathers and then by their husbands. But I do not feel entirely happy with this formulation, and having recently re-read, side by side, the *Classic Slum* by Robert Roberts, and *Hidden Lives* by Margaret Forster, it seems likely that women visualise the social world, and their place within it, in some ways that are different from men. This serious 'gap in our knowledge' still awaits the historian, and perhaps the shortcomings of my account will provoke someone else to set out to fill it.
>
> (Cannadine 1998)

He would have been well advised to also read *Landscape For A Good Woman* by Carolyn Steedman (Steedman 1986) and *Formations of Class and Gender* by Beverley Skeggs (Skeggs 1997) before pressing on regardless. But having done with his disclaimer, he returns to the much more interesting and important – to him – consideration of class in Britain as seen through the eyes of men, and passed off as universal truth, in much the same way as white, male, western academics have always done.

In this account I include narratives containing events and memories associated with my own life and with the experiences of some working class women I have come to know through my work at Ruskin College in Oxford over the last six years – where I have been teaching women's studies. Ruskin is a residential college for mature students which was founded in 1899 in close association with the emerging labour and trade union movements to provide socially and politically relevant education for working class people. The women's words appear as they were sent to me in letters and in written answers to my questions about particular moments and meanings in their lives. For example, Gaynor:

> My sister lives on an awful council estate where I was brought up before I went into care. She is off the danger list for a bit. She is a complex woman and having the five kids means she has lived her life on her wits. She sees having the children as her job since the various fathers have abandoned all responsibility. I could scream with anguish about the situation. But the kids are her guaranteed income, she feels she can do little else other than care for them. To ease the burden whilst she was fighting the cancer I said I'd foster two or three of them, adopt them even, although I'm on my own now as well so I would never be allowed to do it legally. But I didn't realise how much this would deplete her welfare benefits. So we struggle on. Her health's improving and we laugh a lot. Her memory of our childhood is more romanticised than mine. She

> can't admit to a lot of what went on. I've managed to get three out of the five kids to go to school fairly regularly. Although its not what you would call a liberating experience. Schools round here have their work cut out. I think the teachers are quite relieved when some of the kids don't turn up. I try to inspire them a bit – like you and Ann did with me at Ruskin – and I don't take any shit. They know they have to get up at dawn to get one over on me. But it's a hard way of living Jane. And I do believe I had slipped a bit too far off the factory road to recognise the realities for what they are. Maybe it's because I had grown to love college and my books so much that it became more comfortable being up my own arse for a while.
>
> Anyway, I've got involved in local community stuff since coming back. It's mostly women trying to hold this place together. Bea Campbell is right. You know what she means in a place like this – drugs, prostitution, racial attacks, murder. Trying to work through social action with people on the receiving end of no jobs, no hope, and the break down of community, isn't pretty. We had five murders in this square mile in the last 9 months. Crack dealers at the root of it. Bloody sheep ticks! Two unions have their regional offices on the High Street but I'm afraid the more I see of them, the less I want to go back to all of that. Still the same tossers, keeping things for themselves. Still crap when it comes to women's issues. The local labour party want me to run for the Council – only because they think I can win the seat. I've got all the right Irish catholic family credentials I suppose but I don't think that speaking out for a tolerance zone for working women on the streets to keep them safer is quite the brand of community activism the local catholic mafia are looking for.
>
> Thanks for your letter. It put a smile on my face for the rest of the day. I am moving to another flat, within spitting distance of the river. They say its lovely at night – to see the ships and the city across the water all lit up . . .

All of the accounts are from working class women making sense of class and gender, some of them – like Josie – are also concerned with 'race':

> I soon learned that violence was the only way to keep the bullies at bay but as only one of four black children at my primary school, I was usually on my own when it came to doing battle with white boys in the playground – persecutors who never came alone but always in a group. It still amazes me the way that dinner ladies and playground supervisors always had a knack of shifting to the other side of the playground whenever one of us black kids was set upon. Not so surprising was that the white girls simply stood and watched the racist bullying. Some of them objected verbally with what was going on but none of them ever scraped their

> knuckles in my defence. I soon learned that being black was going to make me a victim of violence and that I would have to defend myself as a black person in a white environment. Those who ignored the victimisation, of course, had to live with the white bully boys as their sisters and their cousins. They too had their share of harassment to cope with as 'sissy girlies'. My victimisation provided a temporary relief from the sexist bullying they had to put up with.

The stories do not constitute a universal or a definitive assessment of what counts as education or working class existence. The details may be contradictory but that does not make them right or wrong. Social life is always storied; narrativity in this sense is central to the ontology of social life, involving the active participation of the story-teller in the construction of how she accounts for herself to others – the audience. Calling this information stories does not make it trivial or false, but because of its immediacy, it has the attraction of being both accessible and democratic, providing insights and experiences 'from below', not – as Jean Barr maintains – because 'below' is more accurate, but because making space for voices that are not usually listened to increases the possibilities for creating knowledge that might be useful to those who generate it (Barr 1999a: 16). What it can provide is a richness and variety of detail, loaded with information, about the ways and meanings through which class and gender gets articulated and from which identity and selfhood are constructed. Annette Kuhn argues that 'telling stories about the past is a key moment in the making of ourselves', and whilst the memories included in our stories are personal 'their associations extend far beyond the personal. They spread into an extended network of meanings that bring together the personal with the familial, the cultural, the economic, the social and the historical.' Telling stories is a way of putting on record the lives of relatively powerless women whose 'ways of knowing and ways of seeing the world are rarely acknowledged, let alone celebrated, in the expressions of a hegemonic culture' (Kuhn 1995: 2–4). The narratives included here reveal how variously and frequently official claims made about education, related to economic progress, class mobility, personal confidence and fulfilment, social transformation and empowerment – most of the familiar and tendentious vision statements of the age – do not always work in quite the way that educationalists, politicians and social commentators like to imagine. Mary, for example, relates the quest for knowledge to issues she needs to address as a working class woman, but in the process she discovers solidarity and love in a period of personal extremis:

> Becoming an activist gave me the strength to go out and learn things for myself because I knew that I had experience of working conditions and how my own class of people felt. When my union sent me on education weekends, I just ate it all up. I also know that because we were all sisters and brothers together – we had strength. Being together with these people taught me a lot about life and things that matter. I did not want

> to see the conditions return again that my mother had to put up with or when I was growing up. My mother was born in a workhouse and went to work at the age of eleven to help keep her brother's children, because he had died of hunger. Not only does something like that give you roots and a goal to aim for but it makes you want to shout out, 'What can I do to change things?' And if it's only one thing you make better for your brothers and sisters, then it's worth the struggle. I put a lot of my energies into trade union action. I would stand up to any boss. I was always on the lookout for something else to sort out.
>
> My most difficult problem (I hope this does not sound too over the top, but it's how I feel) has been my fight for life. Knowing that if I give in I will not be able to finish university and I will not get the knowledge from all those books I still want to read and the people I still want to meet. I can't explain how it feels to be told you have cancer. It is such a shock you don't know how to behave. Do you lie down and be ill or do you carry on as though nothing is happening? Or what do you do? I only know I must go on and get as much from life as I can because there are still so many things I want to do – before I call it a day. Trying to keep up is hard. Wanting to be a proper student. Trying not to show how ill I am a lot of the time. Not asking for any favours because I am ill. Trying to be brave – because I'm not very brave really. Most of all, stop crying – as I am doing now . . .
>
> My relationships with other women are special. These are loving and caring feelings that I have for my sisters. Sharing my life experiences with them, and they with me, has given me a lot to think about. I count myself very fortunate that I met and have been loved by Ruskin women. And what has made it all most unique is that we are all so different. Different ages, different cultures, different life experiences. I have learned the working class includes a lot of women, with lots of things in common, despite our differences.

Mary's story should remind those who write about women's lives in academic abstractions that working class women's lives are as distinct and as complicated as any life, despite prevailing pathologies and stereotypes to the contrary, requiring more textured, less deterministic interpretations than have been common in the recent past.

Personal narratives provide the starting point at least. A place from which to reflect upon past experience; to scrutinise the stories we tell about ourselves, which carry agency, meaning and information about the social and psychological positions we inhabit, and the significance we attach to them. Telling such stories can be 'a powerful and practical instrument of conscientization' (Kuhn 1995: 8), a way of exercising critical consciousness and of producing knowledge from the inside about gender, class and education, deriving from personal, particular and shared experience. Not in the pursuit of ultimate truth but in the search for greater, more nuanced, understanding.

There is always the danger, however, that telling stories can be self-indulgent. It is difficult when writing autobiography, not to rely on constructions of individualism, in ways that have gathered credence from enlightenment thinking and liberal humanism, and which have been used traditionally to privilege individualism (rather than individuality), whiteness, masculinity and middle class experience ever since, rather than the small scale details of working class women's everyday and ordinary existence. But it is what becomes of the stories that matters. And what uses can be made of them in the search for political knowledge and theoretical understanding. Women telling stories is a method of learning I have come to value and to seek out in countless conversations and exchanges over decades, in both formal and informal classrooms, wherever I have been. The current popularity of autobiography and narrativity in feminist research is a measure of the significance which now attaches to experience, reflection and psychoanalytic understanding, as a counter balance to the kind of public and external evidence which is available from historical and structural analysis and political economy. Carolyn Steedman exemplifies the theoretical genre perfectly, whilst insisting that, 'Once a story is told, it ceases to be a story; it becomes a piece of history, an interpretative device' (Steedman 1986: 143).

My parents were convinced that education was the route to economic and social advancement for working class children. It was regarded by them as the means of getting on and getting out from under. They placed their faith and myself uncritically within the authority of the system and now, most probably, feel fully vindicated. Convinced that the financial sacrifices they made, the occasional humiliations they encountered, the losses they undoubtedly sustained as they watched their only child move relentlessly beyond their influence and control into a culture and a way of life they could only vaguely understand, were, none the less, what they had struggled to achieve. Grammar school, university, a job for life teaching others and writing about education – always about class and gender inequalities, always in anticipation of social transformation – this journey now provides me with something of an insider's vantage point from which to interrogate ideas, events, and the meanings which can be attached to them; to invite comparisons; to consider contradictions; to make connections. Not in the pursuit of bourgeois individualism, or in celebration of my general ability to pass in the middle class world that was the object of my parents' sacrifices and aspirations, but in recognition of the persistence of my working class consciousness and allegiance, albeit in the context of a livelihood and identity that is now considerably out of place and out of time from where it all began. When you have grown up working class as I have done, you know that the solution to class inequalities is not to fast track selected individuals into the middle class as an inspiration to the rest. Or in the interests of the kind of tokenism which lends credibility to inequalities and injustices within the system. The task remains a collective and political imperative, concerned with dismantling the economic, social and cultural capital which goes with middle class status; with redefining and liberating knowledge; and with redistributing educational resources to the unprivileged and poor, in all their diversity, as a principled act of commitment to the working class as an entirety.

When my parents advocated getting on and getting out from under it was not in the search for status or about greed for the material acquisitions of consumerism, it was, as Carolyn Steedman has observed, about 'people in a state of dispossession . . . gain[ing] their inheritance . . . [and attempting] to alter a world that has produced in them states of unfulfilled desire' (Steedman 1986: 123). It is this continuing legacy of unfulfilled desire and the possibility of intellectual and cultural transformation that informs the commitment of this book. Not in the spirit of working class indictment but in recognition of the constraints which the material, political and educational maldistribution of resources imposes on women's possibilities and opportunities. And which is currently controlled by class and gender interests that remain resistant to widespread social change.

I had thought, when I began to write this, that I had nothing more to say about these matters than I have already said elsewhere (Thompson 1980a,b, 1983, 1989, 1995, 1997), assuming, I imagine, that since my values and priorities have remained more or less consistent, that my interpretation of events would also be much the same. Of course when I begin to reflect upon the journey, and to reorder what has already been experienced, articulated, taught and written by me over time, it seems, in retrospect, to have always been provisional. Circumscribed by and contingent upon the politics, the place, the context in which I was living and working. Providing inspiration and understandings that were as much a product of their time, as of my – not always fully recognised or articulated – shifting subjectivity. And leaving, not surprisingly, something still to interrogate about the process, and to wonder about in the lives of others.

In the attempt to provide what is, I hope, a useful, expanded and textured understanding of what learning means, and what education can contribute to the struggles of working class women, intent on changing the possibilities and the circumstances of their lives, I have organised what follows in three parts. In the first part – called Reflections – I retrace some of my own experiences as a once working class child, moving through education and feminism towards womanhood during the last forty years or so, as a way of rooting theoretical understanding in the authority of personal knowledge. In Part 2 – Connections – I illustrate some of the ways in which theoretical analysis can inform arguments about women's changing relationship to class, community, consciousness and education, in ways that assist in the process of making sense of and understanding the world – in order to transform it. In the final part, Illustrations, I provide three examples of recent educational provision I have been involved in with working class women at Ruskin College, Oxford; in the Rosemount Resources Centre in Derry; and with women on trade union courses sponsored by the General Federation of Trade Unions.

Part 1

REFLECTIONS

2

RETURNING TO THE NORTHERN CITY

Returning to the northern city where I grew up, it now looks superficially the same as any other. Stagecoach buses plough through its one way system. Identikit chain stores, sporting household names, line the high street alongside customised shopping malls, fast food outlets and multi-storey car parks. At night, young men, wearing shirt-sleeves in December, cruise the pubs and clubs in gangs, in search of a laugh, and alcohol and girls. Young women, dressed in short and tight and lacy high street fashions, occupy more space in public places, make more noise than I remember doing, even in the 1960s. There are people begging in doorways, holding up bits of cardboard that read 'homeless'. The main picture house, which became a night-club and a bingo hall for a while, is boarded up and waiting for redevelopment; its redundant Sale notice banging in the wind. An eight screen cinema and retail park now draws the city's crowds to where the fish docks once made Hull a thriving fishing port, landing cod and haddock by the ton from the fishing grounds off Iceland, before the Cod Wars of the 1980s were fought and lost by the Thatcher government. American style diners, DIY stores and cheap electrical outlets, staffed by part time workers, mostly women, compete for conspicuous consumers, offering customer loyalty schemes and interest free credit.

Beyond the underpass, shabby streets of damp and dingy houses mourn the devastation of an industry that shaped the character of this city. Built on danger, tradition, rivalries and superstition, its women lived stalwart, responsible lives, its men played dangerously and recklessly with other men. This is where, in 1970, I first met Lily Bilocca, who led the demonstrations staged by fishermen's wives against the trawler owners about deaths at sea and dangers in the industry, and where I did my first piece of feminist political action in solidarity. It's where I brought the lads I taught, who wanted to become deckie learners on the trawlers, on careers visits at seven o'clock in the morning, to watch the catch being unloaded. We got back to school in time for morning assembly with the scent of fish in our hair, on our skin, in our clothes. The whole neighbourhood was drenched in the smell of the sea and the smell of fishing. These days, the smell is gone; and with it the livelihood of a proud community, leaving poverty. This is where Hull Truck Theatre Company and the Watersons folk group performed agitprop and work songs in the local pubs as the industry began to struggle; where the men sat together with their mates, and the women sat with theirs. Back in the city centre, I watch a swirl of litter blow through the station precinct as the last train heading south leaves from Platform 6.

Hull is a city that I hardly recognise these days but which is full of memories. It is half a lifetime since I occupied the upstairs room of my parents' council house where I grew up and lived next door to a man who worked as a stevedore and a woman who was 'on the lookout', as my mother used to say. Her divorce was something of a scandal in the neighbourhood – although considering the violence she endured I used to think she weathered it with amazing equanimity. Each morning I used to catch the bus to the concrete and clay comprehensive where I worked as a probationary teacher, built on a bomb site in the middle of rows of nineteenth century terrace houses, still without bathrooms or inside toilets in the early 1970s. I sat beside women wearing headscarves going to work at Mackman's Bakery and men in caps and donkey jackets going to the dockyards and the factories.

My mother's friend Mabel, from our earlier, prefab days, moved in up the road. Her husband Des worked as a foreman at BP so they were able to put some money by. In twenty years they had saved enough for a deposit on a bungalow, and moved out in 1974, beyond the city limits, just before he died without warning from a heart attack. It was a working class death. Too much overtime, too much drink, too many cigarettes, too much weight. He had never been to church in his life, except to get married, so it was no surprise that the vicar did not know his name and buried him as Arthur. My mother's friend did not object, or put him right. She had lived her life not wanting to make a fuss. She took a part time job in a dry cleaners after he died and sold the family car. She was of the generation of working class women – quietly seeking respectability (Skeggs 1997) – who never learned to drive and always thought of cars as 'a man's thing'. The house they lived in up the road is boarded up, I notice. Surrounded by rubble. Splattered with graffiti. Hard to let property. No one wants to live on that estate these days if they have a choice. 'Drugs and crime and violence. You take your life in your hands living', Mabel tells me. 'Tried to interest London overspill. Problem families. But they weren't that desperate.'

Mabel is well out of it. On the sideboard, a photo of her daughter celebrates her graduation at 39, from the University of Huddersfield, with a degree in Leisure and Tourism. Outside in the front, her grandson is cutting back the roses and taking care to avoid an ornamental wishing well and garden gnomes. 'In his second year at College. Reading Sports Studies', Mabel is full of pride. I wonder whatever happened to Political Economy and Sociology. Being 'in the business', of course, I know the answer. 'He looks like his grandfather', I say. Inside the television sound is turned down. She keeps it on for company. Mandelson is giving his resignation speech to the tabloid press, trying to explain why he needs a four storey house in London, that costs half a million pounds, to live in on his own. 'Not the sort of Labour Party we supported', Mabel says. I remember she came with me and my mother to a Labour rally in the City Hall addressed by Harold Wilson during the 1964 election campaign. 'Do you remember your mother queuing up for his autograph? And how we laughed when he took his hanky out to blow his nose. It had a hole in the corner. At least he wasn't afraid to call himself a socialist.' Neither was Mabel or my mother, in those days.

I can hardly bring myself to mention politics when I come to visit now. My parents are not impressed by Tony Blair. They like John Prescott, the local MP. Sometimes I detect the same disillusionment expressed by Mabel about hypocrites and spindoctors, and a sneaking nostalgia for the values of Old Labour. But then my mother is the only person I know who cast her vote for the Conservatives in the election that swept New Labour into power, because, as she said, she felt sorry for John Major, and Norma was such a nice woman. She is still the only person I know who has a good word to say about the current leader of the Tory party, William Hague. My grandfather would turn in his grave. My mother does not mention Margaret Thatcher much in my presence. 'But she was courageous, you have to hand it to her. And she didn't go in for back handers and consorting with millionaires'. 'Only Denis!' I want to put the record straight.

The journey back from Mabel's to my parents' house takes me through peripheral estates which Beatrix Campbell (Campbell 1999) writes about, in which the rate of unemployment is well above the national average. I stop to buy some bread and milk in a supermarket that charges the poor more for their groceries than it charges shoppers in more affluent areas, banking on the absence of any competition, and the difficulties and costs of transport, to deliver a captive audience. The rest of the shops are boarded up. Even the pub looks like Alcatratz. A brave attempt at a Drop-In Centre for the unemployed struggles behind window bars and oversized padlocks. I know the women at the checkout well, from somewhere deep inside myself, watching a whole week's shopping slide past along the counter, bought to feed a family of five, and costing less than I would spend on a meal for two at my favourite Oxford Bistro.

There was a time when my mother used to eat last in our family – once my father and I had finished. She said she wasn't hungry or she had already eaten. I believed her of course and my father did not seem to notice. He cycled to and from work every day. He was the breadwinner after all, though he did not earn very much.

If I had the nerve, I would like to join in the checkout conversation, but I do not want to give offence. I wonder whether the women notice my dislocation from this landscape – in my hesitation, my rich clothes, the way I no longer fit the territory as I once did – in the way that most of us can read the subtleties of class within minutes of being introduced. I know all too well the tell-tale signs that help to explain the sometimes look of resignation in their eyes. Women who are getting on with business as best they can, looking more tired and older than they really are. Poorly dressed in styles that are chosen for cheapness and conformity, with part time jobs as cleaners, care assistants, casual workers on the twilight shift. Used to making ends meet with not enough money. Buying tins of beans and cornflakes and potatoes. Stretching the stew. Managing kids alone, managing their men, maybe. Strong women with intelligence and dignity. Always ready for a laugh, some gossip, repeated disappointment. Hassling the Council, their landlords, the Social, the Loan Sharks. The kind of women that keep localities like this intact – without much recognition and usually with a hostile press.

In academic circles where I sometimes move, the 'right to recognition' has gathered considerable momentum in recent years, on behalf of minority rights and identity politics, in which cultural discrimination is usually regarded as the key injustice. But when academic feminism talks about diversity, and about the subtleties of language, discourse, style, identity and psychological complexity, it fails more often than not these days, to consider class as a significant source of difference – despite the sharpened class divisions and increased social segregation since the Thatcher years. Shopping in a supermarket that rips you off because it can; heaving bags along a street splattered with graffiti; beside broken fences, abandoned trolleys and boarded up houses, is not a preferential declaration of identity. It is what happens when class divisions have not gone away, even though it is no longer academically fashionable, or interesting, to talk about them. Being working class in neighbourhoods like these, where deep seated material and structural inequalities persist, does not lend itself to contemporary academic preoccupations with aesthetics, performance, identity and style. Although identity is palpable. Neither is it simply a matter of presentation. As Anette Kuhn remarks, it is

> not just about the way you talk or dress or furnish your home; it is not just about the job you do or how much money you make doing it, nor is it merely about whether or not you have A levels or went to university, nor what university you went to. Class is something beneath your clothes, under your skin, in your reflexes, in your psyche, at the very core of your being.
>
> (Kuhn 1995: 98)

I pay for the milk and bread and get back into my car – rooted in the memories, the sentiments and feelings of belonging, which were born in blood, drawn from the resources of generations who lived this life before me, and from which education, feminism, a decent job have been my liberation.

On the other side of town where she now lives with my father, my mother is watching from the window, their house a continuing reminder of where I come from, although I have never lived here. Partly I am reminded of the past by what is missing from the things she chooses to display. But that is another story.

3

IN SEPTEMBER MY MOTHER FOLDED HER STARCHED WHITE BLOUSE

In September 1958 my mother folded her starched white blouse, black pencil skirt and white frilly apron into a Woolworth's carrier bag, to be put on later in the toilets of Ye Olde White Harte. She did not want the girls at my new school to know that she was a waitress. At that point in her life, when she rode with me on the number 43 bus from the council estate in East Hull where we lived, into town, on to another bus, and out towards the leafy suburbs of the West, on my first day at grammar school, she was working in a pub in town – not far from the Land of Green Ginger in the old part of Hull. It still had a men only bar and a restaurant, which at lunchtime filled up with dark suited solicitors and financiers, wining and dining their way into the late afternoon, whilst my mother tried her best to avoid their tasteless innuendo and condescension. She got good tips, she said, and the uniform was smart. At the same time as she worked at Ye Olde White Harte, she worked during the evening as a barmaid at the Crown, just around the corner from where we lived. Before that she worked part time in a sportswear shop and later as a cleaner in a local authority day centre. None of it was factory work or what she would consider 'common'. But it did not pay her very much or recognise her potential. She did it to fit around her responsibilities for me and at times when my Dad could baby sit. It compensated for the fact that he was not earning very much – although he had a white collar job 'with prospects' (that never materialised) as a clerk in the City Council.

My mother, in a different generation, could have been a scholar, possibly a journalist, probably a teacher. Forty years later, I teach working class women of about the same age as she was then, still juggling part time bar work, waitressing, cleaning or tele-sales at the same time as rushing home to pick children up from school and put the tea on the table, before starting on the housework and turning their tired attention towards books and essay requirements for their college course. Whilst women's part time employment might now be recognised as a major component of the gendered labour market, rather than be inaccurately dismissed as 'pin money', as it was in my mother's day, those who do it have not noticeably benefited from greatly improved remuneration or social mobility so far as the class system is concerned. It remains to be seen whether returning to education on their own account will make the kind of difference to my current students' lives that was denied to my mother's generation. Or whether the postmodern contention that the concept of woman has no existence as an objective reality outside preconceived assumptions and existing discourses, and is better understood as the ontological manifestation of shifting multiple identities, will make life any easier for those who habitually balance conflicting and competing versions of themselves as about the only way possible to live as a woman. And particularly as a working class woman, for whom the luxury of philosophical analysis can seem rather remote from the urgency to improve material conditions and address the range of ordinary and everyday oppressions which women regularly experience.

In the days when my mother waited at the tables of professional men, she transferred her hopes and aspirations on to me, convinced that a good education would put me further up the ladder and out from under in the class sense. I was her only child and consequently the only one capable of assuaging her unfulfilled desires. Our relationship was such that I would do everything I could to please her, to be good enough to represent the 'gift from God' she claimed me to be. To be charged with perfection is a hard task mistress and one that has kept me on my toes ever since, making me more self critical than any adversary would dare to be, and more impatient than is always comfortable with those I feel should know enough, and are privileged enough, to do better.

As a child my few and feeble attempts to challenge my mother's view of purpose and reality were usually half hearted and always defeated. As a consequence I received even more of her attention and tried even harder to satisfy her expectations. And not just hers. I felt from an early age that I was the one entrusted with the responsibility to carry on the struggle, articulate the cause and right the wrongs perpetrated against my communist grandfather, killed by unemployment in the 1930s, by the absence of a National Health system and by poverty when my mother was still only fifteen. The debt I owe to his memory, instilled in me at my mother's knee, signifies the roots and resources which have directed much of my subsequent life. She left me in no doubt about my relationship with destiny as she told me stories about my grandfather's passion for equality and his affection for Robbie Burns, Karl Marx and Keir Hardie. I learned to recite by heart the romantic ballads she loved, and to identify emotionally with their anti-heroes – Young Lochinvar, Jock o' Hazledean and the Highwayman. The gendered nature of my introduction to principles, commitment and courage in the pursuit of a cause did not register at the time. They were the symbols she had to hand. What I retained was the passion for justice, the glamour of struggle, the dignity of marginality, the need to take sides and to stand up fearlessly for truth. But also, being a working class woman, living an ordinary working class woman's life, she had other ways of stamping her presence upon my future which were more mundane.

When I was about fourteen, and hassling her to let me leave school, she marched me to the new supermarket which had just been opened on the site of our old corner shop. It was small by today's standards, but part of the relentless trend towards convenience shopping at the expense of small localised concerns which has now become commonplace. Girls I had known at junior school, who did not pass their eleven plus, and who went to the local secondary modern school, were already *in situ*, dressed in green nylon overalls and white hats, stacking shelves. Relieved, no doubt, to have an alternative to the horrors of Humber Pickle (the pickled onion factory that made your eyes run all the time and sent you home stinking of vinegar) and Metal Box (which was so noisy you could hardly hear yourself speak and cut your hands to shreds unless you were extremely vigilant) but looking none the less distracted by the boredom of their lot. Already planning their escape via boyfriends, an engagement, marriage and a baby. 'If you don't get down and do your homework – it'll be stacking shelves in Frank Dees for the rest of your life', became my mother's most constant challenge during my remaining years at school.

In the white working class area where I grew up, girls had roughly three choices. They got married to someone who lived round the corner whom they had known at school or met through their brother. They worked in Frank Dee's Supermarket, Humber Pickle or Metal Box, and then got married – to someone they had met at the Locarno ballroom on a Saturday night. If they were clever and passed their scholarship, they left after 'O'-levels to become a nurse or did 'A'-levels and went to university or training college to become a teacher.

I decided to make the best of being working class in my middle class grammar school by perfecting my fast bowling skills twice a week on Fenner's playing field with my faithful father and relieving my feelings of class confusion and alienation by becoming very good at team games and joining the East Hull branch of the Young Socialists. Being good at sport built my confidence and gave me legitimacy in the school. Identifying as political satisfied the resilience and emotion I brought with me from my roots. I was not too bad at lessons either, as it turned out, though no one at school seemed to register the fact. On the whole I went along with the rules, understood what I was asked to learn, did my homework, passed my exams.

Grammar schools for girls in the 1950s and 1960s were fairly predictable in their academic expectations and fairly understated in their recognition. They promoted industrious attitudes to learning in which neatness, consistency and attention to detail far outweighed any requirement to be original or passionate. It is hardly surprising that subsequent research looking at the gendered nature of achievement during this period has tended to comment on women producing consistently more competent work than men, but men achieving the unexpected and exceptional results which come from greater risk taking and adversarial independence (Byrne 1978). Grammar schools were not on the whole expected to produce great leaders. That was still the remit of boys' public schools. Girls' grammar schools were still rooted in the minor professional and moderate gender aspirations of middle England in which higher education and a career still took second place to a good marriage.

At school in the early 1960s I did not know what it meant to struggle with big ideas or feel exhilarated by the excitement of intellectual insight or creative achievement. I was not encouraged to challenge orthodox accounts of history or speculate about literary texts outside of received conventions but I learned how 'to do it right' so effectively that I knew precisely what the academic and gender rules I wanted to break were when subsequent political experience and university in the late 1960s awakened my critical approach to the interrogation of knowledge and ideas. School provided the grounding in the kind of academic capital which I have since found invaluable, if only to reject much of what it represented and stood for.

However, as Annette Kuhn has commented, 'although brains, sticking to the rules, doing well academically and passing exams went a long way, they were not, as it turned out, quite the sum total of what was required' (Kuhn 1995: 87). It was in other areas that working class girls like us operated outside the magic circle occupied by class mates from more privileged backgrounds. The 'extra something' that was lacking was much more subtle and less explicit than any of the myriad requirements laid down in the curriculum of examining boards or in school rules and regulations. It was an atmosphere that permeated the ether and lived in the fabric of the culture. You either knew all about it already before you joined the school or you did not. Probably at that age it was not the kind of knowledge that was easy or possible to articulate, but it was strongly felt in being an outsider, not quite fitting in, wanting to keep some things secret about where you came from, in case they were subjected to ridicule or criticism. Not that many of the pupils or the teachers ever did make fun of my parents or my mother's attempts to improvise my school uniform in an effort to afford it – they were too polite.

Braving the taunts from the kids at the bus stop on my estate was always more hazardous and hostile than any ridicule I ever received from those who did not share my class position. But then, they did not invite me home to tea, either. And when my mother offered to take me and some of my friends on a bus trip to the Yorkshire Dales, three middle class and condescending fathers appeared on our council house doorstep unannounced to investigate her suitability. That too was part of the culture. Something I now understand as being symptomatic of the predominantly petit bourgeois system of values the school took for granted and which can be summed up by the notions of social confidence and cultural capital, deriving from middle class attitudes and behaviour endemic in the backgrounds of the children whose presence dominated the life of grammar schools in the 1950s and 1960s.

There were a number of ways in which my otherness from the ethos of the school was experienced. In mock elections I was the only one prepared to stand as a Labour candidate and got a reputation as a trouble maker because I wanted to queue all night for tickets for the Beatles – not the kind of thing which girls from the grammar school were supposed to do. But it was more than this. It was about being different.

I did not think very much about the class system until I went to grammar school. And it took several more years to put a name to it. Up until that time I did not know anyone who lived in a detached house which their parents owned, whose parents had a car, or who went abroad for their holidays. Suddenly I was surrounded by such girls who really knew what it meant to be rich. On the estate where I grew up, in a two bedroomed, end of terrace, council house in the 1950s, most of the children were not what I would have called poor. We lived in new houses built after the war and went to primary and junior schools which gave us milk and biscuits at break time and hot dinners with meat and custard as a matter of course. Some children wore woolly hats to cover bald, purple scalps until their hair grew back after being treated for ringworm. But it was no big deal. Most of them seemed to have a father and a mother in their lives. I knew only one girl who lived differently to us with her mother and gran in a house rented from a private landlord and who told us some complicated rigmarole about the war to explain the non-existence of a father. We thought he was a hero and she was therefore rather special. Which could have been true.

We were the recipients of the post war social settlement made between government and the respectable working class. Good quality housing, the National Health Service and a welfare state, in lieu of decent wages or any social power. In education what was being offered by the 1944 Education Act, in the provision of free secondary education for all and the invention of the tripartite system of grammar, technical and secondary modern schools, was not equality but equality of opportunity, in which a test taken at eleven theoretically exposed all children to 'the opportunity' of being educated in the school most suited to their ability. In practice, of course, children in middle class catchment areas were more likely to be coached for success in the test, were more likely to relate to the ways in which the tests were subsequently revealed to exhibit middle class cultural bias, and were more likely to be under pressure from education conscious parents to succeed. In my school most children were not even given the opportunity to enter, on the assumption that those already in B, C and D streams in a working class catchment area would be wasting their time. It proved to be a system which, for the most part, served to reflect and reinforce pre-existing social class divisions, rewarding some and penalising others whose existing cultural capital already matched the profiles of schools designed to achieve different outcomes. This was not a settlement designed to deconstruct the class structure or to redistribute the resources and privileges of the wealthy middle class, but rather, to appease and socialise us into continuing with our own reproduction, without becoming too resentful, with just sufficient of our number permitted to climb out from under, to lend the illusion of social mobility, and to give credibility to the classless nature of a so called meritocracy.

In those days, houses on estates like ours were a prize, rather than, as they have now so frequently become, a punishment, acquiring all the characteristics of dislocated warehouse sites, in which vast armies of the urban poor are barracked together, increasingly without work and increasingly without hope. Mothers like mine stayed at home or did part time jobs in domestic and catering services. Fathers went out to work as dockers, labourers, factory hands, and mine – cycling 16 miles a day – went to an office in the town where he was the last man left standing to succumb to a calculator and casual clothes.

My father was a Luddite when it came to new technology. He did not trust it. He could add up rows of figures in his head and still can. Others used to bring him the results produced by their calculators to double check. Promotion passed him by. He was grateful to be there – wearing a collar and tie – and was not one to push himself. When he retired at 60, partly through ill health, he was doing much the same kind of job which he had acquired thirty years previously. In a later generation, men like my father have not always been so fortunate. New technology has been harder to compete with and to defeat, and the notion of a job for life, even if it was the same one you have done all your life, has become a thing of the past. My father was part of what they call 'the old school' in local government, in the days before reorganisation. When he went to work my father always wore his only suit, with the cuffs and collars of his shirts turned by my mother to prolong their active life, beneath a plastic mac or yellow cycle cape. He returned home each day for dinner (i.e. lunch) to where my mother cooked mince and mashed potato followed by pudding. When she got the cleaning job in the day centre, my father cycled to my gran's house instead – a back to back terraced house in Ceylon Street, built in the nineteenth century and still operating without hot water in the kitchen, an inside toilet or a bathroom in the 1960s.

But none of this was poverty. On one occasion we went on holiday to Filey in a caravan and had various day trips by 'Bodies Motors' to York, Bridlington and Whitby. I did not know at the time that when my father got his first job in an office, my mother had to sell my pram to pay the rent because he moved on to monthly wages and their savings ran out after ten days. I did not know that the distempered walls were because my parents could not afford wallpaper, or that the rugs, made out of old rags by my mother as she sat beside the fire on winter evenings after work, were an alternative to buying carpets. Or that when I went to grammar school, the cost of the school uniform wiped out summer bus trips, Christmas presents to everyone but me, and almost all the savings they possessed. Fortunately for them they only had one child to worry about. My mother knitted me a jumper which I thought was wonderful until I found myself to be the only one not wearing a crisp commercial job from Gordon Clarkes, the school outfitters in the High Street. I would not have believed that navy blue wool with orange and yellow (the school colours) in the V could turn out to be so obviously the wrong kind of shades. But I knew, by the time we began scouring the market stalls for lengths of yellow and orange cotton, that the summer dresses stitched meticulously on my Auntie Peggy's new Singer sewing machine would be a further indication in the uniform department that I was not quite what the school had in mind.

My mother and father rarely visited the school. Not because they did not care about my education. On the contrary, it was their top priority. When my mother resumed bar work in the evenings parents' nights were out, and in any case meant two bus journeys in both directions. My father used to come to cricket matches from time to time and stand by himself out of earshot of the other parents. Once I persuaded him to play in the fathers' team against our first eleven. He was the only man not wearing proper whites and was put in at number ten although he was the best batsman I had ever known. We did not have a telephone to consult with school mates and their parents about homework, or a car, and any letters arriving from the school were a great source of anxiety and concern until they had been decoded and carefully responded to on blue Basildon Bond note paper, bought specially for the task. Not much in the way of cultural capital to ease my passage through – but no great trauma either. Usually the most difficult manoeuvre was how to get out of the house and on to the bus in my school uniform without the boys from Mirfield Grove – the same ones I used to play cowboys with and roller skating at my junior school – stealing my beret, emptying my satchel in the gutter or shouting sexual obscenities as I hurried past.

At school there were no boys – and in this respect, it felt like heaven. It was possible to throw the javelin and run in relays and practise fast bowling in the cricket nets without anyone turning a hair. When I got six Lancashire wickets for eight runs in my first appearance for Yorkshire Schoolgirls I was the only one in the side from a grammar school. The rest were *really* posh. I got my photograph in the local paper and a fan letter from a train driver enclosing a poem about the magic thud of wet leather on willow. This was not what girls from my class background could usually expect but it was not because the teachers who taught me were particularly feminist. Feminism was not a word that was widely used in Hull in the early 1960s although by the end of the decade, Lily Bilocca, the spokeswoman of a campaign led by fishermen's wives against the abuse of safety regulations in the fishing industry, had been joined by women from the university and recent graduates, myself included, to form one of the first outposts of the Women's Liberation Movement outside London. Some of my teachers were old enough to remember when women got the vote. And all of them were beneficiaries of the struggles undertaken by earlier feminists to have higher education and recognised careers. Most of them were unmarried. Several lived with women friends and kept dogs in preference to children. If this was some kind of code or lifestyle choice, I was oblivious to its symbolism. As girls, we had the usual run of crushes on games teachers and French assistantes but the word lesbian was never mentioned. I do not think I knew that being a lesbian was even possible, not until a long time after I had begun to call myself a Marxist and later a feminist. Not until I was almost 30, in fact.

Our teachers were very pernickety about rules and regulations. Not discipline – in the current sense of moral panic aroused by 'unruly children' reared by 'feckless single mothers' – but in the pursuit of values and behaviour to consolidate our class/gender identity. We had to walk down the right hand side of the corridor only. We could not talk in any of the lobbies. We had to stand when a teacher either entered or left the room. We could not eat sweets or remove our berets in public places. We could not smoke, dye or back-comb our hair, wear jewellery or make up, or talk to boys when wearing school uniform. We were not allowed to take paper rounds or Saturday jobs. We could not wear stockings until we were 17 and only shoes with laces and flat heels. Skirts, when kneeling, had to be precisely one inch from the floor. Hockey boots had to be polished. Gym shoes whitened. Homework handed in without delay or any excuse.

Self-constructions of sexuality were discouraged and repressed, except in so far as they contributed to delaying sexual gratification by the distraction of team sports and academic endeavour. To be fair, contraception, losing virginity, unwanted pregnancies, abortion and premarital sexual experience of any kind was still surrounded in taboo, stigma and illegality for young women in the late 1950s and early 1960s, especially if they were deemed respectable and middle class. Constructions of working class promiscuity and sexual degeneracy carried age old stereotypes applied by patriarchal and middle class commentators upon working class lifestyles which, because they were largely ideological and gendered, did not help towards the sexual liberation of working class girls any more than their middle class counterparts. A woman's right to choose and define her own sexuality needed second wave, and especially radical feminism, to make the connections between the control of women's sexuality and patriarchal power relations, providing a greater choice for some, at least, in these matters. At school a state of androgynous innocence was the official intention, years spent in waiting for the inevitability of marriage and motherhood at some later stage. It was a relief, as a working class girl, to have my initiation into the requirements of compulsory heterosexuality (Rich 1980) artificially postponed by the exigencies of education, class and gender ideologies, although not all my school friends escaped as lightly as I did. Illegal abortions and enforced adoptions were a part of the unspoken culture of girls' grammar schools like mine, and of the sudden and unexplained disappearance of those who contested or fell foul of the school's class and gender requirements about virginity and sexual modesty.

Most of the working class girls I grew up with went to Flinton Grove Secondary Modern School, just round the corner from my home. Between the ages of 11 and 15 they learned basic academic, domestic and clerical subjects in preparation for a brief sojourn in the labour market before marriage and motherhood. Boys and girls were segregated for vocational training and 'late developers' had to wait the best part of a generation before Second Chance and Access Education (Taking Liberties Collective 1989) discovered the extent to which their educational potential was wasted by a system intent upon conscripting and preparing them for manual and menial jobs, compulsory heterosexuality and the traditional division of labour in nuclear families.

Although boys did not attend my grammar school, the influence of men was in the very fabric of the place. The history we learned was all about men. The French and English literature we read was written by men. The mental arithmetic we had to practise in our heads was about men on train journeys doing miles that had to be calculated, and men laying carpets which had to be added together in square yards. Latin was all about Caesar and the Gallic Wars. Geography was about sheep farmers in Australia. Dog eared texts, smelling of formaldehyde, showed men in white coats doing experiments, whilst disembodied hands, that were clearly male, clutched test tubes and set light to Bunsen burners in ways that identified physics and chemistry as an obviously masculine preoccupation. School houses were named after famous men – Andrew Marvell and William Wilberforce. Morning prayers followed the rituals of boys' public schools. The school song was lifted from Eton: 'Follow up, follow up, follow up, follow up, follow up. Til the field ring again and again. With the tramp of the twenty two men . . .'

It was the kind of education for girls which directed A stream pupils towards university and careers – preferably as teachers – but in ways that left unchallenged the world we were about to enter. Men's knowledge and values had already determined the curriculum and shaped the dominant notions of discipline and team spirit. When I left I had learned to believe that men's lives were much more interesting and important than women's. I wanted such a life. I did not think that I would have to beat men at their own game or compete with them. I thought I could merely join in. I knew that it would mean renouncing the company of women for the most part, as friends and confidantes, because women, on the whole, did not go to university, or want careers, or expect, in those days, to travel the world having adventures and to be making history. I had learned to believe that women were boring because their concerns and responsibilities were trivial. All they seemed to want was to get married and have children. Certainly my school had saved me at an earlier age from the kind of preoccupations which informed the lives of girls who lived on my estate, as it proceeded to remove me from my class. But it was only a matter of time until I came to understand that being schooled 'like a middle class boy' was not in itself sufficient grounds to join the world of men as an equal at a later stage. When the real purpose of men's control of education was revealed to me at university, it quickly became obvious that getting married and having children was still a major requirement of the arrangement. The real reason for learning all about men was in order to feel sufficiently impressed and flattered to want to marry one at a later stage. An education which had taught me to define the world through men's accounts of knowledge and experience appeared as much an initiation into assumptions about the superiority and inevitability of patriarchy and heterosexuality as if I'd gone to the local secondary modern school and learned to type someone else's letters, starch and fold a pillow case, iron a shirt and bath a pink plastic doll in lieu of 'really useful knowledge' (Johnson 1979) that might help to change the world.

Quite a lot has been written by women like myself – who are feminists and now middle class – but who were once working class and who got their break via scholarships and grammar schools in the 1950s and 1960s. We were the generation of young women that went into higher education when working class and especially black women were still a small percentage of a major minority. And just at the point when the social upheavals caused by civil rights, protests against the Vietnam war, hippy culture and student politics – in the west, at least – were challenging conventional wisdom, and taking to the streets in defence of workers' rights, civil rights, sexual liberation, anti-imperialism and pacifism. We were part of the generation that thought we had discovered women's rights and which committed ourselves to women's liberation, before we rapidly came to realise that our initial discoveries were along paths already well trodden by other women over centuries, paths that had got lost along the way or become overgrown as patriarchy continued to reinvent itself. What we discovered was a hidden history, lost in distant places, effectively suppressed, but waiting to be rediscovered and re-enacted, once the time and place were conducive to its re-emergence.

4

THE COMPREHENSIVE SOLUTION

In 1969 I returned to Hull from university to teach in a school which at the time I thought would neutralise the worst educational consequences of the class system by putting children from all social backgrounds together under one roof and calling it a comprehensive school.

Ours was a flagship of the comprehensive movement. The headmaster was something of a media performer, who regularly took part in televised spats with Tory sympathiser and subsequent government minister, Rhodes Boyson, then a headmaster in London. At our school we pursued a particularly progressive version of the kind of education which comprehensive devotees expected to overcome the experiences of failure, unfulfilled potential and negative expectations associated with working class children's experience in the secondary modern schools to which they were invariably consigned. A decade of sociological research had revealed the connection between social class and educational failure. Some attributed primary responsibility to ill-informed parenting, restricted language codes, and cultural poverty associated with working class families (Davie *et al.* 1972). Others examined the ways in which streaming and the hidden curriculum of values and assumptions operating in schools meant that teachers unconsciously favoured middle class children and discriminated against working class children (Douglas 1964). Schools were depicted as training grounds, sorting offices and selection agencies for the class and capitalist systems (Bowles and Gintis 1976; Whitty and Young 1977). Educational prerequisites fostered by, or absent from, the home-front were consolidated by schools into patterns of achievement and failure that were extensively class related. This was an analysis that relied heavily on the evidence of quantitative research methods and some participant observation in a variety of schools. Considerable attention was paid to class background and institutional cultures, rather less to the white and gendered nature of most of the research. Almost no significance was attached to the consequences that might be mediated by differences deriving from 'race' and gender. The solution to working class under-achievement was seen to lie in the abolition of selection. The Conservative party and Tory local authorities fought long and hard on behalf of their middle class constituents in defence of grammar schools, but Labour government initiatives, backed by Liberal left wing academic research, accelerated the pace of comprehensive reorganisation.

The school in which I began my teaching career was at the forefront of progressive thinking. Children were taught in mixed ability groups. Streaming by ability – even setting – was considered an anathema and symptomatic of all that was evil about fostering competitiveness and individualism in those who succeeded and a sense of failure in those who lost out. Not only was academic ability being contested by these innovations, but values of egalitarianism and social integration were being offered as a preferred alternative to social division. The wearing of uniform was declared optional. Prize days and corporal punishment were banned. Children were integrated into a house system that attached considerable importance to pastoral concerns. School assemblies were secular. Prefects were abolished. Classes were held in the evening for adults from the local community about planning, housing, educational and political issues. The vision was that of a community school in which class differences would become irrelevant and all children would be enabled to fulfil their individual potential to the best of their ability, in the spirit of mutual co-operation, and with tolerance and respect for others. Tory critics dismissed the good intentions as social engineering. In retrospect, they were informed by liberal humanist beliefs about encouraging self-actualising individuals to flourish in positive and enabling, rather than negative, environments, more accurately than a Marxist recognition of the economic and structural determinants of social class. As socialist teachers we met on Sunday evenings at the Haworth Arms pub to debate the intransigence of the class struggle. But on Monday mornings we pinned our faith in individuals being able to rise above the disadvantages of their material circumstances with the assistance of comprehensive education.

The school in which I taught was an inspiring and difficult place to be. The motivation and commitment of the teaching staff was strong. It was an optimistic time when many of us – ourselves the beneficiaries of decent council houses, grammar school places and redbrick universities influenced by the politics of the New Left – set out to change the world for the class we had come from through comprehensive education. The enthusiasm displayed by the local community was stimulated by the attention of the media. And by the appearance on what had been a derelict bomb-site of a futuristic concrete and clay coloured building, large enough to amalgamate three run down and jaded secondary modern schools built as Board schools in the previous century, and closed down to make way for social change.

It is hard to know whether the school where I learned to teach would have been able to satisfy the different demands of working class and middle class parents, or to integrate children from across the class divide because, of course, the location of the school in the midst of back-to-back terrace houses without basic amenities, lodged between a maximum security prison, the railway lines and the city's main arterial road to the docks, was not conducive to producing many middle class children from within its catchment area. In practice its pupils were drawn from the poorer end of the unskilled and working class, who in transit from other schools, had failed, or not been entered, for the eleven plus, and who were planning on leaving at the first possible opportunity, after they reached the age of fifteen.

Jobs in bakeries, factories, as unskilled labourers, deckie learners on the trawlers, shop assistants and office juniors were still in reasonable supply, with several boys each year being offered apprenticeships in the workplaces where their fathers already had connections, irrespective of their academic performance at school. Few aspired to move outside the area or into white collar and professional jobs that might require further qualifications because by that time their sights had been set on what was familiar and possible. Ten years later, of course, it was a very different story. These were not children who were readily persuaded by a philosophy that encouraged them to respect each other, take pleasure in school work for its own sake, denounce rivalry and competition or behave well in the full knowledge that punishment was virtually non existent. Rival gangs of boys from contributing schools continued their pre-comprehensive hostilities. Girls used the opportunity of optional uniform to arrive in the kinds of cheap and provocative outfits defined by teenage fashions of the period, including the display of high heeled shoes, garish jewellery and pan-stick make-up which they used to anticipate their entry into adulthood. In 1969 there was little understanding about how these were manifestations of gendered identity as much as class, played out in oppositional response to what schools had come to represent, and in relation to a realistic assessment of what was expected from boys and girls within traditional working class communities.

Gradually, as former secondary modern pupils moved on, their younger brothers and sisters arrived without prior experience of other regimes beyond primary and junior school. Though not, of course, with different cultural backgrounds or gender expectations. This was now the moment to expect notable transformation as the consequences of pupil centred, optimistic comprehensive ideologies and methods had a chance to take effect. Certainly the pupils benefited from some imaginative and committed teaching in a school that was self-conscious about valuing and not diminishing what children brought with them from their culture and their background. Curriculum content was chosen to be culturally relevant. Emphasis was attached to exploratory, imaginative and creative skills, as distinct from simply cognitive development. Children were encouraged to find out things by investigation, work at their own pace, help each other rather than compete, be motivated by interest not by compulsion. I spent hours preparing handouts, work sheets and group work exercises to eliminate the old orthodoxies of class teaching, blackboard copying and rote learning. I struggled between classrooms with armloads of various resources and equipment. I integrated music, slides, photographs and film in a multi-media commitment to popular culture at the same time as surviving grammar schools, direct grant and public schools continued to preach the kinds of values, and teach the sort of knowledge, which has contributed to keeping the educated middle class in positions of authority and power, despite cosmetic changes to the class system.

More of the kids I taught stayed on at school than would have chosen to do in the tripartite system. Once the school leaving age was raised to 16, many more achieved qualifications than in a previous generation. In time the school developed a healthy sixth form, with more working class children than ever before achieving 'A'-level success. But schools have never been sufficient in themselves to change the unequal distribution of resources in the wider society. Sometimes being treated like a worthwhile human being at school, being encouraged to ask questions and to expect a choice when it came to finding work, was not always the most realistic preparation for the unskilled labour market, especially when the local economy began to anticipate national economic trends, and the plentiful supply of working class jobs started to dry up. Growing unemployment, increased poverty and community distress all served to restrict the kinds of support and recognition that parents could allocate to their children's education.

In mixed ability classrooms teachers needed to develop extraordinary management skills to make sure that active and exploratory learning did not degenerate into a tyranny of structurelessness. Making sure that more and less able pupils were consistently motivated, that quiet pupils were not overlooked, that pupils with learning difficulties were not stigmatised, that boisterous pupils were not allowed to disrupt the learning purpose of the class was a Herculean task that required enormous skill and stamina on the part of teachers. And all this in the context of the early 1970s when there was very little understanding of the ways in which schools provided a very different experience for working class boys compared to working class girls. In 1969 feminism was being re-invented but it would be a further ten or fifteen years before a feminist analysis of sexism in the school curriculum (Spender 1982a), boys receiving preferential treatment from teachers as an issue of malestream focus (Spender 1982a) and classroom management (Stanworth 1983), training in social maleness (Mahony 1985), and different school responses to the cultural dynamics of sexuality and gendered adolescence (Lees 1986), made any kind of impact on the ways in which education was discussed and practised.

Comprehensive schools also provided particular and different kinds of experiences for black and ethnic minority children (Mirza 1992; Bryan *et al.* 1985) in which the opportunities for cultural ignorance, low expectations and negative labelling from predominantly white and middle class teachers were legion. Although comprehensive schools in progressive local authorities, including the Inner London Education Authority, were at the forefront of political and educational debates about equal opportunities in the wider society, the consequences of structural inequalities exacerbated by 'race', class and gender, the intransigence of social attitudes and the implicit ideologies that supported them, were always going to be deeply contentious and contested territory. As the New Right mobilised around the election success of Margaret Thatcher in 1979, it was the progressives' commitment to equal opportunities in schools – about issues of sexism, sexuality, learning difficulties, racism and multiculturalism – that were subjected to the greatest scorn in an effort to discredit the 'loony left'.

Consequently, the return of successive Conservative governments throughout the 1980s once again made comprehensive schools, and the credentials of their teaching staff, into a site of struggle. Consecutive Tory governments had no intention of abolishing the comprehensive system – so long as there were plenty of opportunities for middle class parents to avoid the neighbourhood schools and to opt out of those parts of the state system where working class children were concentrated. But the redesignation of catchment areas and the guarantee of parental choice to those with enough cultural capital to exercise it, meant that the schools which children could attend were increasingly determined by the structural and geographic divisions which keep middle class and working class neighbourhoods largely separate from each other.

Changes introduced into the national curriculum to reinforce the national (dominant) culture, the management of schools using approaches and connections associated with business enterprise, and the ways in which teachers are now required to be accountable for what they do through inspection and by the publication of examination results and league tables, have all helped to consolidate the reputation and attract the best resources to schools serving middle class constituencies. Judgements made about failing schools are usually those in areas of multiple social deprivation, in which communities in various degrees of crisis expect little from the schools, and in which teachers struggle against enormous demands made upon their energy and expertise. These are not the kind of conditions in which progressive teaching methods can be sustained without considerable commitment and additional resources, or where academic league tables can be expected to motivate those who have no expectation of an academic future. These are the kinds of schools from which white working class boys especially leave with the least education and the fewest qualifications (McGivney 1999a).

The Thatcher years changed the political climate so far as optimism about comprehensive education was concerned. The attack on jobs, benefits and public services in working class communities throughout the period made them into the kind of areas in which hope spent on education seemed increasingly misplaced. And whilst teachers, like health workers and social workers, had their professional competence and integrity relentlessly undermined by the judgements and impositions of the Thatcher government, the morale of those employed in hard hit neighbourhoods became systematically destroyed. Just as the residents who were able to leave, got out, so too did local authorities experience increasing difficulty in replacing senior staff in the most needy and difficult schools. Just as local government and the trade unions floundered against the pace of restrictive legislation and the promotion of economic reprisals, as a way of reducing opposition to government directives, so too did education have little choice but concede to demands for further change and competition as a condition of its survival. It is a policy that has rewarded schools in affluent areas, at the expense of schools attended by working class children, and one which has expected teachers to put corporate loyalty before ill conceived notions of solidarity with disadvantaged children and communities. As such, it is the working class who have borne the brunt of progressive and reactionary developments alike, at a time when their schools have been the battleground on which competing ideologies of Left and Right have struggled to establish their credentials.

5

GLORIA HAD A WORD FOR IT

In 1979 Gloria Gaynor released the feminist anthem 'I Will Survive'. Margaret Thatcher became Britain's first woman prime minister and so far as I had made any decisions about my life, I was going to be one of those women who decided not to have children. However, in 1980 I became a lesbian, and in 1981 I found myself responsible for co-parenting three children. There are a number of stories that could be told about this particular journey which are not relevant to this discussion, but what I did discover was quite a lot about what it feels like to be a parent, wanting the best possible education for the children I loved, at a time when four consecutive Conservative governments shaped the political and social climate and controlled education policy and schooling.

The children went to a medium sized suburban comprehensive on the edge of a medium sized city. They were two girls and a boy among a small handful of black and ethnic minority children in an overwhelmingly white school, serving a predominantly lower middle and working class catchment area. The school's location on the edge of a substantial working class district and rural hinterland, recruited children from the kind of families that were either traditional Tory voters, whose local MP held one of the largest election majorities in the country, or from the self-employed and skilled working class targeted by Thatcherism with offers of council house purchase, share ownership in the privatised utilities, and the possibility of self improvement via increased affluence and individual enterprise. These were voters who were happy to laugh at racist and sexist jokes, blame trade unions and benefit scroungers, be whipped up by the tabloid press against 'left wing loonies', and, being situated not a stone's throw from the sea, turn out with union jacks to cheer as our boys set sail from Portsmouth to save the Falklands and smash the Argies. Certainly Old Labour had done little to capture the hearts and minds of this particular constituency, despite its mainly working class composition, making its residents the archetypal voters who helped to secure eighteen extraordinary years of Conservative government.

Not that my children were critical of their classmates' families. Like most children, they wanted to be liked, and to be the same as everyone else in the gang. Given they were born of mixed parentage, living in a socialist, middle class by occupation, and lesbian family, they probably had more than their fair share of marginal millstones to overcome in their efforts to be ordinary. And whilst the adults in their life were all articulate in print, and radical in their outspoken political opposition to racism, conservatism, militarism, sexism and homophobia, what we wanted for our children was much the same as every parent wants who values and sets store by education – academic qualifications, social awareness, personal confidence and feelings of self-worth that we are led to expect from positive experiences of schooling.

In the event, the years which the children spent at secondary school were not ones that any of us would wish to repeat, but which provided me with considerable insight – from a different perspective – about the lived reality behind some of the debates I was already involved in academically and politically.

By the 1980s, feminist and black analysis of sexism and racism in the education system had come of age (Mirza 1992). The influence of feminism on sociological studies of the period highlighted the dominance of men in the education structure (Deem 1978), in determining what counted as knowledge (Spender 1982b), in securing the best resources and most attention (Spender 1982a) and in rehearsing the kinds of patriarchal repertoires which contributed to masculine aggression and physical prominence in the world beyond the classroom (Mahony 1985). Assumptions about girls were predicated on gendered expectations relating to more or less domesticated, and more or less inferior positions in the labour market and public sphere. Classic studies of girls' identities and sexuality revealed the barrage of negative attention they could expect to receive from boys, and the kinds of strategies they employed to weather the experiences of adolescence and schooling with some degree of control and self approval (Lees 1986).

Enough was known from government reports and from national surveys and large scale empirical studies to show that young black people had very different, and discriminatory, experiences in education and the labour market, compared to white teenagers (Rampton 1981; Swann 1985). Initially the consequences of gender were not recognised or acknowledged (Mirza 1992). Looked at in retrospect, much of the research was fatally flawed by racist assumptions – about racial inferiority and the need for assimilation in the 1960s (Mullard 1982), about social and cultural inadequacy in the 1970s (Coard 1971; Little 1975; Milner 1979) and about stereotypical gender traits in the 1980s (Fuller 1982; Phizacklea 1982; Dex 1983; Sharpe 1987). The suggestion that black women, for example, possess natural and superior strengths which as lone parents and effective heads of families, they employ to overcome the consequences of structural sexism and racism, and which act as a particular inspiration to their daughters, may well have been a well intentioned corrective by white feminists, reeling from accusations about ignoring black women's experience, but they were seen as naive and unhelpful by the very women they were seeking to compliment. According to Bryan *et al.* such interventions

> tended . . . to portray black women in a somewhat romantic light, emphasising our innate capacity to cope with brutality and deprivation, and perpetuating the myth that we are somehow better equipped than

> others for suffering. While the patient, long suffering victim of triple oppression may have some heroic appeal, she does not convey our collective experience.
>
> (Bryan *et al.* 1985)

The superwoman image attached to black women in the 1980s, coming on the heels of earlier pronouncements about inferiority and inadequacy, tended not only to stereotype but also to individualise arguments about achievement in schools, and to distract attention from the persistence of structural and institutionalised racism. Mirza sums up the weakness in such arguments like this:

> Rather than focussing on the family, parental social status, economic and social disadvantage, IQ, poor self concept and ethnic self esteem, commentators on the issue may have to address the far more controversial matter of fundamental social inequality in British society.
>
> (Mirza 1992)

Amina Mama comments on the ways in which the concepts 'ethnicity' and 'culture' were also played off against each other in theoretical discourses and state ideologies in the 1980s in quite negative ways.

> The culturization and ethnization of race as a state orchestrated process, which, by focussing on the language, food, habits and clothing of black (African, Asian or Caribbean) people, masks and denies the fact of discrimination. Systematic and institutionalized racism is thereby reduced to cultural misunderstanding and is so depoliticized. Even more mystifying is the manner in which class politics have been superseded by the new identity politics of gender, ethnicity, sexuality and disability.
>
> (Mama 1992)

Just like sexism, racism in education operates in a number of ways. It may be direct or indirect, conscious or subconscious. It can work through explicit stereotyped assumptions made by teachers about black children, or it can be institutionalised in the routine structures and practices of the school, as for example, in its negation or mis-representation of the history and cultures of black and minority groups. Stereotypes abound. Black girls carry the stigma of being unfeminine on the one hand and sexually available on the other (Mirza 1992). Asian girls are viewed as either docile, and therefore easily overlooked, or exotic and seductive (Brah 1992). Sexual harassment experienced by black and Asian girls from white boys in school is likely to assume their sexual availability, but at the same time, denigrate their sexual attractiveness according to crude racist stereotypes.

There is a tendency among teachers to see most problems experienced by black girls as being the result of strong and stroppy attitudes encouraged by strong and stroppy mothers, whilst any problems experienced by Asian girls are attributed to intergenerational conflict, with Asian parents presented as authoritarian, conservative and supposedly opposed to the liberating influence of schools (Brah 1992). There is, of course, no reliable evidence to demonstrate that conflict levels are higher in Asian families than in white families or that black working class mothers are any more 'undisciplined' than white working class mothers. However, culturist explanations tend to reinforce racist assumptions about the superiority and relative enlightenment of western cultural traditions over non western values.

In general there is a tendency for girls to receive less academic attention in schools than boys. Assumptions made about particular religions and cultures not valuing education for girls may contribute to lowering teachers' expectations still further (Brah 1992). Children requiring extra support with English can find themselves presented with a restricted curriculum as if they are remedial learners. Insistence on traditional dress can cause ridicule.

But in other respects, girls come in for a lot of attention. Most of the distress experienced by the girls in my family resulted from verbal and physical sexual harassment, which was generally tolerated within the pupil culture and not addressed by teachers. Complaints made by us about serious incidents of sexual assault were treated with alarm by the school, and on one occasion resulted in the girls in my daughter's year being cautioned by the Deputy Head not to hitch up their school skirts or unbutton the top of their school shirts if they did not want boys to call them slag, grope their breasts, or try to jump on top of them in the playground and corridors. So far as I know, we were the only parents to complain about sexual harassment, and yet unwanted sexual attention and sexually aggressive contact, overlaid with racist connotations, were the single most relentless and destructive experience of both my daughters' experience of schooling, affecting in turn their academic achievement, their sense of self and emotional well being, and their subsequent relationships with the opposite sex.

Neither was racist sexual stereotyping confined to the attentions of fellow pupils. Because patriarchal and racist assumptions about black female sexuality still go largely uncontested in the dominant culture, it is not surprising that they are also present in school staff rooms and among ancillary staff. The sacking of the school bus driver on grounds of sexual assault was a fitting and appropriate response by the school to one particularly nasty incident, but it did little to challenge the ubiquity of a sexualised and misogynist culture that remained intact and which was hard to address through individualised complaints. As a consequence, my eldest daughter spent the best part of her GCSE year as a school refuser, working at home with tutors provided by us, in an effort to keep her in touch with the education system. We removed my youngest daughter to a not particularly good girls' school, but where the atmosphere was caring, the teachers were considerate, and where she was at least able to avoid most of the worst aspects of sexualisation and harassment for a couple of years, before returning to a mixed sixth form college. Two pragmatic solutions which our income and know-how were able to effect, but which were not a choice open to the majority of parents.

At some stage or other in their secondary school careers, all three children were involved in under-age drinking, under age sex and illegal drug taking, as were the majority of their class mates. Something, it would seem, that a loving family, replete with educational capital, positive encouragement, regular contact with teachers and endless family discussions about the likely consequences of drugs, sex and rock and roll, could do very little to counteract. These were Thatcher's children, for a while, dedicated to individual freedom, but fearful of individuality, with happiness and anxiety related to commodities, and political idealism undermined by the prevalence of spiritual nihilism in the music and drugs culture of their generation. It is hard to say whether or not their experiences would have been less negative and more educational (in an academic sense) if they had attended a more middle class school, or we had taken up the solution offered by Thatcherism to middle class parents of opting our children out of the state system entirely. I know that racism, sexism and bullying of a sexual kind are not confined to one class as distinct from another. The manifestations may be different. The damage done to individuals may be just as harmful. More affluent teenagers may have even more resources to commit to popular addictions. But schools which are more able to focus on educational outcomes, because of a high incidence of appropriate cultural capital and a vocal middle class presence, do not live with quite the same degree of tension between the purposes of education and the resistance of working class adolescent culture. It is in this context that premature conscription into institutionalised heterosexuality is most encouraged by co-education and by the increasing commodification of teenage sexuality in popular culture. On the whole the commercial messages available about relationships are not based on notions of equality between the sexes and it is a brave girl who can stand apart from pressures to conform to patterns of sexual behaviour that privilege male power, despite thirty-odd years of second wave feminist activity in this respect. Girls have to find ways of dealing with boys in large urban comprehensives, which fulfil the apparent obligation to their peers to be cool, but which also enable them to exercise some independence of their own.

The consistency with which they now appear to outperform boys in examinations and qualifications, says a great deal about the extent to which they get on with what they are required to do, whilst boys continue to exercise teachers' time and attention in an effort to interest them and control their behaviour. But girls would do a lot better without the cut and thrust of classroom sexism and sexualised attention. In this respect, gender rather than class seems to be the decisive factor. Sadly co-education has been one of the reforms advocated by progressives and conservatives alike in the state system since the war. It is interesting that it is not a development that has been so enthusiastically pursued in the public school sector, where single sex education remains the most popular with parents and provides the most academically successful provision for children from professional and managerial class backgrounds.

6

ONCE A FEMINIST . . .

At about the same time as I began school teaching, I became involved with others in setting up a Women's Liberation group in Hull. From the beginning our group included and was in close touch with women who contradict prevailing assumptions about the absence of working class women from the formative development of second wave feminism. One of our first commitments to political action was to support the campaign of fishermen's wives, led by Lily Bilocca, about safety at sea. We were also in close contact with the Women's Industrial Union, established by Pat Sturdy in Burnley, with aims to democratise trade unions, make them less sexist and

> to be more like a Union-cum-club [to] look after members' rights at work and help with their problems out of work . . . to stand together . . . to stand firmly with kindness, firmly with consideration. Only this way can we hope to show the men folk the error of their ways and stay uncorrupted ourselves.
>
> (Sturdy *c.* 1971)

In the event the optimism of Pat Sturdy and her co-workers was misplaced and met with considerable hostility from the official trade union movement, revealing the difficulties of trying to build up a strong workers' organisation for women outside official union structures.

I forget at which Women's Liberation conference I met May Hobbs, the main spokeswoman for the Cleaners' Action Group, but she had already established close relations with Dalston Women's Liberation Workshop – a Marxist feminist group – and began to send us cyclostyled copies of *The Cleaner's Voice*, which got distributed to 1,000 night cleaners in London offices. In an undated copy, probably written in 1970/1971, she says,

> As most of you know the STRAND is up to its old tricks again by sacking one of our members . . . so we had a picket on one of their buildings during the day, and we now have the support of the postmen, clerical workers and even some of the print workers in fighting for our cause, to

> be able to belong to a union without the intimidation of the managers and bosses . . . I don't know why some of you are so frightened. If we act together, they cannot beat us, because who's going to do the work? The miners, car workers, postmen and even the power workers never get their rights by being frightened. The contractors are saying cleaners never stick together. That's why I suppose they think they can exploit us. Well, for Christ's sake, let's show them we can be united and fight for our rights.
>
> (Hobbs *c.* 1971/2)

The same copy carries details of a branch of the Cleaners' Action Group being set up in Grimsby, and a trouble shooting visit by Hobbs to speak to thirty cleaners at Norwich University where she encouraged women

> to hold the meetings when they wanted them, and also to make their own decisions . . . without the porters present . . . [so] they could discuss more freely what they wanted the union to do for them. They said you couldn't do anything because you had the men porters jumping up the whole time, which was not fair. It was a very good meeting in that the cleaners got involved in it themselves – half of them hadn't spoken for ages. And now they are beginning to start to get militant and say they want certain things done and will make sure their union branch is run properly.
>
> (Hobbs *c.* 1971/2)

There is also a letter from 'a sympathetic telephonist' about:

> the large number of black women night cleaners [who] face even more problems than other cleaners. Not only do they suffer the lousy conditions which night cleaners are subjected to, but they have to put up with racism too. There has been a deliberate attempt by the contractors management to use race as a means of discouraging union militancy. Black girls are victimised through sackings and through giving them the worst jobs, and the bosses try to frighten them by such remarks as 'You will be sent home when the Immigration Bill is passed', or 'There won't be any black cleaners in a few years'. The black cleaners have shown great resistance to these threats and have been among the most militant in the union. And the bosses have not been able to divide the cleaners against each other as they hoped. Black and white women have come out together in support of their fellow workers. We must resist every attempt by the companies to victimise cleaners because of their colour, for an attack on one cleaner is an attack on all. Nobody's job is safe where one woman can be sacked. In joining together in a union, cleaners have shown that they know that their real enemy is not other cleaners but the boss, and it is against him that we must unite.
>
> (*The Cleaner's Voice c.* 1971/2)

The Transport and General Workers' Union was very reluctant to take the cleaners seriously or to get involved in recruiting women to join the union. In the end it was members of Women's Liberation Workshop groups – mobilised by the Dalston group – that helped to distribute leaflets and provide the support that May Hobbs and the Cleaners' Action Group really needed. Sally Alexander, who was active in the campaign, talks about why and how the Dalston group got involved:

> The women cleaners are mostly between the ages of 20 and 60, but there are a substantial number over 60. They are almost all married, divorced or widowed, with several children, the youngest under school age. Lack of nursery facilities forces them out to work at nights. The women are either the sole providers in their families or their husbands are low paid. Some do two cleaning jobs, one in the day or early evening as well. Others take different part time work during the day. A large percentage of the women are immigrants; West Indian, Asian, Greek, Spanish, Irish. Immigrant women are uncertain of their rights, cannot always speak English very well, and are the most easily intimidated. Cleaners work in small groups in different buildings throughout London. This isolation is accentuated by the different nationalities, or rather the attempts of the supervisor or firm's manager to victimise one or two 'troublemakers', and to provoke racial tension. In fact, the women work together very well, but you never meet a black supervisor, although over half the cleaners are black . . .
>
> When Women's Liberation first began to help the cleaners we were very conscious of our naivety and ignorance and sought the advice of experienced trade unionists. Some women in Left groups tended to be combative in their attitudes towards the union, we felt perhaps we might make more progress if we adopted a conciliatory approach. We listened as male trade unionists inside and outside the Transport and General Workers' Union patiently explained the problems of organisation . . . What they almost all emphasised was that women are notoriously hard to organise because they are home-orientated, they are not interested in union work, and they are easily intimidated . . .
>
> The cleaners are not disinterested in union work. They are sceptical of trade unions' effectiveness. The scepticism has been nurtured by the trade union's neglect. When the officers fail to reply to letters or phone calls, do not arrive for meetings, ignore their most deeply felt demands, paying out a shilling or more a week becomes an unnecessary strain on a tight budget . . .
>
> Male workers will have to radically change their attitude towards women. Trade unions more or less are the working class movement in this country, and they are bastions of male privilege. At every level in the hierarchy of the labour market women occupy a weaker position than men. The unions are doing nothing to alleviate this situation . . .

> At present women are designated a secondary position within the class struggle because they are casual workers, because they are low paid, un or semi-skilled, work part time because they are wives and mothers etc. We are not asking to participate in the class struggle: the Women's Liberation movement must redefine it.
>
> (Alexander *c.* 1971/2)

It was for reasons like these – to do with class and gender issues – that I first became a feminist, and I did so because of the influence of women like Lily Bilocca, Pat Sturdy and May Hobbs. Whilst I am constantly reminded in the literature and in conventional wisdom about the emergence of second wave feminism, that it was a white, middle class affair, which was alienating and irrelevant to working class women, this was not altogether my experience. Certainly it was middle class women who quickly went into print about their ideas and their experiences, and began the process of building theories. The theories which emerged – initially from the social sciences and subsequently cultural studies and humanities – engaged critically with prevailing discourses in ways that contested the gendered nature of their content, their production and their authority. It is not so surprising. At that time, about a year after leaving university, I had amongst my already large collection of academic books – about sociology, politics, history, and English – a mere handful written by women. Most of what I learned at university from books, I learned from men. After an education which was also steeped in malestream knowledge, it was a bias I did not question until after the event.

These were books which, on the whole, tended to concentrate on events and ideas that were of specific interest to the men who wrote them – passed off as universal truths – and which viewed the world through the eyes of the predominantly white and middle class men they turned out to be – even when, occasionally, they were writing about women. The same exclusions and exclusivity applied when the dominant ideas that got published were to do with class and 'race'. Not only did academic books reflect white, middle class men's concerns, they were strangely detached from their own ways of knowing, as if it were possible to produce objective knowledge about an independent social reality, without recognising that the very process of doing so, influenced what the reality became. Such a legacy, in the guise of objectivity, frequently served to obscure the interests of academic writers in promoting particular ideas and arguments at the expense of others. What was kept from the reader – and often, also, from the writer – was any recognition of the dominant voices; the interpretative devices, the contingencies and social interactions; the problematic and diffuse relationship between facts, meanings and interpretations; the various compromises that helped to shape the final product.

These concerns became some of the specific issues about the construction, ownership and distribution of knowledge which feminism began to challenge and which have contributed to a broad based sociological and postmodern discussion about social construction and deconstruction, discourse and reflexivity ever since. The more theoretically sophisticated academic feminist analysis has become, however, the less it has been able to speak *to* women outside of academia – although in some contexts it is still speaking *about* them. The recent developments in feminist theorising, which has moved away from earlier preoccupations with Marxism towards more culturally and literary informed influences,

> parallels a class movement, whereby feminist theory becomes more 'up market', drawing on the cultural capital of those who have had access to 'high culture' and higher education: in some cases feminist theory has become a vehicle for displaying 'cleverness' and masking the inequalities that enable 'cleverness' to be produced and displayed.
>
> (Skeggs 1997)

But over time, women's writing has also included more diverse, more reflexive and more imaginative voices than might originally have been anticipated. In the early days, it was still middle class and educated women who were more likely than working class women to get published and to see the publication of ideas as being part of the struggle for women's equality and liberation. These days more – and different – women get published, but fewer of them connect their writing to the struggle for women's liberation.

The absence of working class and black women's perspectives from the first books that came out of second wave feminism says everything about class, whiteness and access to education. It does not mean that working class and black women were not involved in the struggles taking place – especially in the workplace and against racism and racial violence. As survivors of domestic violence, working class and black women, in my experience, played an enormous part in helping to establish and support the network of Women's Aid refuges that were established in the 1970s and 1980s. And as activists in working class communities, black and working class women were prominent in tenants' organisations, self-help groups and local campaigns on behalf of women's health and child care issues.

But it did not take long for the re-emergence of feminism to trigger a reactionary backlash. When the Festival of Light held a rally in Hull in 1972, attended by 500 people and addressed by Mary Whitehouse, to campaign against obscenity and in support of higher moral standards, with slogans like 'Protect your family life', 'Help to stop the rot' and 'Decency requires your name' – feminism was part of the rot they wanted to stop. Of course our group rose to the challenge with a counter demonstration and with banners demanding 'free contraception' and 'a woman's right to choose' about abortion. The local press reported:

> a mini counter demonstration on behalf of the Hull Women's Lib movement was closely watched by police. These marchers, carrying banners demanding free contraception were kept away from the main procession [and] when the marchers gathered in front of the College of Technology, the liberationists' placards were hidden from the view of the platform by

> Christian supporters. The police asked the liberationists not to antagonise supporters of the Festival of Light . . . [to whom] . . . Hull's three MPs Kevin McNamarra, James Johnson and John Prescott sent messages of support.
>
> (*Hull Daily Mail 1972*)

In our response by letter to its local organiser, we claimed it was also an obscenity:

> to hear 'good solid Christians' mouth insults such as 'harlots', 'sluts', 'whores', and 'you filthy bitches' at one moment, and then sing for the glory of God at the next. It was an obscenity to see the same hands that were 'pointing up for Jesus' aggressively reaching out for women who disagree, and in a few cases, assaulting those women. In a court of law one such attack would be described as indecent assault, but we will refrain from using 'lewd language' to illustrate it. The Hull Women's Action Group has discussed the Festival of Light and its implications at length and feels more strongly than ever that it has repression and not light at its roots. It is a danger to real freedom and growth of human potential and most especially to the liberty of women.
>
> (Letter 1972)

In an effort to keep in touch with the growing Women's Movement nationally we sent delegates to all the important Women's Liberation conferences of the early 1970s, including the first national conference held at Ruskin College in 1970. Like many developments at that time, it happened almost by accident. A handful of women had been attending one of the Ruskin history workshops organised by Raphael Samuel, to bring worker historians and academics together. As usual, it was entirely dominated by men and the work proceeded as though women had no part in history at all. But this time, the women historians decided to do something about it. Instead of agreeing to just another history workshop focusing on women, they decided to organise a national Women's Liberation conference. They expected 300 women to attend but nearly twice as many turned up. There was a crèche for children run by men – which in those days was a novel experience. Discussion ranged from sex discrimination to alternatives to the nuclear family. Considerable dissatisfaction was expressed with the conventional orthodoxies of male dominated, left wing politics:

> The struggle against capitalism and imperialism had never been examined from this perspective . . . the women were not less committed than others to the class struggle and the liberation of Vietnam, but they were determined to exert their own political place . . . For the average [male] Ruskin student, it was a traumatic occasion, especially on Sunday, waking to find slogans [saying 'Sisterhood is Powerful'] daubed all over the walls.
>
> (Campbell and Coote 1982)

Sally Alexander, a Ruskin student at the time, later described aggressive men,

> enraged at their College being taken over by all these women, all these children, at the mess, at the disruption, at the slogans being painted . . . They couldn't go into the television room and watch sport . . . The complaints about the television room and the mess were a cover for something which seemed really disruptive and threatening.
>
> (Wandor 1990)

At the time, we were very impatient and we often blamed ourselves and each other about the slow pace of change – as if thousands of years of patriarchy and two hundred years of capitalism (both of which proved to be more complex than we yet realised) could be defeated overnight. At the Birmingham conference in June 1971 an unsigned state-of-the-movement paper asked us to 'face our problems', given that 'after nearly two years of life . . . there can't be anyone in the movement who is satisfied with the way things are'. These dissatisfactions were identified as being:

> the enormous gap between the scale of our ends – a total social revolution – and that of our means – the numbers of our movement and the effectiveness of their deployment; the yawning gap between the content of the movement – the revolution in consciousness which we are striving for – and the necessary but limited reformist demands of its four campaigns (for equality in education and job opportunities and in pay, for 24 hour nurseries and abortion on demand); the huge gap between the members of our movement and the women in the country whom we wish to change and activate; and the gap inside our movement between our desire for unity and success in spreading our ideas of liberation and the actual diversity of ideas. After two years the movement is fragmented, chaotic and is already in places becoming demoralised. Some people are already leaving because they think they've solved their personal problems, others because they are fed up with a sense of lack of direction.
>
> (Conference Paper 1971a)

At the Skegness conference in October 1971, the spokeswoman for the Maoist inspired group called the Union of Women for Liberation, Comrade Maysel Brar, reminded us that it would be

> necessary for all of us to rid ourselves of our bourgeois and petit-bourgeois attitudes, preconceptions and prejudices and be prepared to examine scientifically the cause of the oppression of women in order to understand how that oppression [could] be ended and the full emancipation of women [could] be achieved.
>
> (Conference Paper 1971b)

Once this 'basic understanding and correct orientation' had been internalised, we were instructed to

> dedicate ourselves wholeheartedly to work for the liberation of all women and for all the oppressed and exploited peoples of the world, accepting the long struggle and many difficulties and sacrifices involved.
> (Conference Paper 1971b)

On no account should we imagine that

> this movement for women's liberation [might be] a vehicle for personal and individual 'solutions', to be dropped as soon as one's own hang-ups are resolved or when the going becomes too difficult and the movement's inability to act as a panacea for all ills becomes apparent . . .
> (Conference Paper 1971b)

According to Comrade Brar, we had a choice, whether

> to follow the feminists who seek to build a bourgeois women's movement to secure emancipation for the chosen few, ignoring the majority of women of this country and the working class and oppressed peoples; to follow the false leaders of the working class, the revisionists, Trotskyites and social democrats (the so called Labour party) whose policies support imperialism and seek to undermine the working class struggle for proletarian revolution and the dictatorship of the proletariat; or to work to mobilise women and raise their proletarian consciousness, to help build a revolutionary working class movement in this country to fight along side the proletariat and oppressed peoples of the world for proletarian revolution and the dictatorship of the proletariat.
> (Conference Paper 1971b)

I am almost certain that Comrade Maysel Brar was not herself working class, although she clearly regarded women's liberation to be part of the class struggle, albeit as a kind of 'add on' towards achieving the dictatorship of the proletariat which she represented as male. In the 1970s class was still used as a concept which romanticised and gave value to male working class identity – in which being part of the dictatorship of the proletariat was just one of its various heroic manifestations. The same projected status and representation did not apply to women in quite the same way. Class – then as now – was largely experienced by women as exclusion. The exclusion occurred because women did not have access to the economic resources, the political resources or the cultural ways to be anything other than working class. For women, being working class was attached historically to all that is dirty, dangerous and without value (Skeggs 1997) and was not widely regarded as the stuff of revolutionary potential or inspired leadership.

The group which called itself the Union of Women for Liberation clearly wanted to lead the movement for women's liberation, however. Earlier in 1971 they expressed their concern about the first national women's liberation demonstration on 6 March and the failure of some of those present to display 'the correct orientation' in their analysis of the causes of women's oppression. In particular,

> the line – very prevalent in the movement at the present time – that women's sexuality is 'the cause of her oppression', which had led the street theatre group to include in their performance a fat woman giving birth to an unending stream of cut-out paper babies for the duration of the march, the babies to be passed all the way down the demonstration over the heads of the marchers; women marchers being slapped with sanitary towels; a scene showing a little girl being pushed behind a tree when she wanted to pee while the little boys 'made fountains'; a scene in which 'Mr Right' strapped on his 'tool' before assaulting the same little girl, now adult, on their wedding night . . .
>
> (Position Paper 1971)

They felt strongly that these were not the images by which the Women's Liberation movement should be remembered.

> We say most emphatically: No . . . The impression given is that the women in the movement are disgusted with and rebelling against women's sexuality – which is not the case. We are disgusted with and rebelling against the oppression of women which is primarily economic . . . in so far as women are treated as sex commodities in this society that is because under capitalism all workers, men and women, are treated as commodities and for that reason it is capitalism which disgusts us, not its victims.
>
> (Position Paper 1971)

Campaigns around abortion and contraception, promoted by the International Marxist Group (IMG) and the Communist Party of Great Britain (CPGB) were also denounced by the Union for the Liberation of Women as a diversion from 'the real struggle . . . which is against monopoly capitalism', and built on concerns that the IMG and CPGB had ambitions 'to assume control of the movement, so as to impose their line on the movement by underhand means'.

Of course, others took the view that the control and definition of women's sexuality was not a petit-bourgeois distraction but a central issue in the struggle for liberation. The women's group attached to the otherwise male dominated Gay Liberation Front, for example, wanted to make a distinction between real lesbians and more dubious, political lesbians. Three 'types' gave them cause for concern.

> There are considerable numbers of women who are continuing to live with and/or struggle with men, either in mixed communes or collectives

> or in couples. These women apparently believe that men can be educated out of their sexism, or 'reconstructed'. Many women have stopped relating sexually to men and have settled into a state of comparative a-sexuality; they masturbate a lot (this is not to say that masturbation is not something that every woman must be able to do, like changing a tyre, defending herself, or picking locks – but it is not 'just as good'). Other women have not only stopped relating to men but consider themselves political lesbians. This means their full commitment – as they see it – is to women, but most of them do not have sexual relations with their sisters. Frequently political lesbians have expressed fear of being 'dominated' by a lesbian, while other criticisms include sexism and role-playing among lesbians. The women's movement must cease being a reformist head trip (political lesbian plot) and get on to the real revolution. COME OUT!!!
>
> (Gay Liberation Front Women's Group *c.* 1971)

These were concepts and suggestions which both terrified and excited me. At twenty-something I still felt more at home with Marx than masturbation, and had never, so far as I knew, ever met a lesbian – real or otherwise.

Thirty years on, the language and preoccupations of these densely worded and closely argued tracts, on faded and cyclostyled foolscap, are very illuminating. They sound ungenerous, and relentless in the extreme. They are also overly influenced by the culture of male dominated and New Left splinter groups which many of us previously frequented and which were forever split by political betrayals and fabricated coups as a measure of their self-proclaimed significance. Looking back through the records of our women's liberation group meetings, the recruiting flyers, the campaign literature, the agendas and the minutes, it is clear, in those early days, that some women brought with them a kind of adversarial orthodoxy from such groups, whilst others brought the more personalised and somewhat confused anger of educated wives, now recently married, with young children and interrupted careers, who strongly identified with Betty Freidan's recognition of 'the problem with no name' (Freidan 1963) and wondered, endlessly, in terms of the frustration of their day to day existence, if 'this was all' they could expect. In neither respect did these different tendencies speak easily to the day-to-day lives of working class women.

The different priorities and different reasons for joining our group are revealed in long and difficult discussions about what we should be called and where we should meet. Initially, as the Hull Women's Rights group, we were swayed by the confidence and authority of a leading academic and social historian at Hull university, who clung to her belief in a particular version of suffragette history. Our links with the Union of Women for Liberation did not sit very well with meetings in the petit bourgeois sitting rooms of large Victorian houses in Cottingham, however, in which space had been negotiated with men who couldn't quite keep out of the way, if only to make sure that everyone knew, and approved of the fact, that they were ostentatiously putting toddlers to bed. Nor was it the kind of ambience in which to meet with Lily Bilocca, May Hobbs or the Burnley Women's Industrial Union, or to confirm our practical commitment to the class struggle.

Equally, because these early meetings frequently turned into what were soon to be called consciousness raising groups, women's distress about the infidelities and hypocrisy of their 'right on' husbands was difficult to reveal in the apparent stability of their comfortable homes, surrounded by the homely sounds of children being carried up to bed – especially in the presence of unreconstructed Marxists, who still clung to the belief that recounting 'personal troubles' constituted bourgeois self indulgence, so long as the working class were not liberated from their oppression by capitalism. A hand written note from the young Hilary Wainwright captures something of the intensity and the innocence of our convictions:

> BP mentioned to me that you are somewhat pissed off with the women's lib group in Hull and quite interested in forming a socialist woman group or at least, something on similar lines. Would it be helpful if I came over to talk to you about it? Give me a ring – reverse the charges – my parents are away!
>
> (Wainwright *c.* 1971/72)

Inevitably our group went different ways. I do not know what happened to the more liberal feminist and more affluent wing who still wanted to meet in each other's houses. I am not sure how they renegotiated patriarchal relations on the home front when patriarchy was not a concept they found useful. The rest of us met in the back room of a pub in town and were joined by large numbers of all sorts of women over the next two or three years; some of whom stayed, some of whom had agendas around sexuality and 'race' which our residual Marxism did not adequately address. We called ourselves the Hull Women's Action group – to emphasise our determination to demonstrate and do 'serious' campaigning. In retrospect, I think we did things that made sense to us at the time, and which seemed possible. But possibilities change, the context shifts, identities are made and re-made in ways that are both complicated and contradictory. Thirty years on it would be interesting to discover what has become of the women we were then. In my experience, it has been the politics of everyday life – what Di Leonard and Christine Delphy call familiar exploitation (Leonard and Delphy 1992) – that has turned out to be the most persistent and difficult front line for women to negotiate, rather than the picket line; although both are intimately related.

Eventually, I also moved on. In Southampton in 1976 I got involved with Women's Aid and spent a good deal of the time when I should have been 'at work' teaching in the university, doing political work at the refuge with women and children who were the survivors of male violence. It was not reading academic books, or following the agenda of activists in the Women's Movement, that converted me to radical feminism, but what I learned about the construction of male sexuality and patriarchal violence from women at the Southampton refuge, the majority of whom were working class.

Horrific stories and relentless evidence of multiple humiliations, dreadful attacks and vicious cruelty against women – at the hands of husbands, partners, sons and other male relatives in their lives – did not discriminate on the basis of age, class or ethnic background. However, working class and black women were more likely to end up in refuges because middle class women are more likely to have other alternatives. The first refuge for battered women was opened in Chiswick in 1972. In 1976 exposing the prevalence of men's violence towards women and children was still treated with shock and ignorance by ordinary members of the public, myself included. It did not take long for the complicity of the state, the legal profession, the police and doctors to be revealed. Once the flood gates were opened and the extent of male (domestic) violence began to be counted, I found my feminism reconfirmed – and radically reconfigured. I began to call myself a radical feminist which, in those days, took the rather uncomplicated view that patriarchy and its various institutions was the enemy, and relationships with men served to bolster patriarchal power.

I came to think of lesbianism as being the logical extension of my feminism, and that withdrawing intimate, sexual and emotional support from men was the most absolute and effective way of acting to undermine the power of patriarchy. This was not the general conclusion of women at the refuge, I have to say, although some did become lesbian in relation to the closeness, solidarity and political preoccupations we shared with each other at that time.

It was a liberation for me to realise that sexuality and sexual orientation were no more natural than gender roles, and that all three were socially constructed within heterosexual institutions, shaped by patriarchal precedents and priorities. Making the political – and I thought logical – choice to become lesbian seemed emotionally quite straightforward at the time. It has, of course, become much more complicated in the light of experience – both personally and politically. But it is not a choice I have regretted. Fortunately I now understand there are other positive reasons apart from politics – to do with desire, emotion, intellect, friendship, affection and choice – about loving women, that are just as important as de-stabilising patriarchy.

I have also come to accept that the opportunity to make such a choice reflects a degree of privilege. For the majority of working class women the most common struggle regarding sexuality is to do with respectability. Working class women are marginalised by their class position and have been devalued and stigmatised historically because of it. Sexuality that is dangerous and perverse has been associated with black and white working class women and lesbians. Heterosexuality – because of the ways in which it is normalised in society – offers some opportunity at least to consolidate respectability. To be lesbian is not an identity to be claimed, it is a condition that adds to a woman's positioning as sexual and therefore serves to intensify her marginalisation.

For working class women, battles around sexuality are not fought through claims to identity but by negotiating power in everyday encounters in institutionalised settings. Specific forms of heterosexuality are produced in social and cultural contexts, in education, through work, by 'race', gender, class and place. Heterosexuality is regulated by law, custom, ideology and practice in ways that make lesbianism illegitimate and, for many, absolutely unthinkable. So long as heterosexuality remains such a strong marker of normalcy and respectability it will always induce investments from those whose positioning within respectability are most precarious.

For these kinds of reasons most women at the refuge did not feel they had a choice about their sexuality or their sexual politics. Mostly they were escaping from domestic violence at the hands of individual men. They were not looking for a discussion about the social construction of sexuality, or about alternatives. Their concerns were very practical ones – to do with safety, finding somewhere to live, sorting out some money to live on, getting their kids back into school. Others could not reconcile their ambivalence around desire. Some were more optimistic about the possibilities of changing men. Mostly they came to their own conclusions and solutions to the problems associated with men's power. Coming out, then as now, required a particular kind of distancing but the reprisals which happened in my own life as a consequence of doing so only served to confirm the courage of my convictions and to influence the personal choices, the struggles, the writing and the work I chose to prioritise as a consequence.

Radical feminism was not a distraction from the class struggle, but it strengthened my growing conviction that patriarchy was 'the main problem', and encouraged me to give my commitment to working class women, rather than men. This led to living in a lesbian family; forming strong friendships with women; looking for insights and creating knowledge that validated women's lives; taking part in feminist political campaigns and challenging male violence and sexual oppression. It also meant helping to create educational spaces for women in women-only courses and the setting up of a Women's Education Centre in Southampton, in which issues of personal and political transformation were given priority, alongside emancipatory learning, 'really useful' feminist knowledge, and the commitment to social and collective ways of getting women out from under (Taking Liberties Collective 1989).

All my energy at this time was spent with women, especially working class, black and poor women, who seemed to me to have fewer choices, less resources, and altogether harder lives to lead. I believed in doing everything I could to help women who were re-assuming control over their own lives and finding ways towards greater economic and social independence. I hoped they would make changes for themselves, but also in solidarity with other women. I hoped they would renegotiate and create relationships involving greater equality, some autonomy and no oppression; based on active choices rather than dependency, duty, obligation or guilt. And many of them did.

When seventy or so working class women and their children marched on the offices of the Director of Adult Education at Southampton University, whom they held responsible for trying to take back control of the curriculum and for withdrawing funds, crèche facilities and part time staffing from the Women's Education Centre, it was said they were gullible and had been manipulated (Taking Liberties Collective 1989). In fact, it was a well planned and effective piece of political and social action, born out of a strong commitment to the Women's Education Centre by its members, and was backed up by a national campaign that involved letters of support from academics, adult educators and former students of the Centre from all over the country. It might be interesting to accumulate 'the power to manipulate women' in ways that men have always done, but it is hardly credible. Rather, the repercussions of the demonstration were very revealing about the political limits of liberal adult education's tolerance of students, especially when they became self-confident and angry enough to challenge the authority of those who thought they knew best about what kind of education should be available to working class women.

One of the lasting achievements of this period – apart from the stories of hundreds of women whose lives were changed, often radically, as a consequence – is a book published by women from the Centre, set in the context of a much broader argument about working class women's experiences of education, and written by those whose voices, even now, do not always find their way into academic and professional publications. This is how the Taking Liberties Collective concluded what they had to say, at a time when Thatcherite economic and social policies, and the related backlash against women's liberation, were taking their toll on grass roots feminist activities:

> Those of us at the sharp end of poverty, racism, male sexual abuse and oppression need support from other women if we are to take effective collective action. One woman's poverty, abuse or socially induced mental illness is not 'her problem'. It is a problem that touches us all. As long as any woman can be smashed by fear or force or prejudice or hatred, we can all be smashed. We are all being smashed. What strikes some of us down today will strike others down tomorrow. Unless we get ourselves together. The resistance we can make on our own against false ideologies, the dangerous indoctrination of our children and the limitations placed on our freedom to take up space in the world, are nothing compared to what we can do together. If we re-group, re-kindle the outrage we feel on behalf of each other and remember that there are better ways to run the world, we have more of a chance. Our options are clear. If we don't take control of our own lives, we shall remain in the control of others.
>
> In terms of women's education, which has been the focus of this book – and which, by the way, we've now proved we can write, despite the odds – of course we realise that education on its own won't change the world. However, a critical, empowering, woman-centred education that links 'what we know' with 'what we need to know' is an important tool in our collective struggle for personal and political freedom. Not

> 'men's education' or 'men's education for women', but education in which we make the knowledge, we are the teachers and we are in control, can help all of us women, whoever we are, to learn together in ways that will inspire and strengthen us in our continuing struggle for women's liberation.
>
> (Taking Liberties Collective 1989)

Looking back, these were heady days, despite their many crises and numerous battles. But as the 1980s became the 1990s, the kind of feminism – and grass roots women's education – that was born out of class, race and gender struggles, and which was related to changing the world for women, rather than simply learning and writing about it, has become a part of the educational mainstream and renamed Access or Training. The price of moving from a frequently embattled and precarious marginality towards the relative security and enhanced respectability of better funding, accreditation and progression routes has been incorporation and the decline of radical energy at the cutting edge of adult learning initiatives for women. Personally I have been fortunate to continue working with working class women in much the same way as I have always done – trying to relate women's struggles in the home, in the community, in the work place and in the academy to the creation of 'really useful' kinds of knowledge that develop understanding but also inform and enable collective action for educational and social change. In this sense, the women I have met at Ruskin College, in Derry and as activists on trade union women's courses, for example, and whose lives and struggles I write about later in this book, have been a constant source of inspiration to me, and a recognition that whilst many old oppressions (persistently) remain the same, others need to be addressed in the context of changing times and new opportunities.

Part 2

CONNECTIONS

7

CLASS MATTERS

'It's Official' the *Observer* newspaper headline announced on Sunday, 29 November 1998. 'We're All Middle Class Now'. What the paper was referring to was the new eight tier table of social classifications based on occupations unveiled by the National Statistical Office, most of which were presented as middle class. Being working class, it seems, is no longer relevant. In Tony Blair's New Britain we need never mention the working class again. In postmodern Britain the term is no longer accurate unless like 'race' and 'woman' we place it between inverted commas. Like the National Union of Mineworkers and Wapping, working class has become reminiscent of a heroic past, of industrial labour and organised struggle, of means tests and the General Strike, of trench warfare and national welfare, of council houses and terrace houses, of men in cloth caps and women in head scarves, of apprenticeships and secondary modern schools, of HP sauce and rugby league. It reminds us of noble intentions and socialist dreams. In which all the heroes were men and all the women were mothers. Having moved out or moved on or moved up – the class rhetoric now makes people feel uncomfortable or guilty (Mahony and Zmorczek 1997).

In the battle for the hearts and minds of the working class – leading to four successive victories at the polls by the Conservative party between 1979 and 1997 – the popular tabloid press assisted in the ideological construction of a number of generalisations and myths. In the 1980s these included the view that 'loads of money' was available to anyone who was prepared to step on the face of the scrounger next door to get on. A move which involved buying council houses at a knock down price and private houses at a seriously inflated price – made easy by 'loads of money' being available as credit and as mortgages. It involved share options being targeted at small investors as privatised utilities – like gas, electricity and water – came under the hammer. Market economics helped transform the notion of standardised markets (based on labour intensive production systems) into mass niche markets via systems of franchising, flexible specialisation, new technologies, Japanese business practices, deregulation and globalization (Hall and Jaques 1989). As the economy was being effectively restructured and hundreds of thousands of people were being down-sized in the guise of increased efficiency, greater flexibility, modernisation and lean competition, the mystique of an economic bonanza was being cultivated by the creation of conspicuous consumption – offering apparent freedom and more choice – to a generation which was becoming addicted to shopping as a principal ingredient of happiness, success and leisure activity.

Those whose traditional livelihoods and related communities were the casualties of this so-called 'enterprise culture' were presented as both the dinosaurs and impediments to Britain's recovery as a world economic power. The vilification of Arthur Scargill (President of the National Union of Mineworkers) as the epitome of all that was bad in trade unionism, together with political 'loonies' like 'Red Ken' Livingstone (leader of the Greater London Council until its abolition), and 'militant extremists' like Derek Hatton (Labour leader of Liverpool City Council), shifted the focus of criticism, as it was articulated by the government and reflected in the tabloid press, on to 'the enemy within'. Occasionally this was reinforced by bouts of xenophobia directed at foreigners in general and at Argentinians (regarded as the enemy in the Falklands War) and Iraqis (regarded as the enemy in the Gulf War) in particular. The intention was to take people's minds off the widening economic gap which was developing between the living standards of the rich and those who still had jobs, in comparison to the growing numbers of redundant workers who were being systematically wasted by unemployment.

But no one could disguise the less palatable dimensions of New Right economics completely. Already several steps ahead of Britain, right wing academics in the United States (Murray 1989) had already developed the arguments necessary to depict the growing presence of an underclass as symptomatic of pathological deficiencies among certain social groups – including lone parents, unemployed youth, minority ethnic communities and recent immigrants – to be fecklessly dependent on welfare, to the extent that they would prefer to 'take drugs', 'do crime' or 'claim hand outs', rather than to 'pay their way' via proper jobs or voluntary work that might improve their job prospects.

At a time when British politicians, right wing think tanks (Cockett 1995) and postmodern academics were declaring the death of grand narratives – such as social class – in favour of lifestyle and consumer groups and identity politics, the notion of an underclass was taken up with surprising enthusiasm, in much the same way as it had already been used in the United States, and would subsequently be used in Australia and New Zealand, to stigmatise the poor and to define them as somehow responsible for their own demise (Morris 1994).

It is more than a decade now since John Major, when he was conservative prime minister, promised to deliver a classless society (20 November 1990, press conference). This was not to be a society without classes but a society providing the means for people to advance by ability, regardless of their class origins. It was to be 'an opportunity society' in which the role of government was to 'provide the ladders' enabling citizens to rise to 'whatever level their own abilities and good fortune may take them from wherever their starting point' (Major 1996). In fact Major's classless society was little more than the well worn commitment to meritocracy, based on the illusion of mobility for those with ambition and ability from low class backgrounds. Its focus was on the individual rather than the collective and yet, as Adonis and Pollard argue,

> the condition of classes is far more important than the mobility between them. Minorities are on the ladder; majorities stay put . . . the capacity of individuals to climb at all depends upon them not being more than a ladder length from their destination. And there is always downward mobility . . . the further the fall, the greater the grievance and despair . . . for all its drawbacks, the word underclass captures the essence of the class predicament for many at the bottom: a complete absence of ladders, whether basic skills, role models, education or a culture of work.
>
> (Adonis and Pollard 1997)

Margaret Thatcher's apocryphal view of society was that 'there is no such thing', and her view on class was 'the least said about it the better' – on the basis that the more you talk about something, the more you give the idea credibility in people's minds. Margaret Thatcher said a few odd things in her time as prime minister but this was probably a more perceptive remark than most. Although, not mentioning class has not made it go away. Widening educational participation does not solve class oppression. Individual solutions do not solve the problems of class relations in capitalism. You cannot get rid of class conflict (or sexual oppression or racism) with therapy. Conditions of structural inequality have not disappeared but the discussion about it has been dying, politically and academically, for the best part of twenty years. And it is the working class who have lost (Pakulski and Waters 1995).

The class war was not decided simply by the defeat of the miners during Thatcher's years in government but the battle for the Yorkshire coalfield was a defining moment. The twin traits associated with Thatcherism – ruthlessness and individualism – finally managed to make the working class no longer dangerous. They were bullied and incorporated, turned into an underclass and silenced. New Labour does not speak for them. It speaks for those whom the current deputy prime minister, John Prescott, calls 'the beautiful people' and for the professional classes whose autonomy and professionalism were attacked by Thatcher. The Old Labour solution to poverty and structural inequalities, based on upping the taxation of the better off, to increase spending on the badly off, whilst strengthening the role of the state to mop up unemployment, is most definitely not the political platform that won Labour the 1997 election. Blair's version of a stakeholder society, a third way, a New Britain, is to persuade more people to think of themselves as middle class. Speaking in 1996, he said,

> our task is to allow more people to become middle class. The Labour Party did not come into being to celebrate working class people having a lack of opportunity and poverty, but to take them out of it.
>
> (Blair 1996)

Since at least the 1980s, the choice on offer to the working class, whatever political party has been in power, has been to get on their bikes, retrain, move from welfare into work and pin their faith on 'Education, Education, Education'. New Labour's New Deal, put like this, is pretty straightforward: strive to join the middle class or rot in the badlands of the underclass.

The 'amazing disappearance of the working class' works quite well as a theory if you have a full time job yourself and feel enthusiastic about New Labour's political 'third way' (Giddens 1998). It is convincing – just about – if you take the view that the chronological passage of time inevitably produces change, which is automatically progressive, and you do not risk testing your hypothesis in the real world. For example, in those areas where manufacturing and heavy industry have disappeared, especially in the North, in Central Scotland, South Wales, Northern Ireland and large parts of the Midlands – where hospital cleaners, factory workers, shop assistants and building workers go about their daily business; where socially, housing has never been more polarised, and where housing tenure is now, more than ever, an accurate predictor of health, income, educational level and the likelihood of unemployment. A child from an unskilled manual class background is still twice as likely to die before the age of fifteen as a child from a professional family, whilst the life expectancy of children from the unskilled manual class is seven years shorter than for children from professional classes. In most respects health inequality is now greater than in the 1950s because of increased class segregation in housing and the widening gulf between rich and poor (Adonis and Pollard 1997).

In their book *A Class Act* Andrew Adonis and Stephen Pollard argue that, in addition, Britain still has a 'two nation' education system in which in England especially, schools are so rigidly divided between public and private sectors that the word apartheid is not an exaggeration. Measures based on 'A'-level performance consistently reveal that performance in private schools is on average a quarter better than in their state counterparts. In 'A'-level league tables the top state school comes in at seventy-first and the best English comprehensive falls outside the top 200. Behind these figures lie enormous disparities in funding – affecting buildings, teaching resources and teachers – and a rigid separation of the public and private sectors. In 1997, 610,000 children, belonging to one million parents in the higher professional, executive and managerial classes, were in private schools; children who will be among the best educated of their generation, and 90 per cent of whom will go on to university, frequently Oxbridge (Adonis and Pollard 1997).

The introduction of comprehensive schools in the 1960s and 1970s was masterminded on behalf of the then Labour government by Tony Crosland – himself a former public school boy and Oxford don – who saw himself as a progressive engaged in the class struggle on behalf of the working class. In 1971, 35 per cent of state schools were comprehensive; by 1981, the figure was 90 per cent, by which time almost all direct grant schools had become part of the private sector. Labour party policy at the time was that grammar schools – the 'fucking grammar schools', as Crosland called them – should be abolished in the interests of equality of opportunity and a classless education system.

Even supposing that the class system could be changed by education, the policy was flawed from its inception because nothing was done about the private sector, to which

> the professional classes decamped en masse rather than submit to comprehensivisation. In many cases they simply took their grammar schools with them into the private sector – particularly when Shirley Williams . . . moved to abolish the direct grant scheme, under which the state contracted to buy places in leading private grammar schools.
>
> (Adonis and Pollard 1997)

By the end of the 1980s private schooling had become a lucrative business enterprise and something which the upwardly mobile, metropolitan middle classes actively pursued along with other material manifestations of their improved social and economic standing. In the 1990s the introduction of league tables further boosted the fortunes of the private sector. 'In 1996 the headmaster of Cheltenham College was sacked because the school was not high enough in the league tables – it was a defining moment' (Adonis and Pollard 1997).

At the beginning of the twenty-first century, the divide between state and private schools is wider than at any other time since 1945 and the pattern is being repeated within the state system. The introduction of comprehensive schools has tended to replace selection by ability with selection by class and house price. Those who can afford to buy their houses have more choice about where they live than those who are dependent upon the rented sector and social housing. It is within this material difference that housing and education's 'two nations' still exist. Working class people send their children to the schools that are available when parents lack the money, the time, the influence or the knowledge to send them anywhere better. They are consequently the class that has borne the brunt of both élitist and progressive educational policies, as well as some of the worst school buildings and housing imaginable, in places where low income people, and those dependent on the state for benefits, are concentrated in circumstances of increasing social exclusion. Council housing is now the location where younger people, including young unemployed men and single parents, live together with the old and those dependent on state benefits (Social Exclusion Unit 1998). Despite the legacy of Thatcher's 'home owning democracy' and the dramatic increase in owner occupation over the last two decades, 32 per cent of the population – almost a third – still rent their properties. A fifth of all households in England and a quarter in Scotland live in council properties. People in 'good' housing areas live longer and enjoy better health and health care. People in 'bad' housing areas experience poorer health, suffer more long term illness and more symptoms of depression (Adonis and Pollard 1997).

In practice, therefore, middle class children go to middle class comprehensives in catchment areas made up of middle class neighbourhoods, whilst working class children attend the inner city comprehensives and schools on large peripheral council estates from where their parents cannot afford to move.

> The tragic irony is that for all the good intentions, the destruction of the grammar schools – in the name of equality of opportunity – only had the effect of reinforcing class divisions. Those who can afford to flee the system desert to the private sector: those who have the money to escape to a leafy middle class catchment area leave the inner cities; and those who can't are left to pick up what is left over for them.
>
> (Adonis and Pollard 1997)

During the last twenty years or so, Thatcherism, market economics, the new world order, and the collapse of communism in Russia and eastern central Europe, have all contributed to the demise of Marxism as a world view, and of structuralism and political economy as academically respectable positions. But just because Marx did not get it right about the end of capitalism and the future of socialism, it does not mean he did not have some useful insights and some principled beliefs (Allman 1999). Neither does it mean he was wrong about the importance of material reality in people's lives, as formative influences on their fortunes and perceptions. It might be utopian, and therefore unrealistic, to imagine, as Marx did, a state of social and economic equality – from each according to his means, to each according to his needs (*sic*) – but structural determinants beyond market forces, coincidence or free choice, are still, it seems to me, critical to the persistence of the extreme inequalities which ensure that the self same groups always end up in poverty and with poor education, bad health and unemployment. This is not the kind of language or the analysis that is currently fashionable, however.

Part of the problem is that the working class are no longer considered to be interesting or sexy. The men have stopped being 'heroes' and have turned into 'criminals, vandals and drug dealers'. The women are becoming mothers 'far too young', on their own, and principally – it is alleged – to 'secure council houses'. The cynical use of single and teenage mothers, unruly children who are 'out of control' and excluded men, to represent a threat to 'traditional family values' and the social order – by both Conservative and New Labour governments – has been used to generate support for policies on law and order, cuts in benefits and restructuring of the welfare state. The allegations of 'scrounging' and 'dependency' as somehow synonymous with working class existence are now so bad that even working class people do not want to be associated with the term (Skeggs 1997). My parents regularly read versions of themselves – the working class – distorted in the tabloids as workshy, and presented as trivial and stupid in television soaps, in ways which they have come to regard as 'the truth', even though the representations bear no resemblance to their lives, or to the lives of any other working class people they know. So powerful is the message, it helps to construct perceptions which define realities, and which in the process change patterns of interpretation and social meaning. It is much more common to find left wing academics and Old Labour supporters espousing working class credentials or allegiances than any number of working class people not wanting to be associated with dreadful, pejorative stereotypes about immorality and dependency. The vilification of the underclass by successive politicians and right wing commentators in recent years, as a warning to others, has achieved much of what, presumably, it was intended to do: the demise of collective action and community values in the face of individualism and pragmatism as a political credo. But not entirely. When I asked Trisha – a women's studies student at Ruskin College – about being working class, she described herself like this:

> To me being a working class woman means exclusion. Even before puberty, I always felt trapped, out of place. At that time I didn't know why or by whom – but I do now. The 'arch villain's' plans for me were no less than a working class grow bag for factory fodder or cannon fodder, depending upon boom or slump, my reproductive years to be spent in the grip of wedlock, my home a sort of farm for free range peasants – in Wythenshaw, the largest working class estate in Europe. Of course, I resisted. It's my nature to do so, and I was encouraged by my mother and my uncle. My education began early – my mother encouraged me to get an education and my uncle encouraged me in another way. It was him who told me bed time stories that angered and inspired me – about the slaughter at St Peter's Fields in Manchester and about the General Strike of 1926. And about my grandmother, working in their mills full time at the age of twelve.

Elaine also has a strong sense of being both working class and a woman, and of developing considerable pride in what that means:

> I have always seen myself as working class. I was born and live in a public sector housing estate and in common with the majority of people who live there I have to sell my labour in order to receive an income. My family work through necessity, not choice, and in most cases in very poor working conditions.
>
> As a woman in Northern Ireland, the view of myself is also reinforced by the political situation. My community in general has seen itself as being under siege – from which a strong sense of pride and solidarity developed. As a community we saw ourselves as a coherent social unit – working class and under attack. For me this encouraged not only a sense of being working class, but also having pride in it. Because of the war in Northern Ireland and the particular economic circumstances in Derry, once the shipyards declined, the main source of employment was in the shirt factory, and that was women's work. Unemployment in my lifetime

> has always been more of an issue for men than for women. Men were the ones who stayed home, whilst women worked and were the providers. It is true to say that this responsibility did not translate into women being viewed as the head of the household, which was still the role allocated to men. Although some work is still available, the shirt factories have also closed down now and many women no longer have paid employment . . .
>
> In the midst of 'the troubles' women took leading roles in protests. Women were very often the ones who organised and led demonstrations – they rattled bin lids and spoke at meetings . . .
>
> Eventually I got involved in community development, particularly with women, who are the most active in our community. I have brought to my work a sense of pride in women, in my class, in my community and culture. As a paid worker I am underpaid and exploited but my horizons are widened. My aim is to empower individuals and the community as a whole to have a voice in the direction of the future.

But despite the evidence of women like Trisha and Elaine, the negative stereotyping and pathologising of working class people remains. It is not altogether challenged by the Marxist concentration on material life as being the source of power and political relationships, and of consciousness and ideas. Whilst this has provided an alternative analysis to that of 'blaming the victim' and helped to connect repressive ideologies to the ideas and interests of dominant groups, it is an emphasis which has tended to subsume mental and emotional life to the exigencies of economics. The implication that mental life flows directly and exclusively from material conditions has served to simplify the inter-relationship between structural determinants and personal constituents of emotional behaviour, in ways that have frequently acted to attribute psychological simplicity to working class people, as well as homogeneity (Steedman 1986). Whilst the recognition of shared interests and class solidarity in the face of a common enemy has been an important organising principle and political philosophy which I have no wish to discredit, accounting for the working class 'as a mass' seriously mis-represents women, and actively denies to the individuals involved their own particular stories and their own individual histories.

On the other hand, the opportunities for developing class solidarity in working class organisations and communities of mutual interest have suffered greatly from 'the death of politics' and 'the democratic deficit' during the Conservative years. Parliamentary politics have ceased to engage with the social meanings and lived experience outside the concerns of corporate party interests, in much the same way as Chomsky shows how large sections of the lower class, black and recent immigrant groups in the United States are effectively disenfranchised by a system which pays no attention to their concerns, and then defines them as apathetic for showing no interest in the democratic process (Chomsky 1992).

The present House of Commons is arguably more uniform in its appearance, socially and ideologically, than any since the Great Reform Act of 1832. The arrival of Labour women in significant numbers in 1997 helped to shift the gender balance – despite sexist references to 'Blair's Babes' and the sense that some kind of fatwa has been imposed upon them to secure their silence on matters female or feminist – but their presence has not altered the fact that more than four-fifths of today's MPs come from professional, executive or managerial backgrounds. If the old aristocracy has mostly disappeared from the Tory side, so too have Labour's authentic working class trade unionists – down to one in five of all Labour MPs by 1996 (Adonis and Pollard 1997).

Parliamentary politics has become an all consuming career because an increasing number of its practitioners have made it so. By 'raising the threshold for participation, they have only further discouraged – or disabled – the non careerist from taking part' (Adonis and Pollard 1997). Not only has the practice of parliamentary politics become less accessible to ordinary people, the perception on the part of growing numbers of citizens is that they cannot influence what the politicians do. Both parties now advocate a classless, 'one nation' society and swap identical buzzwords to do with choice, freedom, individuality, responsibility and opportunity whilst 'acute social segregation and the lack of aspiration among the lower classes coexist with a pervasive sense of political impotence and it is hard to believe that the two are unconnected' (Adonis and Pollard 1997).

During the years of Conservative government between 1979 and 1997 working class politics, expressed at local level through local government action and trade unions, suffered from a reduction in influence and incorporation, punitive and repressive legislation, the disciplining and demoralising effects of unemployment and increasing poverty, privatisation and deregulation. Middle class and left wing intellectuals and academics, involved in socialist and feminist politics in the 1960s and 1970s, lost some of their momentum in the 1980s, brought on by the crisis in the Left and the backlash against feminism. Individuals who were burned out, overcome by cultural pessimism or who could not get enthusiastic about the future of radical politics, increasingly turned to personal solutions to occupy their energies – or they gave up. And whilst teachers and academics make up the single largest occupational group among the membership of both Conservative and Labour political parties, 'politicians of all hues and, it must be said, many educators demonstrate little interest in deepening the quality of life, in extending democracy through enlarging our capacities for thinking, criticising, creating and controlling' our own lives (McIlroy 1993: 18). When such a retreat is mounted it becomes even more important to remember 'whose experiences are being silenced, whose lives are being ignored and whose lives are considered worthy of study' (Skeggs 1997).

Hope lies, as ever, in the resilience of those on the front line – especially women, whom Beatrix Campbell (Campbell 1984) calls 'the true radicals' – in creative anger, disaffection, oppositional culture, and the will to resist that which is manifestly unjust (Thompson 1983, 1989, 1997). It helps, of course, to be organised rather than idiosyncratic, and collectivist rather than individualist, if social change is the desired objective. Far more people currently belong to self-help groups, community organisations and social movements than are members of political parties (McGivney 1999b). Their political potential comes from the creation of subversive space for participation and dialogue in relation to issues with which they are concerned. According to Anthony Giddens,

> they can force into the discursive domain aspects of social conduct that previously went undiscussed, or were 'settled' by traditional practices. They may help contest 'official' definitions of things; feminist, ecological and peace movements have all achieved this outcome, as have a multiplicity of self help groups.
>
> (Giddens 1994)

Within academia many have turned to postmodernism for inspiration, a theoretical view of the world which dismisses class as 'a relic from a modernism which has no applicability to the supposed ability to travel through differences, unencumbered by structure or inequality' (Skeggs 1997).

In the social sciences and the humanities this has led to what often gets referred to as the 'cultural turn', in which empirical and factual information is now examined less in relation to quantity and objectivity, and more in relation to experience, nuance, meaning, transience and ambiguity. Social experience is now regarded as being not only contradictory and gendered but also complex and shifting, and as such, less certain and more provisional than the legacies of enlightenment thinking would have us believe. The way is cleared for considerable freedom of choice and for conspicuous manoeuvre.

For (working class) women, however, possibilities are still negotiated through power structured relationships in everyday life. Postmodernism's interest in identity and the body, for example, needs to understand that working class women carry the stigma of being everything that is 'mad, bad and dangerous' and their negotiations take place within profoundly unequal relationships and institutions (Skeggs 1997: 160). Working class women do not easily assume that their identity is interesting or their bodies are valuable. These are theories that have largely been developed about other kinds of bodies in different material conditions. Bodies which are more privileged, which occupy social space and which are able to move through it in very different ways. For many working class women the issue remains the struggle to become respectable in the face of restrictive and pathologising stereotypes. In such circumstances the likelihood is not to imagine multiple shifting identities so much as being able to pass and to 'fit in' with respectable society.

In social geography the places where people live and work are increasingly viewed as spatial texts that may be interpreted differently by different readers, who are positioned and differentiated from each other by their gender, class, ethnicity, age and life experiences (McDowell 1999: 227). In other words, it is not simply that places, like texts, are different, they are also experienced differently and perceived differently by different people. In describing her feelings about coming to Britain from a small island in the Seychelles, Sylvette says:

> I can't really explain how alone, homesick and thoroughly humiliated I felt when I first came to Britain. I wouldn't go into shops because of my strong accent and the cold staring faces. I walked the streets afraid to look into white people's eyes, a habit that stayed with me for a long time until I built up my self confidence. As a black woman living here in Britain I have to do battle not just with racism but also sexism and class prejudice in a country that no longer needs or wants me. In the past I was needed to clean other people's houses, wipe their children's noses and provide emotional support in return for poverty wages. The economic climate was ripe at that time for Britain to import black people from the colonies to do the kinds of jobs that white people didn't want to do. In my case I was paid £5 a week when I came here in 1972 to carry out all the household duties and responsibilities for the family who employed me for seven days a week. When the British economy began to decline and we were no longer wanted the National Front marched down the street where I lived demanding that we should be sent back home because we were taking white people's jobs.
>
> I have tried to educate my daughter on issues of racism. I tried to prepare her psychologically to survive in the racist country in which she was born. There are moments as a mother when I wished she did not have to witness my humiliations. There was also times when I was left with no choice but to retaliate, or else abandon my daughter with a lost feeling, and I with a loss of confidence . . .

We did not need postmodernism to recognise that women see the world through different eyes and experience the world differently, as a consequence of being positioned differently within it. This has always been the understanding of feminist scholarship. Women's relationship to men, their development of subjectivity and identity, their relationship to the places in which they live, all derive from complicated negotiations, mediated by attachments to (at least) class, gender, ethnicity, age and sexuality, and by conscious and unconscious emotional processes involving internalised patterns of belief, ideas and feelings. These are differences which articulate with structural and racialised inequalities – of resources, power and opportunity – which result in women's subordination to, and oppression in different places, in different ways, at different times.

Whilst it is now widely understood that the forms taken by women's oppression vary historically and culturally over time, and are additionally complicated by the intersecting consequences of class, imperialism and sexuality, which have different kinds of significance depending on where women are coming from and how they are positioned, the insistence on changing such relationships of power and inequality is what finally distinguishes feminism from the postmodern analysis of difference.

The concern to elaborate theoretical complexity in relation to women's lives requires a fair degree of openness and imagination in its approach, as well as considerable sensitivity to the nature of individuality (as distinct from individualism) and commonality in the understanding of human agency. The point, so far as feminism is concerned, is not to abandon the recognition of shared oppressions, common interests and related conditions that exist in spite of individual differences – because the feminist project is both to understand the position of women in the world, and to act politically in order to change it. As such, intellectual and political developments are best regarded not as descriptions and categories waiting to be filled, but as a process in which ideas and possibilities remain open to challenge and negotiation, within the very real constraints of structure.

In considering the lives of working class women, the feminist concern to understand what it means to be working class and to challenge urgently the material and social constraints of what is currently available is, of course, no small undertaking. It relies on a close examination of class/gender relations, on dismantling much of the basis of everyday social relations, most institutions and power structures, as well as the ideological and emotional foundations on which current class/gender divisions stand. This is because structural inequalities are deeply embedded in the distribution of economic and social resources, and also deeply rooted in our sense of ourselves as individuals – men are one thing, women are the opposite – which derives from centuries of capitalist economics, western intellectual thought and institutional structures. As Doreen Massey has argued,

> deeply internalised dualisms . . . structure personal identities and daily lives, which have effects upon the lives of others through structuring the operation of social relations and social dynamics, and which derive their masculine/feminine coding from deep socio-philosophical underpinnings of western society.
>
> (Massey 1995)

In this context women are seen as being not only different from men, but inferior. In terms of gender, the western intellectual tradition has attributed femininity with qualities that are less highly valued than those of masculinity, and added them to similar gradations of superiority and inferiority that are built around attitudes to race and social class. The 'natural order' in most working class communities is still widely assumed to be one in which men should supply leadership, provide protection and resources, and exercise authority. The spectacle of women gaining independence, more influence and greater opportunities, which place them beyond the control of individual men – albeit it in relatively circumscribed conditions of single parenthood, casual labour market activity or educational achievement – poses threats to the old order and demands a different and renegotiated settlement between men and women.

Trisha well understands the many contradictions involved in such negotiations:

> My lover, for example: he's a staff rep at the Town Hall. He's black so he's fighting racism. He's also fighting for his own economic survival and trying to support his two mixed-race children, emotionally and financially. He's fighting to hold onto his identity (serious Rasta, this man). And at work he's fighting against cuts in living standards. He needs care – and he's one of the very few men I've ever met who deserves my care – but he's too laden down to give me back the care I need.
>
> Then there are my four children. At different times they present me with different problems. I try to concentrate on the one who is in most need – in crisis. At the moment that's the 33 year old. He's homeless, unemployed and a drug addict. With him I'm struggling against (second generation?) 'domestic' violence on the home front. I struggle to help him overcome his intention (genetically inherited or learned behaviour?) of dominating all of the women around him. Maybe I should write some more about this and you can tell me where class fits in! He stopped trying years ago. His position is that, although he has the skill to build good homes for those who can afford them, he can't afford to buy one of the homes he can build for himself, because the wages in the building trade have been forced so low. In other words, he can't afford to buy the product of his labour on what they want to pay him. He's one of the dispossessed of this country; white, working class, male. He feels betrayed by the 'leaders of the revolution', i.e. the British labour movement. I'm struggling to stop him killing himself slowly out of desperation.

Against the backdrop of enormous economic changes in recent years, played out on a global scale, but contingent on the lives of small localities, men and women increasingly meet each other as changing individuals in a shifting landscape. As gendered individuals, men and women are rarely known quantities, who enter and leave relationships with others uniformly and intact, but are more accurately seen as activists in ongoing and contested negotiations about relationships and meaning. Gender identities and relationships are not simply allocated and worn like a second skin, or performed according to a given script, they are improvised, constructed and re-constituted through discourse and everyday activity and behaviour.

Although I believe the basis of women's continuing oppression is firmly rooted in the characteristics of late capitalism and in the excessive control still exercised by men in relation to women's minds and bodies, significant social and economic changes in recent times have delivered to some women (in the West, at least) reliable contraception, divorce legislation, more economic independence, better education, and altered attitudes to monogamy, intimate relationships and family arrangements. All of which are the ingredients of transformation. So enormous have some of these changes been, that commentators such as Anthony Giddens have suggested that 'a transformation of intimacy' has been the result (Giddens 1992).

Women have clearly had the most to gain from such developments and from being considerably relieved of the fear of unwanted pregnancy and from men's control over women's fertility. Giddens argues that a new form of social contract between men and women is now possible, based on emotional expression and bodily intimacy, creating a different concept of sexuality – in which negotiation rather than imposed power and struggle is the basis of the new relationship. The evidence for his optimism is not yet widespread, however. Especially in circumstances in which men who fear women's increased economic and emotional independence are as likely – more likely, because of residual patriarchal tendencies – to use violence against women in an effort to retain control (Halmer and Maynard 1987; Hester *et al.* 1996). But his ideas are helpful in reminding us that gender relations and sexuality are social constructs, rather than biological determinants, and as such, are subject to modification and re-negotiation, even though the political and social constraints can be enormous. It is a possibility which Beatrix Campbell – from an entirely different political perspective – also anticipates when she writes about imagining a more democratic settlement emerging between men and women, as older and increasingly contested arrangements lose their focus and significance, partly through struggle, partly as a consequence of social change (Campbell 1999).

8

WOMEN IN WORKING CLASS COMMUNITIES

Definitions of what is meant by the term 'community' are contentious to say the least (McGivney 1999b). The usage might include a range of potential meanings including geographical, occupational, political or cultural dimensions. The term has frequently been used ideologically and ambiguously (Thompson 1980b) and remains a 'notoriously slippery and contested concept' (Martin 1987).

In the past, ideas about community and class were seen as related – and frequently synonymous, but only when describing working class communities. Such communities, it was said, developed a special kind of 'community spirit' born out of solidarities of common interest, shared troubles and strategies for survival (Willmott and Young 1962). Strong feelings, deriving from the sense of belonging to a particular locality or group, shared histories and common conditions, frequently provided the networks of friendship, mutual support and local knowledge that kept groups of people together in difficult times. Or so the story goes. Personally I think it depends who you ask. If it is the case that those who live in close connection and alliance with each other give meaning to connections and the politics of daily life in the language of community – then it should be taken seriously. It may be that the term is used in an idealised and emotional way to describe what is best about common histories and shared understandings, but that is all right. It still allows for conflicts of interest and difficulties to have their place in negotiations between people who also have a lot in common.

It might be that the term is also used to emphasise cultural, religious and ethnic solidarities – a kind of collective statement about identity. Often the term is used in this way by minority groups who know they inhabit a marginal and outsider position in relation to the rest of society – as a statement of mutual identification and belonging: for example, the black community and the gay and lesbian community.

My scepticism about the appropriateness of the terminology is triggered when it is applied to groups of people by those who are not part of the group being described as 'a community', in ways that are contrived or which imply some kind of cultural or social homogeneity. Applied to working class groups and minority ethnic groups, for example, there is a real danger of undue simplification and of stereotyped generalisations being made. The recognition that the language of community often gets used by social commentators and politicians, to enhance the image, and distract attention from material conditions that might more accurately be addressed in terms of racism, dispossession, poverty and powerlessness, is not new (Thompson 1980b). It surfaces, for example, in the notion that having 'a sense of community' is some kind of legitimate compensation for extreme social and economic inequality, or that, having lost it, serves to explain why sink estates are the terrible 'antisocial ghettos' they have become. There is rarely the same ideological need to romanticise or pillory middle and upper class neighbourhoods, in this way, even though – in terms of money, jobs, education, cultural capital and values, for instance – their residents also have a lot in common, and quite often operate fairly antisocial and exclusionary practices to make sure they retain them. On the other hand, because the word 'community' has appealing connotations, powerful institutions sometimes make use of it as a gloss to refurbish a less positive image: for example, the business community and the academic community.

As well as ideological considerations there are also, frequently, moralistic overtones implied when those who are relatively privileged use the language of community about others who are less so. I am thinking of the communitarian ideas of Amitai Etzioni, for example, which have clearly found considerable favour with Tony Blair and New Labour in Britain, just as they did with Bill Clinton in the USA, and with right wing British commentators like Melanie Phillips and Janet Daly.

The urgency with which those in pauperised neighbourhoods are being exhorted to 'restore civic virtues', 'live up to their responsibilities' and not merely 'focus on their entitlements' in order to 'shore up the moral foundations of society' and 'recreate the spirit of community' might be seen as a rather one-sided and hypocritical apportioning of the responsibility and blame for structural inequalities and social conflict (Etzioni 1995). It is not an exhortation which is being made to the richest tenth of the population, for example: those whose net incomes in Britain, after housing costs, grew by 68 per cent between 1979 and 1995, whilst those of the bottom tenth fell by 8 per cent, at the same time as the proportion of children growing up in households living below half the national average income increased from 10 per cent in 1979 to 32 per cent in 1995 (Social Exclusion Unit 1998).

Whilst recognising that the meanings which people identify as being important to them is an imprecise science, and full of contradiction and complexity, in the end, it is probably safest to refer to groups of people and localities as 'communities' if that is the language used by those involved. Communities like cultures or ethnicities are not static totalities. They are fluid arrangements of different individuals, values, ideas and practices – in which the boundaries shift and blur around the edges all the time. Neither can their ontology avoid influencing, and being influenced by, those who are not their members. For example in Britain, minority ethnic communities are frequently viewed as 'outsiders' by the dominant culture, and are clearly affected by the implications and consequences of this in a racist society. But they, by their very presence, also have an influence on, and affect, the 'insiders' too, in ways that are not always immediately obvious. In the short term, the dominant culture might become more or less racist as a result of minority ethnic communities being present and accounted for in white British society. In the longer term, as minorities settle and are born in Britain, they actively contribute to the process of redefinition about what it means to be British in a period of significant social change. This is especially relevant at the present time in relation to the loss of empire, globalisation, the weakening of the nation state, devolution, and the strengthening of links with Europe – all of which are leading to the emergence of a new and different kind of British identity. Of course, there is also a power dynamic involved, about whose definitions carry significance and meaning, although it is not inconceivable, in the context of an increasingly multicultural society, that diversity and equality might be able to coexist.

Whilst it is important to recognise that the term 'community' is frequently used ideologically by dominant groups in society, in order to obscure institutionalised structural inequalities, and to apportion blame for the creation of the circumstances in which they find themselves to those who have least resources, education and power – it is also important not to underestimate the implications of communities becoming inward looking and reactionary. It is commonplace in Britain to encounter racism, for example. Racism is not the prerogative of any one class or group more than another, although white racism – in its institutionalised form within mainstream culture, social organisations and the state, and in its numerical proportions – is clearly the most prevalent and powerful.

In working class neighbourhoods, racism collects and generates ideas and practices which sabotage the strengthening of political alliances across interconnected oppressions, to the advantage, always, of more powerful and privileged social interests and agendas, which are also racist. But also, in working class neighbourhoods – more so than in middle class and more affluent neighbourhoods – people of different nationalities, ethnic groups, 'races' and cultures are actually engaged in living the kinds of changes, on a day-by-day basis, which are needed to create the different attitudes, practices and allegiances necessary to the emergence of a less racist and more equal society.

In this sense, working class communities can be seen to operate both within and against racism, revealing at least two parallel tendencies. One is the sharpening of antagonisms, evidenced by increasing levels of racism and of institutionalised resistance to either recognising or addressing the consequences of what racism means. The murder of the black teenager Stephen Lawrence in London by a gang of white youths; the seriously 'bungled' police investigation; the court case; the public inquiry about the failure of the police to secure prosecution; and its aftermath, for example, all reveal many of the problems associated with persistent racism. The second tendency is the, almost coincidental, drift towards multiculturalism, as a feature of people from different racial and ethnic backgrounds now inhabiting the same geographical location.

Whilst Britain has a long history of invasion and settlement by different groups, considerable rivalry between its constituent nations, and a shorter but significant history of colonial relationships, lived at a distance, during the last 400 years, the British have never seriously defined themselves in terms of ethnicities. The identification of minority ethnic diversity did not really surface until the 1950s, as though this was a process that started when recruiting offices were opened in the West Indies to enlist manual workers for the health service, transport and manufacturing. When it became clear – probably in the 1970s – that initial assumptions about assimilation were inappropriate and not going to work, the drift towards some kind of – almost grudging – recognition of other cultures began (Mullard 1982). If it were not for the parallel tendency towards intensified racism, it is possible that, over time, this drift might eventually arrive at a qualified acceptance of multiculturalism. It would be quite a different journey, however, from one that is more positive and self-conscious about 'the process of becoming' a multicultural society. Just as black British and minority ethnic groups in Britain are already helping to redefine what it means to be British, there is also a need to shift public consciousness and to frame legislation designed to break down the barriers which deny some groups access to full citizenship and Britishness so long as racism continues. An altogether bigger and more concentrated effort needs to be led by government that is concerned to value, and be seen to promote and legislate for, a multicultural society. This is a very different emphasis from current notions of gradualism and drift.

In either event, the kind of society we eventually become – in terms of recognising diversity and building new kinds of solidarities – whether it be through conflict or dialogue, or a combination of both, will largely be worked out in working class communities, where the possibilities and day-to-day realities of creating other ways of living together are real and not rhetorical. It could be that the 'resources of hope' attaching to the emotional and social idea of community might help to build these alliances, and there is some evidence at least that the journey has begun.

This is not the only society-changing activity which those in the poorest neighbourhoods are taking on, however. The Blair government is now asking people to take responsibility for 'turning around' the communities in which they live. The challenge is directed at those living in some of the worst housing estates and pauperised neighbourhoods which, over the last twenty years particularly, have become home to the poorest among the working class, those dependent on state benefits and the long term unemployed, including young single mothers, badly educated and unskilled young men, some ethnic minority groups and those among the elderly who have no independent resources of their own (Social Exclusion Unit 1998).

The prospect of 'turning around' neighbourhoods like these can scarcely be imagined unless the process is related to major long-term policy commitments about the reallocation of resources and support – jobs, education, health care, hope, safety, quality of life – and about real partnerships between government and local people in which those on the front-line have serious involvement and real control over what happens to them. This is a journey which has a long and inauspicious history, during which time successive governments have busied themselves from the 1960s onwards with schemes concerning Urban Aid, Community Development Projects and Educational Priority Areas; then Urban Development Corporations and Task Forces in the 1980s; the Single Regeneration Budget in the 1990s and New Labour's National Strategy for Neighbourhood Renewal and New Deal for Communities in 1998. Let us hope, after a number of false starts, it is a journey which is at last gathering some greater commitment and momentum.

What usually gets overlooked in all of these discussions, however, except by feminists, is what happens, and what it feels like being part of something called 'community', from the standpoint of gender. Men and women experience these things differently. It is something Beatrix Campbell pays attention to in ways that raise interesting questions about working class masculinity and femininity (Campbell 1999). For example, how different versions of working class masculinity and femininity are associated with, reflect and affect, socio-spatial relations in working class localities, and how the changes which are taking place in working class neighbourhoods are also contributing to the re-negotiation of gender relations.

It is well known that more affluent and middle class residents can afford to live in places characterised by greater amounts of open space, personal privacy, access to good schools for their children and private capital resources. Poor and working class people, on the other hand, have their choices considerably curtailed. They are more likely to be found in areas that are marked by decline, blight, noise and pollution, where the housing stock, schools and material resources are poor in quality. Inequalities in economic resources and standards of living are, in this sense, closely related to and exacerbated by the very structure and arrangements of urban life (Social Exclusion Unit 1998). What is less obvious are the ways in which polarisation, based on social class and ethnic divisions, are also informed by gender considerations that exhibit enormous physical and symbolic significance in the material and cultural construction of masculinity and femininity.

Classic studies of working class communities have paid legendary attention to male solidarity and mutual identification, associated with heavy industry and physically dangerous occupations like mining and deep sea fishing (Dennis *et al.* 1956; Tunstall 1962). It was argued that reliance on each other in the workplace spilt over into close personal, social and political links outside of work; affecting almost every other aspect of life; creating a 'sense of community', in which 'structures of feeling' were embedded. Looked at from a feminist perspective, many of the 'good old values' associated with working class communities relied heavily on the invisible labour of women's economic, domestic, social, sexual and emotional energies. Within the most infamous and celebrated of these studies, gender differences and gender relations were noted, but rarely considered problematic, worthy of interest or requiring explanation. The association of men with waged labour and women with the home was largely taken for granted by Orwell and Hoggart who put it down to tradition, and then talked about tradition as though it were nature (Orwell 1937; Hoggart 1959). They did not wonder where women's subordination and dependency came from, or think to look for it in sexual inequalities on the home front.

Writing about the fishing industry in Hull, Jeremy Tunstall caricatured sexual politics in a way that was both male-centred and misogynist:

> The fisherman's wife organises her life around the task of bringing up her children – and this inevitably becomes in many ways more important than her other main task of looking after her husband during the [time] when he is ashore . . . when a fisherman comes home he disrupts the normal routine. At first this is welcome, he comes bearing gifts for the children. His coming is the main event by which the passage of time in the home is marked, he brings the family into focus . . . After he has been ashore a while the fisherman feels that certain pressures are being exerted on him to go back . . . The man inevitably finds himself differently regarded by his wife after a week or two from how she regarded him after a day or two . . . Does she only want him when he has money? When he is there more than a few days why does she grow weary of him? Why is he going to sea just to pay that ungrateful wife and her children? Legalised prostitution? One sees the point and it explains why fishermen say so often and so savagely that women are just 'money grabbing bitches' and less polite things. 'My wife is all "Gimme, Gimme",' one man commented.
>
> (Tunstall 1962)

The strength of feeling and of belonging to a place, associated with established working class communities, and which may well have contributed to keeping them going in the past, has been passed between generations in the traditions of hard work, struggle and sexual divisions that helped to shape the labour and trade union movements, and which, in a very real sense, came to be synonymous with what counted as organised, working class politics (Thompson 1968). But these were also the politics forged in masculinist organisations that were exclusionary, segregated and frequently off-putting to women. Women in working class communities have tended to experience life rather differently.

Now, as in the past, working class women's politics are more likely to come out of their radicalism in the domestic sphere, and especially in relation to housing, health and children. Fighting local authority landlords about tenants' issues; campaigning for play schools, nurseries and youth clubs; organising mother and toddler groups, self-help groups, drop-in centres and holiday play schemes; tackling vandalism, drugs and drug dealing; targeting women's health care, isolation and depression, domestic violence – all provide examples of militant self-help activities undertaken by women at the crisis points where sex and class oppression meet (Taking Liberties Collective 1989; McGivney 1990; Thompson 1995; Barr 1999b). This is political activity among groups frequently starved of the resources necessary for self-help and political action – money, authority, education, contacts in high places – in which activism is a gesture of defiance, however parochial, against traditional constructions of femininity, respectability and subordination.

No one who knew Lily Bilocca (see page 11) would recognise her from the description of fishermen's wives painted by Jeremy Tunstall. When she challenged the trawler owners for their failure to fit radios into boats working the dangerous seas off Iceland, which made it impossible for the crew to summon help if they were in difficulty, she met the resistance of employers who did not want to disclose the location of fish stocks to their competitors. She also experienced the total displeasure of fishermen whose interests in health and safety was secondary to the bonus payments they could earn, and whose terms and conditions of employment were not for women to negotiate. When Pat Sturdy (see page 35) tried to establish an Industrial Trade Union for women outside of the organised trade union movement, she encountered considerable resistance from those men who thought women in trade unions acted to depress wages, to reduce trade union militancy and to neglect their natural and proper duties as wives and mothers. Neither did they like the idea of single sex unions which men were not allowed to join. May Hobbs (see pages 35–7) got very little support from the Transport and General Workers' Union in her efforts to recruit black and white night cleaners to the union. In the early 1970s, recruiting women, part time workers and black workers was not seen as a priority by white male trade union organisers In practice, trade unions were highly separatist organisations which habitually, if not deliberately, excluded women.

When looked at from the standpoint of women, much of the mystique associated with romantic notions of working class unity becomes exposed. Working class men's politics has not paid attention to the same issues as women's, and involves no conflict with their masculine identity. In fact, it often enhances it. Women's femininity, on the other hand, is rooted in domestic life, which is also fuelled by men's sexual prejudice and privilege. According to Beatrix Campbell 'men and masculinity, in their everyday, individual manifestations, constitute a systematic bloc of resistance to the women of their own community and class. Both individual men and the political movements men have made within the working class are culpable' (Campbell 1984). Working class men's sexism, together with racism and craft chauvinism, have all served to spoil the Labour and trade union movements, leading to a form of collusion with capitalism in the interests of white, working class men's wages and privileges, and in ways that have distorted the Labour movement's capacity to deliver sexual equality or socialism (Thompson 1999a).

Most women know this. Working class women both accept and resent men's domination, but without independent resources, they are not in a strong position to do much about it – although they continue to try. When 'what counts as politics' is defined as being the politics of everyday life in households and communities, it is women who are usually the most thoughtful, imaginative and adaptable. It is women who seek out the most democratic and conciliatory ways of working. It is women who are impatient with rhetoric and bullshit that does not lead to action or change. It is women who are more likely to embrace changes and to become transformed by their own experiences of change (Campbell 1984; Taking Liberties Collective 1989).

After the Second World War, suburban housing estates built by councils for the 'respectable' working class, employed for the most part in manufacturing and craft industries, provided space, some trees, built-in cupboards, grocery deliveries from the Co-op van and plenty of responsibilities to keep them fully occupied. Such communities were the places from which men left in the morning to go to work and to which they returned in the evening to be fed and watered, before going out again to get organised (in union and party meetings), to get improved (in night classes) or to play (in pubs and social clubs) with other men. Less boisterous versions of the species, like my father, went into their sheds to make things from wood, or chatted over the garden fence to the man next door as they planted potatoes and cultivated chrysanthemums. In the 1950s, a period which Beatrix Campbell, with tongue-in-cheek, refers to as 'the golden age of fathering', when working class fathers were in their 'proper place' as breadwinners, and positioned in authority over working class families, it was estimated that such men spent on average eleven minutes a day with their children (Campbell 1999). Their typical role in the family was characterised by their absence and by the authority that derived from their financial role as breadwinners. Their masculinity was constructed in relation to the political economy of paid work, and in masculinist organisations like the local Labour party, the factory, the union, the pub, and the football terrace. These were institutions which, like the Stock Exchange, the Church of England, the Conservative Association, public schools, the Inns of Court, the Army, and the police force also served to construct masculinity in separatist organisations – not in relation to femininity – but in association with other men, in conditions of greater or lesser exclusivity, secrecy, latent militarism, rivalry and social solidarity.

Women of the respectable working class made the new estates their homes and got on with the business of bringing up their children, looking after their houses, servicing their men, relating to their neighbours and finding community with other women engaged in the same pursuits. Their economic dependency preserved the authority of men on the domestic front, as did the emotional and sexual servicing of men from within ideological constructs of femininity and motherhood that were based on taking care of others first, conjugal fidelity and obligations, domestic labour and the psycho-social development of identity and emotions within patriarchal power relations (Oakley 1983; Leonard and Delphy 1992). Respectable working class women like my mother also fitted part time paid employment into their busy domestic schedule because, contrary to popular belief, the average family wage, earned by the average male breadwinner in the 1950s and 1960s, did not meet the needs of the average working class family.

Women's lives in such communities were closely connected to those of other women who were living the same kinds of lives. Working class women, in a material sense, often had more in common with each other, than with the men they were married to. My paternal grandmother and her daughter regularly conspired to keep information, which was important to them, out of the consciousness of my grandfather, who was a bully and an autocrat. But the privatisation of family life usually served to discourage discussion about shared troubles outside the family in the name of loyalty, respectability or, in the case of my grandmother and her daughter, fear. My mother, an extrovert and gregarious woman, with a strong interest in helping others, has always been secretive, to the point of paranoia, about anyone else knowing about her problems. She is still a professional in the art of 'keeping up appearances' and in not 'letting the neighbours' know her business. From such commitment to privacy as a matter of pride, she has consistently failed to seek advice, support or comfort from other women about financial hardship, her only daughter being a lesbian, periods of serious ill health. It was not the loss of working class community, or the aspiration to be better than her neighbours in a material or class sense, which Wilmott and Young and Lockwood and Goldthorpe wrote about in the 1960s (Wilmott and Young 1962; Lockwood and Goldthorpe 1969), but more the values deriving from gendered and privatised notions of femininity, relating to respectability, loyalty and responsibility (Steedman 1986). The same kind of notions which, as well as fear, also served to silence countless other women of her generation, both working class and middle class, about domestic violence and abuse (Halmer and Maynard 1987).

Paradoxically maybe, it was my mother, as a consequence of her working class childhood in Scotland, who also taught me about socialism as an emotion, rather than an organising commitment. My maternal grandfather was a Christian communist, who walked miles to rallies addressed by Keir Hardie and who died of poverty and pneumonia in the days before the welfare state and National Health Service were invented. My grandmother worked as a cleaner in other people's houses, took in laundry, and scavenged in the market for bruised fruit and stale bread and buns to feed her family. In 1926 she helped to pull scabs off the buses in the General Strike. All of which predisposed my mother to keep our small family together, body and soul, to help others when she could, but not to get into political arguments, or enter into discussions about the triumphs and defeats of her everyday life, which women of my (feminist) generation subsequently considered so important to the understanding of class and gender politics on the home front.

Women like me might have been assigned our social class position in relation to our fathers' and – when relevant – our husbands' relationship to the means of production (using a Marxist definition) or in relation to occupation (using a social scientific definition) but I am sure we learnt much more about the meaning and reality of working class identity from the lives of our mothers and from the ways in which they and we negotiated our femininity. My defection, induced initially by education, and subsequently by feminist politics, was not about deserting my class, but rather, deserting the particular construction of femininity it made available to me. Fortunately my feminism also counteracted the worst consequences of being educated like a middle class boy at grammar school, and then university, and enabled me to re-value and reinterpret the work done by the women of my class in an entirely different light. I also came to see that official classifications, and historical and sociological definitions of social class have habitually failed to recognise the ways in which the lived experience of working class men and women is materially and emotionally very different. Profoundly different constructions of femininity and masculinity are created in the hegemonic gaps (Mouffe 1992) and subversive spaces between the private and the public sphere; the home and the workplace; ideologies of gender; the political economy of labour; and the domestic and emotional negotiations that take place within patriarchal relations on the home front. Negotiations which continue and change, by the way, as working class men and women inherit, create, reconstruct, make sense of and give meaning to patterns of identification and ways of relating to each other in shifting and altered circumstances.

Forty years later, peripheral housing estates similar to the one where I grew up have become very different places. The steady collapse of heavy industry, and then manufacturing, has changed the labour market fundamentally, and the gendered economic relations associated with it. In circumstances of growing structural unemployment, the role of the male breadwinner has largely disappeared. Working class women's long march into paid employment, when they can find it, now makes them a numerical majority in the labour market in many working class areas of the country, especially where men's jobs have declined. It is a labour market change which has not replaced men as such, but rather responded to the openings created in financial and commercial services, peripheral assembly work controlled by new technologies, retailing and privatised (social) services. Neither has it been at the expense of men and children. On the whole working class women's work is part time, and taken on the understanding that shared domestic duties and child care on the home front, and state or employer support on the work front, are not expected to be the necessary condition for doing it. Modern working class women, it seems, are reconciled to working in the public and the private spheres simultaneously, as they have always done. Working class men may now be more in evidence in the supermarket parking lot, may 'help' a little more with the housework, and spend on average almost four times longer with their children than they did in the 1950s. But no amount of academic research, even of the popular variety that gets reported in the tabloid press and women's magazines, and which sets out hopefully in search of the 'new man', has been able to amass much evidence to suggest any significant redistribution of domestic work and child care in dual income families (McDowell 1999).

In pauperised neighbourhoods, however, especially in those that once were called 'peripheral', and now get labelled 'sink', few people expect to be in regular and paid employment. These are the communities which the respectable working class, who struggled to get their children into grammar schools, craft apprenticeships and white collar jobs, were able, in the fullness of time, to evacuate.

When I left home after university and my first teaching job to move elsewhere, my parents put in for a council transfer to a smaller development on the other side of town, which during the Thatcher years they were invited to buy, along with a few shares in the privatised utilities to give them a stake in the capitalist system. My mother's union, in an effort to hold on to its declining membership under the assault from anti-union legislation and economic restructuring in the 1980s, also succumbed to the enterprise culture and provided a private health care plan. The respectable working class, like my parents, who had worked hard all their lives, who had never wanted to rock the boat, who always dreamed of getting out from under, were prime targets for the neo-liberal self-improvement and self-help strategies employed by the Tories to disengage the most aspiring from any residual loyalties to the collectivism of the organised working class. Whereas new front doors, elaborate porches, carports and double glazing behind Austrian nets now serve to differentiate privatised council housing from rented property, and to distance their occupants from the residents of pauperised neighbourhoods, it is unlikely that the accumulated privileges of traditional middle class existence have been significantly penetrated by such modifications. Whatever redistribution of council property, shares in privatised utilities, health insurance, and peaceful neighbourhoods have taken place over the last twenty years, they have not been out of resources donated by the affluent and comfortably off, but from within the allocation of housing possibilities and national assets (water, electricity and gas) once held by the state on behalf of everybody. Leaving less to go round for the poor; leaving the material and cultural capital of the affluent essentially undisturbed; and leaving people like my parents disciplined by the promise of something still beyond their grasp, as the goalposts keep on moving, and by the fear of slipping backwards.

In the process they left behind the vacant lets, into which working class families from inner cities undergoing slum clearance and gentrification in the 1960s and 1970s were relocated. When the best council housing stock was systematically sold off during the 1980s, at the same time as private housing prices soared, financial services expanded and the manufacturing industries declined, the houses that were left, and were the least commercially desirable, increasingly became the new detention centres for the poor. These are now appalling, dislocated wastelands, in which material resources are in scarce supply, in which public services have been cut and private capital withdrawn, in which housing stock, health and educational facilities are run down, and in which drug taking, street violence, domestic violence and crime appear to flourish (Social Exclusion Unit 1998). They are not now the places from which men leave in the morning to go to work and return in the evening to settled domestic units organised and normalised by women. They are more the places where men, women and children share, as never before in modern times, domestic and public space, frequently in competition with each other for scarce resources, contesting the changing landscape of ethnicity, class and gender; masculinity and femininity; childhood and adulthood; power and opportunity – in crisis conditions of material, cultural and spiritual poverty.

These are places and people that are easy to stigmatise and to hold responsible for their own demise, in ways that the 'undeserving poor', the 'culturally deprived', the 'disadvantaged', the 'scroungers', and the 'socially excluded' have always been. It is usually the men who receive the most attention, because their behaviour – albeit licensed by constructions of masculinity within a patriarchal society, and formed in masculinist assemblies characterised by rowdiness, exclusivity, secrecy, militarism, and power – is likely to pose the most danger to property and order. Women – as the mothers responsible for dangerous men, as the wives who have divorced them, and the young women who do not want them as fathers for their children – are assigned the most blame and the most responsibility, because they are likely to constitute the cheapest 'solution'.

The changing lives of men and women in working class communities are discussed in some detail by Campbell in *Goliath* (1993). In analysing some of the causes and characteristics of urban and neighbourhood riots in 1991 – especially in Cardiff, Tyneside and Oxford – she considers the political and economic consequences of economic restructuring, unemployment and regional decline in three different kinds of post-industrial landscape, sabotaged by capitalist realignment and the politics of Thatcherism. She is particularly interested in a wider set of questions about the social construction of masculinity and femininity and about what makes young, unemployed men, living in very different locations, turn on people and property within their own localities, to engage in arson, antisocial, criminal and violent activities, directed at fellow residents. She describes how women continue to do business in ways that display enormous resilience, courage and strength; and take on astonishing responsibilities in the face of mounting tensions associated with masculinity.

Campbell attributes part of this alleged 'crisis of masculinity' to the promotion of competitive individualism, economic aggression and social ruthlessness in national politics during the Thatcher years. Throughout this time, older ways of managing disagreements in a disciplined way, between common enemies in the class struggle, and which characterised politics in Britain after the Second World War, turned 'a national tone of what had always been a quarrelsome country' into something that was 'now reckless, butch and dangerous' (Campbell 1993). Campbell uses the term 'butch' advisedly, not simply as an ironic comment on the style adopted by Britain's first woman leader and in terms of the antisocial and violent behaviour of bully boys and hard men on the streets of pauperised neighbourhoods, but also in relation to the bullishness of hard men in the city and in corporate board rooms, where brutal take-overs and asset stripping, sanctioned by the enterprise culture of fast money and financial scandal, made 'lads' out of rich and poor alike. For young working class men, excluded by unemployment and poverty from the good life – and from the status and acquisitions it could provide – the only way to retain some of the accepted attributes of masculinity, she suggests, was through stealing and other forms of laddish behaviour.

She uses Oxford as an example, whose car industry once relied upon the Blackbird Leys estate to supply black and white labour, but which was also an industry closely associated with masculinity. Cars were made predominantly by men, for men, and throughout much of the twentieth century were closely identified, in the popular psyche, with modernity, mass production, conspicuous consumption and mobility. As the numbers of men in the Oxford works declined – from 30,000 to 5,000 in twenty years – the prosperity of the Blackbird Leys estate was devastated. Not only the livelihoods of families dependent on the car works for income, but also political and trade union affiliation, employment prospects and the identity of working class men were all but extinguished. The lads were effectively prevented from making cars, but it did not stop them from stealing them. This is how she describes the activities of young men from the Blackbird Leys estate in Oxford during the summer of 1991:

> The night boys defied the definition of a passive underclass: these young men weren't *under* anyone. Economically they were spare, surplus, personally they were dependent on someone else for their upkeep, usually their mothers; socially they were fugitives, whose lawlessness kept them inside and yet outside their own community. They had no jobs, no incomes, no property, no cars, no responsibilities. But that is not to say that they weren't busy, with their 'own business'. And what they did have was a reputation. In many ways they were the 'invisibles', their reputation derived nonetheless from being seen, from performing. Their vanity showed their valour. They planned, primed and timed a local drama that took place nightly in a small square.
>
> (Campbell 1993)

According to Campbell, 'car crime on the estate was about the relationship between young men and power, machinery, speed and transcendence'. Through theft and through the spectacle and danger of joy riding, young men reconstructed a type of masculine identity for themselves which their fathers had previously created in the workplace, but which economic decline and global changes in the location of car production had destroyed.

Meanwhile women went about their business. Partly in defence of their men, partly in defence of their communities. The ease and frequency with which the bad behaviour of boys gets blamed on mothers leaves women with responsibility for the kinds of masculinity over which they have never had much control. It is the kind promoted by the powerful men in their sons' lives – other lads, their fathers, the police, the politicians, prison officers and the judiciary. Without social systems offering much support or an alternative analysis, working class women continue to manage life for their men as they have always done. A lawyer interviewed by Campbell in *Goliath* explains the relationship between men and women in pauperised neighbourhoods like this.

> When the men get into trouble, or when their wives want them out, it is their wives and mothers who make the arrangements. The men won't go

> to their solicitors, they won't liaise with the housing department, they won't liaise with their kids' schools. It's the women who make the appointments, it's the women who call to cancel the men's appointments, it's the women who make the apologies. We have women ringing up saying the men want to know what's happening to their case, or when he's due in court. What is absolutely astonishing about these tough men is that they have to have their slippers under some woman's bed. The men cannot make out on their own. The reality is that children in this community do not grow up seeing men do any of the coping, caring or standing on their own two feet.
>
> (Campbell 1993)

The response to poverty and unemployment are made manifest in the different ways in which men and women deal with their distress. The criminal response of masculinity is typically exclusive, secretive, coercive and destructive. Its rewards are the appropriation of material provisions, commodities and identity. The challenge which it makes is not to the capitalist or state systems which created the circumstances and crises which men experience, but to the communities in which they live, and frequently to the women with whom they live. According to Campbell, 'the criminal fraternity is nothing if not about the means by which coteries of men constitute their dominance' as patriarchy has always sought to do. Women, on the other hand, respond to poverty and its related distress through self-help networks that are sustained by voluntary action and support groups. More people join self-help groups and than join political parties and the majority of them are women (Giddens 1994). Women's ways of working are more likely to be open, expansive, egalitarian and incipiently democratic (Cockburn 1998). As such they challenge the systems which have bearing upon local and domestic life. Whilst crime and coercion are sustained by men, solidarity and self-help are sustained by women. The contrast and the implications are enormous.

It is, of course, easier to blame women for the crisis in masculinity, than to question the patriarchal ways in which masculinity gets constructed as a potentially dangerous and violent gender, not in relation to femininity, but in relation to other men, over which women have never had much influence or control and certainly no power. It is easier to blame women than to contemplate the social and economic price that has been paid, at a local level, in order to promote free market economics and related social policies at a national and global level. It is ideologically easier to appeal to women, as mothers and lovers of boys and men, to do what capitalism is unprepared to do, what the state is unwilling to do, what patriarchy has no reason to do, because constructions of motherhood and femininity within patriarchy and heterosexuality make it very difficult for women to imagine an alternative.

Having a woman as prime minister did not help. Once Margaret Thatcher announced that she was a prime minister rather than a woman, we knew we were in for another honorary man with no sense of responsibility to her sex or any intention of taking other women with her into power. When she declared that there was 'no such thing as society' she also gave considerable credence to the politics of aggressive and competitive individualism and to the death of grand narratives as a way of conceptualising structural power differences. Once John Major talked about a classless society, and whilst Tony Blair attempts to find 'a third way' through the minefield of 'old fashioned' ideas, based on class interests and class based politics, pauperised neighbourhoods have become increasingly difficult to discuss in the language of previous discourses to do with capitalism, social class and patriarchy.

The strategy advocated by the New Right, traditional Conservatives and New Labour alike, which seeks to 'cure' the crisis in masculinity, especially in pauperised neighbourhoods, is to put such men back at the head of traditional families, where their legitimate authority and status can once again be recognised, their rights and responsibilities as fathers can be guaranteed, and where women can be expected to do what women have always done – attempt to keep everybody going and keep everybody happy (Dennis and Erdos 1992; Halsey and Young 1995). Even if it is at a cost to themselves, in terms of equality and safety, and despite the long march of women out of relationships of economic dependency and sexual oppression. Cuts in single parent benefits, parent education schemes, street curfews on children, fines imposed on parents whose children do not attend school, or who do damage in the neighbourhood, and the rehabilitation of fathers as role models at the head of two-parent families, all serve to impose conventionally gendered, and considerably idealised, family-centred solutions. These are 'solutions' which are expected to somehow resolve the consequences of continuing and long term poverty, in neighbourhoods existing without plentiful supplies of decent or properly paid employment, depleted resources, minimal facilities, collapsed infrastructures, increasing hopelessness and violence taken out against each other. All of them conditions which cumulatively demoralise communities and sap the will to live.

Charles Murray, the right wing American sociologist, infamous for his racist views about black Americans' genetic inferiority compared to whites, has also made influential and equally dubious pronouncements about the disappearance of working class fathers, leading to the moral and functional decline of working class families (Murray 1989; 1990). These are views which have contributed to right wing fundamentalist and, more recently, New Labour preoccupations with the alleged 'crisis in masculinity' and the pathology of pauperised individuals, in preference to addressing the many repercussions of structural dislocation and economic decline, as late capitalism organises to reposition itself for greater control and profit on a global scale. Strange bedfellows, including the former deputy leader of the Tory party Peter Lilley, American communitarian Amitai Etzioni, right wing philosopher and writer Roger Scruton, 'ethical socialist' Norman Dennis, Oxford based sociologist, and erstwhile socialist, A. H. Halsey, and *Sunday Times* journalist Melanie Phillips, have all weighed in with arguments depicting family dysfunction, absentee fathers unmanned by poverty and feminism, irresponsible and promiscuous mothers who emasculate fathers and conceive children simply to secure council flats, and out of control and terrifying children seeking revenge (Phillips 1991; Dennis and Erdos 1992; Halsey and Young 1995). The stereotypes are harsher than those which were prevalent in the 1970s and which tended to caricature the poor as feckless and stupid. Today's deviants are seen as altogether more self-conscious, wilful and deceitful in their intentions; more criminally committed to immorality, fraud, and dangerous violence.

The plan to put men back at the head of the family is also a 'solution' conceived within discourses that are deeply embedded in the masculinist politics of both Right and Left. Discourses which do not offer any insight or possibility about a different or more democratic settlement between men and women, other than that predicated on the political economy of work, and on the construction of masculinity in separatist and masculinist organisations. In the longer term, a different kind of settlement between men and women must be created which has the possibility of transforming both genders.

In a society increasingly said to be 'classless', the bottom 30 per cent of the population, which Will Hutton identifies as being unlikely to expect economic independence ever again in the lifetime of their communities (Hutton 1995), is regularly described in policy documents as socially excluded: those who exist on the fringes of New Britain, as an 'underclass' of homeless individuals, criminal young men, single mothers and their children, the long term unemployed, welfare dependants and a growing elderly population without savings or other independent means (Social Exclusion Unit 1998). Contained within and defined by such categories, it has become common, in the context of post-Marxist, postmodernist and post-feminist times, to dump the language of 'race', class and gender divisions – and the related debates about economic redistribution, the political accumulation of cultural capital, institutionalised racism, socialist alternatives and women's liberation – into the dustbin of history. As if they are passé or no longer relevant. And with them, the recognition of roots, allegiances, common understandings and collective memories that give rise to different analyses, to political movements born out of oppression and injustices, and to social movements concerned with people's survival and resistance.

Described by some as 'the last great modernist', Anthony Giddens' ideas could help to salvage some socialist values, including the intention to redistribute resources, power and life chances and to 'democratise democracy', through 'social reflexivity', 'generative politics', 'repairing damaged solidarities', 'opening up spaces for dialogue', 'combating violence' and promoting social participation and inclusion as a set of 'utopian realisms' (Giddens 1994). Here in different language can be found an analysis of the problems and possibilities of late modernity for the reassertion of human agency in a seemingly overdetermined world. It is one way forward for the Left. In the meantime, the sort of resilience which is kept alive on anger and compassion, and on the very human search for connection, with roots in what Raymond Williams liked to call the resources of hope (Williams 1989) can help to build a renewed and radical consensus around what Jürgen Habermas calls the claims of the lifeworld over and against those of the systems world

(Welton 1995). Both contain assumptions about politics that sit much more coherently with the political strengths of women in working class communities and with the kinds of values and debates that have been forced into the discursive domain by, among others, community activists and the women's movement during the last thirty years.

9

ON CONSCIOUSNESS AND CONTRADICTIONS

In the first part of this book I included various accounts of my own experience. Writing about experience, one's own history, is never a simple or uncomplicated affair. It involves selection, interpretation and memory, 'a complex interplay between the self writing now and the self recalled then, at different stages of personal history' (Barr 1999a). The stages are also constructed in relation to an ordering of priorities, political preoccupations, meanings and emotional understanding, as well as social context, political consciousness and expressions of identity. Together they produce ideas that are shaped by their context, but which also provide a way of thinking through connections, interrogating possibilities in the present and re-imagining the future.

Auto/biographical writing of this kind is another kind of data and can be another way of revealing how individuals and groups give meaning to and make sense of their lives. It can help to expose complexity and contradiction in the human condition and to show how any number of different ingredients are involved in shaping and negotiating what emerges.

Auto/biographical writing is richer if it is able to reveal that there are many and various responses to the forces that determine – some times over-determine – a person's life. By approaching auto/biographical writing in different ways, which derive from different emotions or experiences, it is possible to explore the complex ways in which individuals are sometimes influenced, sometimes resistent, multifaceted and socially reflexive participants in everyday life. Anthony Giddens has said,

> a world of intensified reflexivity is a world of clever people. I don't mean by this that people are more intelligent than they used to be. In a post traditional order, individuals more or less have to engage with the wider world if they are to survive in it. Information produced by specialists (including scientific knowledge) can no longer be confined to specific groups, but becomes routinely interpreted and acted on by lay individuals in the course of their everyday actions.
>
> (Giddens 1994)

Not only does this have tremendous implications for the reassertion of human agency in a seemingly 'runaway world' (Giddens 1999), it also adds an important urgency to debates about consciousness and about informal learning – from life and through social action.

Understanding consciousness and the ways in which we give meanings to emotions and events is important. Michael Newman puts it this way:

> Experience is complex, and reflecting on experience is complex also. We construct and reconstruct our experience, falsify it, break it up into episodes, allocate to each episode particular truths of our own, and so set ourselves in conflict with others . . . At some stage we decide that a particular truth will do for a particular experience and leave it at that . . . Some [people] seem able to break free from the trap of reflecting on their own experience and engage in critical thinking. Critical thinking may take a person's own experience into account but will include much else besides. Critical thinking is reflection on experience of another order altogether.
>
> (Newman 1999)

Usually the relationship between experience, reflection and critical thinking is not so neat. Sometimes it is what is missing from a life, or from the account of a life, which is more revealing than what is reflected upon and made explicit. There are several kinds of absence, some of them material, some of them emotional. There are the things that do not get said, the feelings that are not acknowledged, the absences of information, the events that are not included in the story for one reason or another. These are the absences, discontinuities and gaps which often come to light in the writing process. Sometimes they are highly significant, providing moments of being and illumination. Sometimes they are moments of not knowing, breathing spaces, places of temporary 'nothingness' in which it is possible to make discoveries, learn from experience, work out what to do next; moments Virginia Woolf might have recognised when she wrote, 'it is in our idleness, in our dreams, that the submerged truth sometimes comes to the top'.

Often this process is not entirely conscious, rational or logical. Sometimes it is against our will. Sometimes it provides a connection with the unconscious and with the arrangements of a person's internal world which can be challenging, distressing or liberating. The process is never simple. It reveals the kind of complexity which is not the prerogative of those who are highly educated or socially privileged, although having the opportunity to write about it might be.

According to Carolyn Steedman (1986), one of the problems and consequences of writing about the working class as a category has been to imply homogeneity, and to attribute to the group, characteristics born of generalisations that obscure the psychological complexity of individuals – whatever their class or condition – and which fail to recognise that what might seem like 'common experiences' are none the less experienced differently and uniquely so far as individuals are concerned. Writing about groups as a category also robs them of their individual histories and of ways of discussing and understanding the relationship between their own and other, shared experiences in the creation of culture and identity. As members of a group or as individuals, the working class are rarely asked to write about themselves. Writing about the self – in the context of critical thinking – does not imply bourgeois individualism, as Newman comments:

> we may strive to be monarchs but the truth of our existence is to be found in our lives along with others. It is in the consciously examined company of others that we will most effectively reflect, learn, survive and transcend.
>
> (Newman 1999)

In the accounts I have given from experience there are numerous omissions, some of which are incidental, many of which would be relevant to this discussion if you knew about them. But in the end, I am not writing about me. The themes are women, class and education. I have tried to situate myself in the subject matter of the writing, partly because I have learnt things from experience and from life which inform my knowledge and my argument; partly because I am aware, upon reflection, that the meanings I attach and the significance I apportion to events and interpretations have changed over time – which has a bearing on consciousness; and partly because information about the context of a life declares the investment in what I am writing about.

It is no longer necessary, and was never a very good idea, to treat those who are the subject matter of research as objects, in ways that are divorced from the complexity of human existence and from how real lives are lived, or to effect some kind of neutrality. It is a malestream legacy which has detached itself from its own ways of knowing, as if it is possible to produce objective knowledge about an independent social reality without recognising that the very process of doing so influences what the reality actually is. Interpreted in a limited way, auto/biograpical and socially reflexive writing can be irritating – a checklist of 'what I did and didn't do and why'. It can appear narcissistic. It can even get in the way of understanding how meanings are made and knowledge is produced within particular social structures and social processes. But with careful elaboration, and some sense of critical consciousness, the recognition by a writer or researcher of being part of the process seems to me an altogether more honest way of seeking understanding. These days I always tell my students when they are choosing dissertation topics to 'put themselves in the picture' and I always maintain, in my old fashioned, radical feminist way, that as women writing and researching about our lives, we have a responsibility to add something, however small, to the store of human knowledge, in an effort not only to understand the world, but also to change it. This means putting women's different voices 'on the record', taking seriously different women's lives and ways of knowing, and approaching knowledge and action as praxis. In choosing to write this book in this way I have tried to take my own advice for once.

In re-reading my reflections, what becomes clear is the extent to which my views and actions at any one time are partly a product of their time. To some extent they are shaped by the historical and social context in which I have been living. They owe quite a lot to my social class origins, my ethnicity, my gender and my sexuality. Strong emotional roots in working class politics and culture predisposed me, from an early age, to view the world politically. Being a working class child in a middle class school; a woman in a man's world; a lesbian in a heterosexist society; an activist during a period of Tory government which attempted to curtail active democratic participation in politics; an advocate of education for social transformation, critical thinking and emancipation in an era of technical training and dumbing down – have all given me sufficient experiences of marginal locations and minority status to develop some empathy with others in similar positions. And also, some enthusiasm for contesting conventional wisdoms about women, class, sexuality and education. Allegiance to the women's movement has always created subversive spaces for collective resistance and encouraged imaginative activities within hegemonic gaps (Mouffe 1992). While this adds to the possibilities for active dissent, it also draws upon the significance of non-rational influences on ideas and actions, originating in emotional and unconscious sources and an inner life. It can reveal important knowledge and feelings about the nature of contradiction.

This chapter makes some attempt at least to explore consciousness and contradictions in the light of what I have learnt from my own experience, and is discussed in relation to theoretical insights that are helpful in analysing and elaborating their wider significance.

As a child, I was one of those who benefited from the introduction of free secondary education, and who came from a respectable working class family that put its faith in education as the main route out from under, towards knowledge, social mobility and economic prosperity. However, I also carried with me the legacy of loyalties, strong feelings, unfulfilled desires, commitments drawn from previous generations, as a profound and early influence on my ways of thinking about, and being, in the world. Before I had a language with which to debate my opposition to injustice, my animosity towards gratuitous social and economic privilege and my automatic allegiance to those who have least power in society, I already had the structure of feelings and the roots of consciousness around which to build arguments and ideas that eventually shaped the 'words' to make sense of the 'things' I felt strongly about.

As a young teacher, attached to my working class beginnings, and influenced by the politics of the New Left which I discovered at university in the 1960s, I regarded my job as some kind of political responsibility to be exercised on behalf of others who, unlike me, had not been given the opportunity to escape the limitations of their class destiny. Not for me incorporation into the value systems of the middle class. I thought of my educational inheritance as a weapon to be used in the war against structural inequalities and political oppression. The military metaphors sit uneasily with me these days. Their origins derive from the literature and persuasion of the socialist groups I frequented at the time, which were, in retrospect, extremely masculinist in organisation and composition. It was the language of class conflict and class struggle. When I hear the Principal of Ruskin make frequent and fervent metaphorical allusions to the sports field and the battleground – as in 'kicking something', or more usually 'somebody', 'into touch' or 'taking them to the wire' I know his references, devoid, in his case, of much commitment to political resistance and solidarity, still resonate in smoke filled rooms and originate in the same sexist, adversarial and macho bravado I have come to abhor. In those days, however, I still thought that being a socialist meant using the language of armed struggle. Sometimes I called myself a Marxist (not yet a feminist), regarded Tories as the class enemy, and was scathing about the limitations of liberalism as any kind of political analysis from which to contemplate radical social transformation.

Yet I was romantically attached to progressivism as a force for change, and in the context of schooling, to comprehensive education as a way of redressing social inequalities as well as changing individual lives. I was not alone. Prominent leaders of the Campaign for Comprehensive Education at the time included the Marxist Professor of Education at the University of Leicester, Brian Simon; the Maoist Head of the Education Department at Coventry College of Education, Peter Mauger; and Caroline Benn, wife of the left wing Labour MP Tony Benn. Of course we all viewed education as a 'site of struggle', in which the capacity to fulfil the historic concern of the ruling class to 'gentle the masses' was being contested in an effort to provide the 'really useful knowledge' and critical intelligence with which the masses could anticipate and engage in the 'practice of freedom' (Freire 1973a). Restructuring the education system along comprehensive lines, so as not to reflect and therefore reproduce the class system – as the tripartite system had done – seemed like a good Marxist (structuralist) response to social inequality as we then defined it.

Unlike liberals, we did not pin all our hopes on education to adjust the value system of society and bring about the attitude changes necessary to encourage more equality. We knew that social class originated in material conditions that related to the ownership and control of the means of production and the exploitation of paid labour. The redistribution of wealth, power and resources in society remained top of our list of political priorities. We still believed that the class struggle was most likely to be won or lost at the point of production, and put great faith in communist and socialist militants in the labour and trade union movements – rather than the Labour party or trade union leadership – to develop their class consciousness and exercise some kind of influence over the proletariat in the struggle against capitalist employers and the capitalist state.

But also, having read widely, we knew the importance attaching to education as ideology in the construction and control of dominant ideas and values, making schools into what Althusser called an ideological state apparatus, to be contested, not only in the material but also in the ideological sense. In addition, education represented resources to be redistributed to those who structurally received the least from what was potentially available. A combination of increased economic resources, brought about by the redistribution of wealth, and increased intellectual resources, brought about by the redistribution of educational opportunities would, we believed, be the most effective assets available to the working class in their struggle to overcome exploitation and class oppression. As such, comprehensive schools provided left wing teachers, like myself, with the opportunity to put our political commitments into practice, which was, of course, precisely the anxiety that liberals, traditionalists and conservatives had about us. In fact, it all proved to be much more difficult, complex and contradictory than we imagined, and did not, inevitably, achieve the kind of consequences we anticipated. Although there are any number of immensely good comprehensive schools and seriously dedicated teachers, the way in which the comprehensive system was introduced, without doing anything about private education and the public school system, has exacerbated the division between the two and actually strengthened the class divide. As a result, selection by ability has been replaced by selection by the ability to pay, and within the state system, by access to specific catchment areas through house ownership.

Some years later, as a lesbian-feminist and parent, negotiating the education system on behalf of the children I loved and helped to take care of, I wanted to support a sustained critique of racist, ruling class and patriarchal systems of knowledge and power in schools, and I wanted my children to be happy and to flourish. The former seemed to me a perfectly logical and rational agenda – albeit a minority view, to be supported by passionate commitment, argument and evidence. The latter was dependent on a number of unacknowledged contradictions. In my conscious mind, there was no doubt about it. Racism, ruling class hegemony and patriarchal systems of knowledge and power were wrong and had to be challenged in order to effect change. At home my children were greatly loved and grew up in an atmosphere in which they developed a strong sense of injustice about discrimination and prejudice; in which they were surrounded by people who held similar values to do with anti-racism, non-violence, sexual equality and socialism. At home they were self-confident in their difference from most of the other children they knew, and they were safe. And I, naively and mistakenly in retrospect, imagined this was enough to get them through. But of course at school and outside the home, the pressures and the conflicts of being of mixed parentage and living in a radical feminist and socialist inclined, lesbian family, in one of the whitest and most conservative parts of Britain, did not make it easy for them to be happy or to flourish, and led to contradictory emotions all round, which my contemporary assessment of patriarchy, materialism and political struggle did not help me to identify, or to understand, until it was far too late.

At the time my assumptions about the importance of consciousness owed considerably to Marx. Marxist theory presumes that political consciousness derives from material conditions and makes a distinction between 'true consciousness' in which individuals understand the class nature of their material circumstances and their relationship to others who share the same conditions, and who then act together in the interests of their class towards the goal of liberation, and 'false consciousness' whereby individuals do not understand where – or in solidarity with whom – their true interests lie, and consequently act in ways that defeat the prospect of class solidarity and liberation. It is a model which sets great store by the application of logic to the connection between experience, understanding and action and which delineates a clear distinction between the correct political position and the incorrect.

Freire distinguishes between the kind of 'naive consciousness' that comes from being trapped in oppressive cultures and by experiences that are controlled, constrained and externally determined, leading to fatalism and silent resignation, and 'conscientisation', whereby we become aware – through the development of critical consciousness – of the world as something which can be changed (Freire 1973b). Learners can stop being objects of social history and become subjects of their own destiny.

Paula Allman, taking her inspiration from Marx, Gramsci and Freire, explains human consciousness as something arising out of dialectical relationships with people, events and objects in the social world which can be made to be 'more critical' (Allman 1999). This, she says, 'is the necessary basis for transforming educational relations and developing forms of engagement that can lead to, and eventually bring about, justice for all humankind'. Following Freire she is certain that critical education for social change implies cultural action in which ideas and ideologies also need to be challenged. Following Gramsci, unless the oppressed and exploited have the tools to challenge dominant ideas they risk being locked into the present and unable to imagine alternatives for the future. In the writings of both Gramsci and Freire the language of criticism connects with the language of change in the concept of praxis – the point is to be able to undertake social action as a consequence of enhanced critical insight in order to bring about social change. The language of critique also relates to the language of possibility, in that education for liberation is about increasing people's abilities to reflect critically on their situation, in order to see the possibilities for acting to transform it. As allies in this endeavour, the oppressed need educators committed to the process of dialogue – dialogue that connects theoretical and experiential learning and also theoretical and reflexive practice. Both educators and oppressed groups need a critical understanding of the relationship between ideological struggles and material struggles in order to effect transformation.

The implicit assumption in all of this, however, is that 'accurate information' exists which can be rationally and systematically identified, controlled through understanding and explication, and which in turn will lead to transformation. Critical sociology and academic feminism taught me that what counts as accurate information was produced historically in social situations in which dominant ideas reflected the interests of ruling (white, middle class and male) groups and was in time organised by them into 'recognised bodies of knowledge' (Spender

1982b). This was knowledge that must therefore be contested, as should the ownership of particular kinds of (high status) knowledge; it should be reconstructed and redistributed in the interests of subject (black, working class and women's) groups.

In practice, such endeavour was always in opposition to ruling ideas and mainstream values, and critical of all kinds of conventional wisdom about inequalities and inevitabilities in the human condition. It was a philosophy based on certainty and conviction, leaving little room for doubt. It still forms the basis of my commitment to critical intelligence and the desire to democratise and develop – in the process of education – capacities for critical thinking in those who are usually excluded from the places where definitions and decisions about their lives get made. But it is nonetheless a model which, in its unreconstructed form, relies upon the exercise of logic and rationality, and on assumptions about the unitary, self-regulating human subject. It has not had a lot to say about the emotions or the feelings – especially when they display symptoms of ambivalence, contradiction, anxiety or guilt; and it has had nothing – until more recently – to say about the illogical, the irrational, the subconscious or the unconscious.

The problem with all of this, as I now see – having spent years espousing these views myself – is that they could be read as being simply 'the other side of the coin' of liberal humanism – a world view which is anathema to all self-respecting Marxists and radical educators alike. I say this because both are based on the assumption, in the end, that humanity is characterised and defined by the ability to think (therefore I am) and act rationally, on the basis of reason and logic, in a linear and progressive manner towards an anticipated outcome. Liberal humanism may concentrate on individual choice, freedom and personal responsibility, whilst Marxism emphasises the significance of material conditions and oppressive structural forces in shaping social relations, but both assume an intellectual model, based on the creation and control of ideas as the key to consciousness and as the pre-requisite for informed action. Although liberal humanism and Marxism have different world views, different allegiances, different visions of utopia and are deeply critical of each other, they both derive from the same western intellectual, enlightenment tradition which privileges mind over matter, reason over emotion, attaches greater significance to culture than nature and regards the human subject as unitary, rational and capable of exercising self-control. Both have built their opposing theories on common assumptions about a dualism in the relationship between the individual and society.

The relationship, it now seems to me, is much more complex than this, especially in its emotional content, and the extent to which feelings help to shape the meanings which people attach to the ideological, social and material conditions in which they find themselves. One's identification with a class or set of conditions is rarely static or uncomplicated. It would be unusual to imagine being simply the sum total of one's class, or sex or 'race' or gender. Neither do shared conditions automatically create common understandings or identical psychologies. Conditions also change, as do our perceptions of them, the meanings we attribute to them, the significance we attach to contradictions, and the related identities we adopt, inhabit, and relinquish along the way. I do believe that recognition – as a form of consciousness – is an important element in the relationship between social existence and political action, although I now understand that political and cultural roots, feelings and emotional resources, personal experiences, meanings and ideas, the sense of being both 'within' and 'against' at the same time – and all of them in various combinations – add enormously to material conditions in the making and remaking of the kinds of consciousness that can be used to change lives.

Contradiction is treated by Marxist analysis as a structural weakness, indicating conflict, difference, inconsistency, or the absence of connection between two aspects of social structure or processes within a social whole. Such contradiction is said to be responsible for the dynamic properties of society. The assumption that all phenomena are composed of opposites is one of the three laws of dialectic materialism, which is often applied to history and to the analysis of political and social change. Marx argued that in all modes of production prior to communism, a contradiction eventually develops between the forces of production and the relations of production. The ensuing contradiction is expressed in, and eventually resolved by, class conflict, leading to revolutionary struggle, new relations of production and a new cycle of change. The process is logical, linear, inevitable and cumulative. Michael Newman gives a number of more contemporary examples.

> Using dialectical analysis we can examine certain objects and ideas that may appear to have no connection at all, such as colour and size, or justice and time, and deduce relationships. We can examine pairs of opposed objects or ideas which reflect each other, such as white people and black people, or the First World and the Third World, or small and large. In these pairs, each object or idea implies the existence of the other. The First World depends on there being a Third World, and vice versa. Remove either one and the other concept becomes meaningless . . . White people and black people, men and women, the First World and the Third World – the objects or ideas within these contradictory pairs often exist in an unequal power relation to each other. Dialectical analysis enables us to form an understanding of these power relationships by identifying the parties in the relationship and examining what mediates that relationship.
>
> (Newman 1999)

It is all very neat, very convenient and logical – in liberal humanistic terms, all very yin and yang. But again, the concept of contradiction, used in this way, still draws heavily upon the enlightenment tradition of rational thought and binary divisions. Within liberal humanism, opposites are frequently viewed as complementary, one without the other is meaningless, together they make up the interdependent, organic whole. This has been a particularly useful conclusion for those who have wished to promote and preserve the western industrialised, (hetero)sexual division of labour between men and women, with all its attendant inequalities, as being, nonetheless, 'complementary' when it comes to getting things done. Within Marxism, opposites usually display conflicting interests that put them into conflict with each other, out of which comes struggle, leading to social change. The proposition that something is both the case and not the case at the same time leads to all argument and theory in scientific knowledge being systematically scrutinised in order to eliminate the presence of contradiction, for any proposition which involves or leads to contradiction is a logically impossible account of the world when looked at purely from the logical relationship between statements. Marx built on the alleged logical tension created by contradiction as an indication of friction or conflict, leading to social change. But he wanted to believe that, under communism, all contradictions would be eradicated and the need for further political change would become superfluous.

Despite the influence of my intellectual training, however, I was learning rather different lessons from my own experience, about the ways in which the historic production of grand narratives and self-directing, autonomous, rational knowledge paid little or no attention to the concerns and life histories of women. When I talked with women at the Women's Education Centre in Southampton, in consciousness raising groups and in political campaigns to do with domestic violence, lesbian custody and rape, for example, I learned a lot about the ways in which new knowledge can be constructed through discussion, telling stories, sharing experience, imagining alternatives and trying them out. This was both emotional and practical knowledge as well as revolutionary theory. It did not fit the previous mould. But because I was still caught within its intellectual grip, I did my best to press it into shape.

It seems stunning to me in retrospect, being well practised in both the enlightenment and Marxist intellectual traditions myself, that I could, at the same time, consistently repress major contradictions in my own life and in my analysis of life, which quite escaped my notice or my consciousness for years. Not in the strictly Marxist sense that social discrepancies in wealth and power, for example, are the kind of contradictions that help to mobilise opposition among those who have the least amount of either, and hence the most to gain, from collective social action in pursuit of their redistribution. My self-defined responsibility as a cultural worker, helping to democratise education, to identify 'really useful knowledge' and to develop the capacity for critical thinking among those most socially and politically oppressed, was kept alive on the presumption that such obvious contradictions must fuel consciousness for change, in which radical education can play its part in assisting liberation. I am thinking more in the emotional sense – that when the logical, linear, inevitable and cumulative consequence of pursuing particular kinds of action in pursuit of change did not achieve the anticipated outcomes – that lesbian families can live as easily and normally as heterosexual families, for example – they gave rise to various feelings of ambivalence, anxiety, contradiction and guilt. But rather than doubting their logical, ultimate inevitability, I simply pushed myself to try harder. Even when it seemed as though the inevitable outcomes had been achieved – for example the capacity to deny emotional dependency, possessiveness and the petit bourgeois preoccupation with serial monogamy in favour of multiple relationships in which jealousy and possession are proscribed – it took me a long time to recognise the disparity between espousing the ideas and reconciling the related emotions. The contradiction between an intellectual commitment to sexual autonomy and profound emotional distress to do with insecurity and loss, was always enormous, because few of us, actually, can tolerate the pain and vulnerability which such uncertainty can bring. But it was not to be spoken about or acknowledged until a long time after the emotional damage had been done.

What strikes me now is how pervasive was the energy directed towards criticism and the certainty attached to reason, how vehement was my critique and condemnation of all things dominant and mainstream, and yet how wedded had I unconsciously become to the very ways of knowing that I wanted to condemn. I have often quoted in my writing and my teaching the words of Audre Lorde, and her observation that 'the master's tools will never dismantle the master's house' (Lorde 1981) in order to encourage irreverence, imagination and subversion, and the productive use of 'creative anger', another of Lorde's insights, in pursuit of critical thinking and social change, without fully realising the significance of her perception in relation to my own intellectual commitment. As if the knowledge which comes from experience and struggle in everyday life can only be legitimised when accorded the status of theory, and only then, in the context of rational and sustained debate.

Throughout the 1970s and 1980s humanistic psychology presented one of the biggest challenges to Marxist structuralism, critical sociology and the kind of socialist feminism that made sense to me in the 1970s. In adult education, the ideas of Carl Rogers and Abraham Maslow were used to underpin theories of adult learning, and sat quite comfortably amidst the prevailing liberal tendencies associated with 'the great tradition' (Wallis 1996) and much of the evening class, community education, literacy and basic skills provision sponsored by local education authorities in the aftermath of the Russell Report (Russell 1973). Both Maslow and Rogers were concerned with how individuals develop their human potential most effectively, as a process of individual growth, towards 'self actualisation' (Maslow 1968) and 'becoming a person' (Rogers 1961). This development was seen as an essentially individual and psychological process, which had little to say about social structure or social difference, although the writing of both is full of negative assumptions about difference, usually expressed as distinctions between those who do, and those who do not make it, in the 'serious human being' stakes.

Maslow constantly contrasts ordinary people 'who need others', with self-actualising people who do not. He identifies human needs hierarchically, with food and shelter at the bottom, and self-actualisation – identified as autonomy and not needing others – at the top. Self-actualising people are those who 'make up their own minds, come to their own decisions. Are responsible for themselves and their own destinies . . .' They are eminently more valuable than those who do not

> make up their own minds, but have their minds made up for them by salesmen, advertisers, parents, propagandists, TV, newspapers and so on. They are pawns to be moved by others, rather than self moving, self determining individuals. Therefore they are apt to feel helpless, weak and totally determined: they are the prey for predators, flabby whiners, rather than self determining persons.
>
> (Maslow 1968)

Despite the veneer of egalitarianism in liberal humanism, there is much talk from both Maslow and Rogers about 'higher' levels of motivation and 'superior' human beings. In *Motivation and Personality*, Maslow asks,

> Could these self actualising people be more human, more revealing of the original nature of the species type in the taxonomical sense? Ought a biological species be judged by its crippled, warped, only partially developed specimens, or by examples that have been over domesticated, caged, trained?
>
> (Maslow 1970)

It is surprising, in retrospect, to believe that these kinds of view were so inspirational to adult educators in the 1970s, but illuminating about the intellectual and ideological context in which negative and stereotypical descriptions became the substance of pathological definitions of educational disadvantage, leading to arguments in favour of behaviour modification through education, rather than economic and educational redistribution and positive discrimination in favour of the poor.

What Maslow calls 'self actualising', Rogers calls 'becoming a person' and identifies as the capacity to achieve emotional self-sufficiency and the determination to pursue one's own individually defined goals. The implication is that a process of personal change and individual effort can lead to individual liberation and fulfilment – and ultimately – the abolition of nasty things like poverty or sexual and racial oppression, because having become a person, individuals will not let themselves be affected by them anymore. On one occasion Rogers claimed that the problems of Northern Ireland could be solved if only sufficient trained humanistic counsellors would go there and hold encounter groups on every street corner (Grimshaw 1986). It is not only history that has proved him wrong.

From the point of view of humanistic psychology and liberal humanism, the rational self is replaced by the feeling self as the essence of individuality, for whom change comes through progress to 'more human' ways of being and exercising choices. From the point of view of structuralism and Marxist theories, individuality is determined by material conditions and change comes through the inevitability of structural contradictions leading to increased class consciousness and revolutionary struggle. Both humanism and structuralism, although viewed as opposing theories, share a concept of the human subject which is essentialist, and both reduce complicated and diverse human and social conditions to other conditions, such as structures or freedom of choice.

On balance, structuralism still has much more to offer, in my view, especially now that its political and powerful insights have been elaborated by feminism and post-structuralism to take more account of social diversity and social complexity. Equally the insights to be added from psychoanalytic and psychodynamic theories, about the nature of desire and intention, have enabled the discussion of ambivalence, guilt, anxiety and emotional contradiction to inform a more complicated understanding of the connection between the conscious and the unconscious as a way of considering the dialectic relationship between structure and subject (Alcoff 1988; Kenway *et al.* 1994).

Psychoanalysis, with its focus on emotional and bodily symptoms, slips of the tongue and dreams, adds information from the unconscious to the complexity of human existence, and allows for inconsistencies and contradiction. The psychoanalytic subject is more usually regarded as being non-rational, diverse, multiple, and in touch with emotions that are not always under the control of the conscious mind. Psychoanalytic theory provides a relational and social account of the history of individuals, which is provisional, contingent, and emotionally constructed in the course of relating to significant others.

In her excellent study of class and gender formations Beverley Skeggs is sceptical about what she calls the 'psy' professions, whose prominence she sees as directly related to the demise of class analysis and the lack of attention given to the material-structural features of people's lives over the last twenty years (Skeggs 1997). In writing about working class women, she says,

> the emergence of an authorizing narrative of personal trauma, in which singular difficult experiences come to account for the whole personality . . . [underestimates] the unremitting emotional distress generated by the doubts and uncertainties of living class that working class women endure on a daily basis.
>
> (Skeggs 1997)

The only available 'authorizing narrative' to explain working class women's lives is pathology, which is not a liberating ideology. Constructions of identity derive from everyday negotiations in circumstances of systematic inequality which are 'profoundly located in structural organisation'. They are not free floating emotions. 'They may not be authorized, often uneventful (and rarely spectacular) but they do matter and they are constitutive' (Skeggs 1997).

Put together, the insights which come from structuralism about the considerable influence of social and political structures on people's life chances; and from feminism about experience, sexual politics, social diversity and cultural difference;

and from psychoanalysis about the significance of emotional patterns laid down in the unconscious over time and in relation to others, provide a kind of feminist post-structuralism. Within this paradigm it becomes possible to view the human subject as complicated rather than unitary; formed dynamically rather than essentially; constituted in relation to circumstances and social contexts and in relationship to others; and continually changing, both from one negotiation to the next, as well as over longer periods of time.

In trying to understand the human subject – or one's own subjectivity – it therefore becomes important to pay attention to the social and emotional histories of individuals, as well as their social circumstances; to conscious and rational processes, but also to the kind of investments which they have in particular behaviour or positions in a discourse. These are investments which may not always be rational, conscious or positive; which may be contradictory, but which address, however fleetingly, the fulfilment of desire, and the kinds of satisfaction that derive from expressions of desire. In this sense, talk of transformation becomes not simply an intellectual process, but one that also recognises emotionality, embodiment, and multiple shifting subjectivities in relation to others and to social circumstances.

It now seems more possible to argue that learning takes place from experience and through struggle, as well as from contested ideas and pedagogies in formal education settings (Foley 1999). Its components are practical, emotional and intellectual, and involve shifts in consciousness over time in response to changing circumstances, contexts, and interpersonal relations. Meanings, articulated with the assistance of critical thinking and reason, or common sense, also find expression in the unconscious, in forms that can be contradictory and inconsistent. Understanding and identity are both complicated and dynamic, and operate as a continuing process of becoming. Not 'better' in a linear sense, or 'more human' in a hierarchical sense, but shifting, and subject to reconstitution and renegotiation, in a relational and social sense.

Class, gender and ethnic identities can also be described as 'shifting', in ways that reductionist or heavily deterministic definitions about socio-economic status, 'race' and sexual difference do not adequately address. Since working class women are as complicated as any other group when it comes to investing in emotional positions and negotiating identities, they are not well served by offers of education that are formulaic, uncritical and domesticating, despite the widespread enthusiasm among adult educators for widening participation and extending educational access to working class and black women on this limited, and limiting, basis.

10

ALL OVER BAR THE SHOUTING?

The recent publication *Educating Rita and Her Sisters: Women and Continuing Education* collects together a series of articles about women's education in Britain at the present time (Benn *et al.* 1998). Together with its subsequent review in *Studies in the Education of Adults* (Stalker 1999), it captures some of the contemporary dilemmas facing women's education within the academy. Joyce Stalker's review gives the collection one cheer on the basis of 'a group of super women with whom I would love to spend more time . . . I can imagine that we would have energised discussions, with many points of agreement and of healthy disagreement'. But she withholds her other two cheers on the basis of the writer's 'vague' analysis of neo-liberal legacies and her disappointment with 'the tone of the articles'. It seems to Stalker they lack

> the essential energy of the women. There seems to be an unnecessary carefulness in each chapter; a reticence to be blunt for fear of being called reductionistic, to be sharp for fear of being called essentialistic, to be pointed for fear of being called simplistic.
>
> (Stalker 1999)

She could be right because all of these are familiar criticisms directed at women who still feel strongly about women's education. In the end the book is

> driven into a liberal feminist stance by this cautiousness as well as by an emphasis on the individual, on self esteem, on self respect rather than on the structural, the political and on the socio-economic milieu.
>
> (Stalker 1999).

'Driven' of course is debatable. Most of the contributors to *Educating Rita* have been around for long enough not to be driven anywhere they do not want to be. They are all the survivors of academic careers in women's education – all but two of them in universities. Big, grown up women, who make their own choices, I imagine, including the choice to support the standpoint and the position they articulate in their writing.

It could be, as Stalker suggests, about 'the dilemma of women in academe – how to voice their passionate concerns for women, make clear, poignant political statements and still retain their academic credibility'. Or it could be that what they have written is a full and accurate account of what they think and want to contribute to the discourse in which they are engaged. We must, after all, recognise women's agency – as an alternative to victim status – whilst understanding that in the struggle for agency and change, women have to operate within as well as against the very real constraints of structure. It is, of course, in the tension created between the two – within and against – that challenges exist, and opportunities emerge, to re-negotiate and re-constitute the world for women.

It is not surprising that some of those contributing to *Educating Rita* have chosen to do this in a relatively liberal way rather than a more radical way because liberalism has emerged – or survived – as the dominant professional voice in women's education (Thompson 1995). But the consequence is also slightly more complicated than Stalker's palpable weariness with liberalism suggests. Several of the contributors, I know, would not want to identify themselves as liberal feminists. Indeed a number of them write from an expressed allegiance to a more radical standpoint. Their accounts have a lot to do with being immersed in the prevailing preoccupations of continuing education theory at a time just before the rhetoric and discourse took on new preoccupations in pursuit of lifelong learning (Thompson 2000). It was a context in which continuing education orthodoxy – as it functioned to service the state and the economy – frequently acted to concentrate the debate on matters of continuing professional/vocational education, institutional reviews, performance indicators, quality assurance, funding, accreditation and progression (Thompson 1983; Barr 1996). At the same time, the postmodern – with its emphasis on discourse analysis, deconstruction and language – served to influence some theoretical writing. Whilst it undoubtedly posed some interesting questions, and created additional publishing opportunities for those driven by the requirements of the Research Assessment Exercise (RAE) in universities, it was no more useful than technical rationalism and managerialism in the struggle for 'really useful knowledge' relating to collective social action in pursuit of social change (Thompson 1995).

At much the same time, the kinds of women's education that emerged from the campaigns of second wave feminism in the 1970s, and which used the space available in community-based adult education to develop feminist knowledge, pedagogy and praxis, also entered the academy in rebellious and impatient mood. Like other radical social movements the women's liberation movement represented an urgency and passion for change. In educational terms this involved the desire for knowledge – and the creation of new knowledge in new, more democratic, ways – that would be 'really useful' in explaining how and why women in different contexts, different cultures and different historical circumstances had been silenced, exploited, discriminated against and oppressed. Knowledge that would not only contribute to a critical understanding of the historicity and contingency of different women's position, but also recognise resistance and inform political action for social change (Barr 1999b).

But the discourse of academic feminism became increasingly disconnected from the concerns of more radical feminisms – involving liberation and transformation – despite the continuing material, social, cultural and political inequalities experienced by women in contemporary societies (Thompson 1995).

First came the struggle to establish the academic credentials of a 'new' discipline – within and against – academic institutions reflecting masculinist assumptions about knowledge, specialisms and scholarship, in which structures and systems have remained hierarchical, patriarchal and exclusionary. Then came funding mechanisms which increasingly privileged research and publications over teaching, at the same time as student numbers – related to funding targets – increased, adding to administrative workloads (Barr 1999a). The conservative years were marked by a crisis in the Left and the decline of radical politics – including the politics of feminism and radical education. Driven by government commitment to market economics, enterprise and competition, educational institutions were also transformed by the relentless pursuit of 'what pays' rather than 'what matters'; by efficiency and outputs; by the commercialisation and intellectual commodification of academia; and by managerialism and marketing strategies (Barr 1996).

In the late 1980s and early 1990s academic feminism converted to postmodernism in a big way, turning its attention, in the process, away from issues of structural oppression which continued to shape the lives of black and white working class women still struggling against poverty, violence, racism and gendered inequalities (Nicholson 1990; Barret and Phillips 1992; Brodribb 1992). And this at much the same time as the global scale of structural differences between rich and poor, north and south, black and white, men and women, was increasingly evident.

As capital acted to reposition itself, in order to further dominate and control the global market, and in ways that undermined the sovereignty, (popular) democratic interests and cultural integrity of separate nation states in the interests of accumulating capitalist wealth, the 'logic' of economic advance also involved cutting back public spending in the rich world and structural adjustment programmes in the poor world (Mayo 1997). Although the operation was global, its impact was experienced locally, and its costs were borne by those least able to withstand the consequences – predominantly poor women.

Restructuring the global economy and labour markets – considerably facilitated by electronic and information technologies – contributed to changing the social relations of production and consumption in ways that challenged prevailing socio-political ideas and explanations based on 'grand narratives' about capitalism, patriarchy, imperialism and nationalism (Hall and Jaques 1989; Bauman 1998). Strategic economic obsessions with privatisation, deregulation, franchising, niche marketing, peripheral labour, flexible specialisation, casualisation, built in obsolescence – among other monetarist orthodoxies – depended on neo-liberal notions of competitive individualism, enterprise, consumerism and there being 'no such thing' as societies – only expendable workforces and insatiable markets (Hayes

1994). The language of freedom ('free' markets, 'free' choice, 'free' enterprise) acted as euphemisms for the prevalence of unfreedoms which exacerbated the divisions between rich and poor at both local and global level in the interests of satisfying capital's greed for dominance and the accumulation of wealth.

It has always seemed to me that the widespread intellectual conversion by academia at this time – including academic feminism – to postmodernism 'fitted' very well with prevailing economic and political trends. How useful to have the construction of postmodern knowledge and ideas preoccupied with transience and uncertainty, in which identity is ephemeral, culture means the mass communications business, and worlds fragment and fall apart. How timely that words (discourse, linguistics, de-construction) should be deemed to replace things (material conditions, inequalities, oppressions). How interesting that the particular should assume more significance than the general; that immediate, short lived specialism should be regarded as more sexy than interconnection and intercomplexity. How predictable that the individual (the psyche, the body, the fluctuating identity) becomes the subject of theory rather than the group (the sex, the community, the class, the nationality, the race). What a relief that no one needs to do anything in solidarity with anyone else. How convenient, in fact, for the consolidation of the New Right's economic, social and political project, that those responsible for the construction and distribution of postmodern ideas acted to corroborate preferred New Right versions of reality. Convenient but not so surprising. We know from experience – as well as from the intelligence of Marx – that the dominant ideas of any age are the ideas of the ruling (in this sense, the late capitalist) class.

But not all academic feminists sought refuge in postmodernism. Some became femocrats and some, unfortunately, lost sight of where they started. The price of integration into the academy and of achieving an occasional presence in some influential positions involved further distancing from grassroots feminism – which had wanted 'general' rather than 'individual' advance for women, and had expected feminist transformation of malestream and patriarchal institutions, rather than incorporation, in the process (Taking Liberties Collective 1989).

At the same time as academic feminism became less boisterous and more dutiful, women's community based learning increasingly moved from the margins into the mainstream of adult and continuing education provision, via the access and accreditation industries. Although frequently represented as a 'major achievement' by providers of adult learning, in terms of securing more resources, promoting progression routes and improving the general quality of provision, the move into the mainstream also contributed to de-politicising and individualising women's issues around alleged deficiencies of confidence and self-esteem, rather than discrimination and structural oppression.

In both respects the loss has meant the weakening of connections between working class, grass roots women's groups, social movements concerned with social justice and academics who might work together with them in a committed way.

Something of the loss is captured in the title of the book, *Educating Rita and Her Sisters: Women and Continuing Education*, which made Stalker feel so irritated. No one who is dedicated to sustaining democratic and egalitarian relationships between different women, in pursuit of the kinds of understanding and knowledge that help to address urgent and pressing problems, would position those 'on the receiving end' in relation to those 'articulating the discourse' as *Rita and Her Sisters*. I am afraid it does imply a range of class and cultural assumptions which are patronising in the extreme about those it serves to caricature, let alone to exclude. However, Stalker's declared ennui about the prospect of reviewing 'not another book about women's education' also catches the fear of successful academics (and women MPs) to be 'too identified' with women's issues. Especially in the 'post-feminist' era. Imagine a review beginning by disclaiming the need for 'yet another' book on the Second World War or theories of evolution?

Be that as it may, the chapters in *Educating Rita* dealing with research do need to be approached with caution. We all know how much pressure academics are under to write and to produce research these days, but the critical questions must remain, in whose interest? And to what purpose? In *Educating Rita* those writing about research demonstrate a commitment to social reflexivity and to accounting for their own role in the research process. But the movement between the personal and the definitive is a difficult terrain to negotiate. The reason why feminist researchers must put themselves in the frame (Barr 1999a) is to raise questions about what is missing from allegedly neutral and objective accounts of data collection and methodologies – especially in relation to power, implicit assumptions, interpretations and ethical considerations. But it is a delicate and nuancing business, in my view, which at its best unravels layers of complexity, gives every sense of 'being there', and does not 'get definitive' or effect closure prematurely. It involves important questions about who is heard, how we listen, whom we are accountable to, whom we address and how we address them (Skeggs 1997). It is most important to pay due respect and absolute attention to the meanings, integrity and authority of all those without whom researching women's lives would not exist – the women whose lives are under scrutiny (Bordo 1990).

The danger, of course, is that important principles of feminist and self-reflective research develop their own orthodoxy, in which 'putting oneself in the picture' reads like a speech at an Oscars ceremony – which acknowledges everybody and qualifies everything in sight, but still ends up sounding like an affirmation of one's own pre-eminence. The proprietorial first person – as in 'my' learners, 'my research' (Preece 1998) – can seem as resistant in practice to making serious and equal space for 'others' to be heard as the tradition of detachment which is being contested by studiously jettisoning pretensions to neutrality. Equally, the use of narrowly conceived reflexive practice can become fixed by its own terminology – 'the researched voice', 'subjugated knowledge', 'hired-hand research', 'role model interviewers', 'self disclosure', 'continuum of responsiveness', 'client group', 'excluded categories' – and ends up sounding as closed and objectifying about those being defined as the worst kinds of formulaic research have always done (Preece 1998).

Apart from feeling it is time to move on from postmodernism, the language of deconstruction and academic self-importance, to more constructive research and learning with women on a more equal basis, my main reservation about *Educating Rita* is the near total muting of any voices speaking from the experiences of women other than professional academics. Gaynor, a former women's studies student at Ruskin College – in one of her numerous letters – makes the point like this:

> yes, we need to concentrate on educating ordinary women – women from my class who can fight their own battles – but a bit of real solidarity wouldn't go amiss. Having the educated middle class coming out to 'help us with our problems' annoys me to the quick of my temper. Domestication? No thank you. We demand education, equality and a voice. It is as much our right to speak as it is for others – the middle class missionaries – to do so on our behalf. Sisterhood demands equality, freedom of speech, education, respect for difference – building solidarity and connection among those of us with a common purpose to fight.

The subject matter of *Educating Rita* is not about the commitment to solidarity, however: more about the preoccupations of those who manage research and deliver education to women on behalf of institutions which are in service to the state and the economy. Assumptions about education 'being a good thing' are implicit – albeit education as defined by relatively enlightened and liberal academics. Scarcely any discussion is to be found about the reasons why education – and what sort of education – might be useful to women – and what sort of women – at the current time. The far from neutral relationship between women, the economy and the state is sometimes described but generally taken for granted. The implications to women of hostile institutional structures are sometimes referred to but not radically contested. The language of business enterprise and managerialism is criticised but replaced with the language of liberal humanism and personal development, rather than social purpose and liberation. The notion that theory is most important when it is produced in relation to practice is not seriously explored although I am sure most of the contributors would take the view that all of us need to be able to make sense of the world in order to change it for the better. The concentration on individualism precludes the more radical conviction that education will only empower people if it enables them to act collectively on their own reality in order to change it; and women's education will only be relevant and useful in this process if it derives its legitimacy, has its roots and exists in relation to groups and movements of women in ways that make a difference to their lives (Thompson 2000).

Understanding the historical and contingent nature of institutions and ideas – including the position of women within them – ought to remind us that things could have been different and might still be otherwise. Historicity and contingency ought to allow us to imagine and revise different forms of social relations. In this context the continuing presence of women's education and academic feminism within and against educational institutions could be seen not so much as a disengagement from grass roots credibility and connection, but as a different site of struggle, requiring different strategies of resistance.Women may not have transformed academia during the last thirty years but they have made some real gains, occupied some important territory and continue to operate in spaces that are often marginal, sometimes crucial and always highly contradictory in order to exert some possible – potentially more radical – influence.

But the space remains precarious. It has been seriously undermined, as we have seen, by recent developments, ranging from the tyranny of individualism and neo-liberalism to the orthodoxy of technical rationality. If Thatcherism was bad for women's progress and equality (Taking Liberties Collective 1989) the jury has yet to reach a verdict on the contribution to be made by New Labour. The signs are not encouraging. The last two decades have not been easy ones to survive with feminist aspirations and values intact. The language of feminism and patriarchy remains absent from the New Labour agenda, despite a healthy increase in the number of women Labour MPs (Thompson 1999a, b). Feminist academics have needed to work hard to keep their toehold in the academy – their average pay and chances of promotion remain significantly inferior to men's – but others have fared much worse. Women's poverty, and the numbers of women living in poverty – especially single mothers and elderly women – has been a marked feature of the increasing polarisation in British class society. Women in the global economy are the poorest of the poor, the least educated of the least educated, the least powerful of the least powerful. In the affluent north, too many feminists have developed middle management mentality, or become wedded to the faculty or the therapist's chair.

It could be that there is a distinction to be made between educational institutions as examples of 'an apparatus' and the possibility of making connections between women on the inside and the outside of academia to continue with the struggle for political and social change. To 'give up' the academy to dominant ideas – be they patriarchal, liberal, neo-liberal and now, Blairite – concedes a powerful and tantalising space, a site of continuing struggle, which has resources to be won and ideas worth contesting, reconstituting, transforming and making available to women in more equitable and useful ways. To date academic feminism has gained more from studying women than it has contributed to women's struggle for political change. Feminist academics, however pressed and marginalised they may feel, have benefited more from the intellectual commercialisation of women's lives than women have received in return. Whilst this is not so surprising in a patriarchal, class based, white supremacist society, which distributes power and resources in seriously distorted ways, it can (still) be different.

In my experience – and hinted at occasionally by some of the contributors to *Educating Rita* – women's education can still provide a space for useful, empowering and subversive knowledge with which to challenge conventional wisdom about women and men, generate critical and creative thinking, act in solidarity with women in their struggles against unsatisfactory and subjugating circumstances, and serve to reinvigorate political life and cultural action. I discuss some illustrations of this in action in the final part of this book.

The challenge facing women's education and academic feminism is to sustain and reconstitute the politics of their origins, within the new positions they have taken up, and in the context of present and future possibilities. Educational institutions, especially universities, should be the kinds of place in which women (and others) seeking social and political change can secure the services of intellectuals and the resources of academia for their own projects, and make use of them in contexts which will make a difference to their lives. Really useful academic knowledge can open up ways of seeing that have not been experienced before. It can help to re-interpret what has previously been defined in terms of personal inadequacy or personal failure as political oppression, in ways that assist women in the process of collective empowerment that leads to social change. This means democratising learning and the creation of knowledge in ways which ensure women's continued ownership of their own experiences, their resilience and reservoirs of wisdom – expanded by new insights – to be used in the service of their own communities, rather than in service to the intellectual and commercial self-interests of academics and educational institutions.

Collaboration between women on the inside and the outside of academia, which is democratic and egalitarian, critical but inclusive, which respects diversity but reaches across difference towards the creation of active solidarities, is always worth the struggle. It imagines the possibility that the way things are is not necessarily the way they have to be. It furthers the vision of a radical and democratising women's education, which reaches beyond the academy, to articulate its concerns with women other than academics, and to look elsewhere for evidence of the energy and conviction that will put persistence, resistance, emancipation and transformation back on to the agenda of women's education.

Another view, of course, is that so far as feminism in women's education is concerned, it's 'all over bar the shouting'. We do not need feminism any more because more girls leave schools with better qualifications than boys these days (Arnot *et al.* 1996; McGivney 1999a: 23–25). Equal numbers of women and men enter universities which a generation ago were the preserve of men – albeit to read arts and social science subjects rather more than natural sciences, technology and engineering. The labour market has been feminised to the extent that in some areas – including the one in which I grew up – women actually outnumber men, but only in low paid, part time and casualised employment (Coyle 1995; Dex *et al.* 1996; Walby 1997). Whilst no one talks with much passion or shows much interest any more in equal opportunities as a women's issue, the media, educationalists, policy makers and government are more noticeably exercised by gender issues when they relate to working class and black boys' poor performance in schools, the alleged crisis in working class masculinity and the consequence for the economy and social cohesion of growing numbers of excluded men without the discipline of work or traditional family life to keep them out of trouble (Campbell 1999; McGivney 1999a). Women have 'never had it so good' it would seem. Now it is excluded men we should be most concerned about.

Research seems to confirm some improvements in women's performance in education and the job market, and worrying trends affecting men. A study carried out at Sussex University by Woodfield and Saunders (1998) reveals that, as the numbers of women students are increasing, they are also outperforming men by between five and ten percentage points by the end of their second year. This is not so surprising. It helps to be part of a sizeable group rather than a marginalised minority if you want to make your presence felt. According to Woodfield and Saunders this seems to apply irrespective of age and social background. There is something about being a woman which cancels out class and age, apparently. But of course, far fewer women from working class backgrounds attend universities than women from middle class backgrounds and mature students with domestic responsibilities do not usually have as much time to spend on their studies and themselves as younger women should expect to do.

It is argued that age and social class make more of a difference to men in relation to education. Older men from working class backgrounds score lowest. Men under 21 and older men from middle class backgrounds do better. This confirms what Veronica McGivney reveals in her study of *Excluded Men* (McGivney 1999a). She identifies four groups of men whom the government's lifelong initiatives fail to reach – young men without qualifications and with few skills, men in manual occupations, men from some black ethnic minorities, and older working class men. Apart from the well known class and 'race' factors which affect participation and performance in education, constructions of working class masculinity also play their part in promoting identity and status via more physical, vocational and leisure pursuits. If such groups of men are difficult to enrol in further education and training, they are hardly likely to be found in higher education in any great numbers. Nor has higher education shown much interest in recruiting them – until relatively recently. We should not be surprised that whilst more women than men now get 2.1 classifications in their final degrees, middle class men continue to get more firsts – and thirds.

Research also shows that men are more vocal in seminars and tend to set the agenda of what gets talked about. Women speak less but take more notes. All the evidence suggests women work harder, attend more diligently, and display a greater degree of agreeableness, altruism, sympathy and compliance. They are more likely to accept what they read and what they are taught. This may help to explain larger numbers of men getting firsts and thirds. Their propensity for 'risk taking' and 'the element of flair', so beloved by academics, sometimes pays off and sometimes plummets. Even if they have not applied themselves as seriously as women, it does not stop men from contributing to discussions and expressing their own opinions 'more confidently' in examinations. Consequently they are more likely to do very well or very badly. Having an opinion about something is not necessarily the same as understanding it, after all. Women tend to be more co-operative, flexible, less defensive and better at working in groups – all qualities which favour the trend in higher education towards continuous assessment, seminars and team work.

These are similar kinds of observation to those detected by the *Guardian* in the recruitment of graduates to the labour market:

> Ask any company recruiting 20 somethings and most will now confess that women are more employable than men . . . employers are looking for 'soft skills' . . . candidates with the ability to manage people and relationships . . . team workers, people who are adaptable and flexible.
>
> (*Guardian* 1998)

I am not sure whether we should be celebrating the extent to which education is endorsing the kinds of quality in women which support the economy's current preoccupation with 'soft skilled' personnel in functionary positions, or whether the conclusion to be drawn from all this is that we should try socialising boys in the same way as we socialise girls – or vice versa. Certainly there is some interest in work with boys and men that expects positive changes to occur once they are persuaded to 'get in touch with their emotions'. It seems unlikely that counselling will cure structural inequalities, however, or persuade men and boys to forgo their investment in the varieties of power which are still widely available to them irrespective of their emotional proficiency, and despite their class or ethnic backgrounds.

The employment trends might be read as good news for young, middle class women in professional occupations, although the business and service sectors still identify masculinity as the essential ingredient when it comes to senior positions. Only 18 per cent of managers and 3 per cent of company directors are women, where laddish behaviour in top jobs is interpreted as a sign of leadership and strength rather than evidence of identity crisis and exclusion (*Guardian* 1998). Success at work still depends on structures which assume the value added benefit to men of familiar exploitation and servicing on the home front (Leonard and Delphy 1992) which in a heterosexual and patriarchal society routinely allocates the necessary career accessory called 'a wife' to men rather than women.

There is nothing very new in the analysis of education which finds men taking up more space in the classroom and in discussions than women, or in masculine behaviour being indulgently described as being about 'more confidence', 'risk taking' and 'flair'. Dale Spender, among others, began to draw attention to these phenomena years ago, except she analysed them in terms of power and in relation to the social construction of masculinities in patriarchal societies (Spender 1982a). She also identified women who are quieter, more agreeable, more flexible and more thoughtful about others as displaying characteristics deriving from less social power and from specific gender socialisation within patriarchy. These days, it would be usual to be more cautious about attributing gender traits to men and women on the basis of essentialist assumptions – deriving from either nature or nurture – but it is also clear that gendered behaviour patterns do operate notwithstanding increasing sensitivity to age, culture and class diversity (Abraham 1995).

What is different now is that the climate – and the needs of the economy – have changed. In some circumstances women's ways of being (in the British context) are now more likely to be recognised and rewarded than was previously the case – especially if they fit in with the requirements of school league tables, university retention rates and labour market needs. But the commitment to equality is nowhere near significant enough to change the gendered focus of the curriculum, the gendered structure and segregation of the labour market, the gendered organisation of pay and work – in ways which permeate the tough, reinforced and resistant glass that still acts as a ceiling, or a floor – by which men's economic, social and political power is retained (Franks 1999). As Jeff Hearn points out,

> While changes abound in law, work, citizenship, personal relations, and so on, there has been a widespread, stubborn persistence in men's dominance – in politics, business, finance, war, diplomacy, the state, policing, crime, violence generally, heterosexual institutions and practices, science, technology, culture, media, and many other social arenas. What is perhaps most interesting is that while men's general power as a (the) dominant social category remains virtually unchanged, and may even have become intensified in some respects, men's power is constantly being challenged, fragmented and even transformed.
>
> (Hearn 1999)

Systems of oppression – such as patriarchy – continually struggle to reconstitute themselves and to regroup as a way of heading off potential threats to their power base. In terms of the future, Hearn is pretty sure that

> many men will probably still find ways of holding on to various powers; of being violent, threatening, shouting, seeking to get their own way, whilst leading rather circumscribed lives, working fewer hours and getting paid more than women, living less healthily, dying younger and 'hanging out' with other men.
>
> (Hearn 1999)

Of course, there is no guarantee that women will be endlessly prepared to put up with them if they do, and the curriculum and praxis of feminist education must continue to challenge the expectation that they will.

Part 3

ILLUSTRATIONS

11

DERRY DAYS

Derry is an old and beautiful city dating back to the sixth century, situated along the banks of the River Foyle in surroundings of enormous natural beauty. After the partition of Ireland in 1921, Derry became a border city. It's the place where Amelia Erhart landed – the first woman to fly solo across the Atlantic in 1932. Derry is a working class city, divided geographically along religious lines into Catholic and Protestant areas, from which the middle class have moved out to safer and more desirable suburbs. Working class communities in Derry have grown used to poverty and politics. Eleanor Marx made a visit to Mooney's shirt factory here in 1891 to encourage the growth of 'organisation and combination' among unskilled workers. Following her speech at St Columb's Hall, the local newspaper estimated that hundreds of women workers came forward to join the women's branch of the National Union of Gas Workers and General Labourers. The recession of the 1930s cut deeper and lasted longer than elsewhere in the UK. The post-war boom was shorter lived. By 1970 consumption per inhabitant was only three-quarters of the UK average (Rowthorne and Wayne 1998). In the period between partition and the resumption of Direct Rule from Westminster, Protestants used their influence as capitalists, property owners and administrators in the public sector to make sure the opportunities which did exist went to Protestants. These days both communities face similar problems. The manufacturing industry and jobs in the public sector – which once provided steady employment for men – have been devastated by economic recession and by Conservative policies. Women, as everywhere else, shoulder the main responsibility for unpaid domestic work, take most responsibility for managing family poverty and have the worst choice of low-paid, part-time and 'unskilled' jobs (Cockburn 1998).

Derry has also been the site of some of the most serious repercussions of 'the troubles' outside Belfast. Bloody Sunday happened here in 1972. The local cemetery holds the bodies of those from the Derry Brigade killed in the armed struggle and of hunger strikers who died in custody during the period of Internment and Direct Rule. Republican and Nationalist street murals painted on to gable ends mark the entrance to the Bogside and Free Derry Corner. As I write this in June 1999, a hoarding expresses 342 days of solidarity with those still under siege in

Drumcree as tension mounts towards another marching season. In the Waterside area of the city, Loyalist street murals depict Loyalist paramilitaries invading the Bogside carrying a union jack, whilst an IRA man lies on the ground with a stake through his heart. On the corner of Queen Street and Asylum Road, where I am staying, the police barracks are fortified with metal sheeting, barbed wire and security cameras – still looking like a bunker in a war zone despite the paramilitary cease-fire and the precarious optimism of the peace process. In the world of Irish politics, it has usually been the middle and more affluent classes, with financial and ideological interests to defend, who have acted as professional politicians, but it is the working class who have done the fighting and sacrificed their lives.

On the domestic front – across both communities – gender battles are still being negotiated and decided. Culture, religion, sectarianism and 'the troubles' have all contributed to a traditional form of gender division in which men have retained predominance, authority and control, although women are seen as strong and central to sustaining family and community life in terrible and traumatic times. The strength of sexual stereotyping is reinforced by other factors – all of which are inter-related. These include the psychological and material consequences of poor employment opportunities for women; poverty, and what is sometimes called 'time poverty' caused by the prevalence of women's multiple roles; the absence of women in influential positions; and the absence – until very recently – of a platform for the expression of women's interests (Women and Citizenship Research Group 1995). In addition the fear and experience of sectarian, police and military violence on the streets – which is widely associated with active masculinity, heroism and martyrdom – has compounded the difficulties of discussing domestic violence in the home. In conditions of 'armed patriarchy'(Edgerton 1986) personal violence also erupts easily but is rarely related to oppressive patriarchal relations, women's economic dependency or men's traditional attitudes to the exercise of power.

Debates about gender politics and feminism have received less attention in Northern Ireland than in the rest of the UK in the face of more pressing and historical definitions of politics and priorities. A small, embryonic women's movement struggled throughout the 1970s and 1980s but was split by religious and political divisions. It was isolated from the larger, more confident movement in the south, largely because Irish feminism closed its eyes to the situation in the north, wary of inward looking and church dominated tendencies in Irish politics and introverted nationalism. At the same time British feminism was notoriously indifferent and deeply ignorant about the conditions facing women in Ireland. As second wave feminism was gathering momentum in Britain, the big issue facing Northern Irish women was the war. Some might have wanted a women's movement and feminist social change, but they also had the war to live with. In Northern Ireland, on top of poverty, discrimination, British imperialism and patriarchy, the gendered nature of the war blighted and restricted women's choices even more (Mulholland and Smyth 1999).

It would be wrong to regard women as bystanders in 'the troubles', however, or to underestimate women's involvement in sectarian conflicts. Eilish Rooney argues that 'those who see the state of Northern Ireland as reformable, see "the troubles" as an avoidable additional burden on women's lives. They generally applaud how women cope with and confront violence' (Rooney 1997). And yet women throughout the period of 'the troubles' have been active in protests, in organising demonstrations, in establishing support groups for prisoners and their families and in becoming political prisoners themselves. In some respects women have been active 'in the background', carrying goods from place to place, hiding guns and other weapons and smuggling letters in and out of prison. But they have also played a more visible and prominent role in the Civil Rights marches and have lent support to those on hunger strike. They have attended military funerals and gathered together in large numbers during peace rallies. They have campaigned on behalf of the peace process and voted for peace in massive numbers in the wake of the Good Friday Agreement. Whilst working class women in Britain have been portrayed (inaccurately, in many respects) as apathetic about politics and about political participation, those in Northern Ireland have become widely involved in the struggle to defend their communities and to extend the democratic rights of ordinary people – but in ways that do not fit the usual definition of what counts as politics.

The concept of 'life politics' used by Anthony Giddens (1994) captures the essence of what I mean – although the radical feminist conviction that 'the personal is political' made the same point a quarter of a century earlier. Life politics refers to the range of circumstances, conditions, struggles and commitments which affect people's everyday existence at home, at work, in their communities. In Derry this has meant getting up in the morning, raising children, doing the business of everyday life in a war zone. But it also includes making ends meet, holding down a job, experiencing the effects of discrimination, taking part in education, negotiating changes in personal and social relationships, dealing with statutory authorities, feeling involved or excluded from what is happening in the wider world. These are typically the concerns which acquire significance and meaning in the private sphere, which may be experienced as 'individual problems', and which are often constructed as the consequence of 'personal failure' or 'the way life is'. They involve issues which are so 'ordinary' they become accepted and taken for granted – especially if people feel they do not have much control over their own lives or much room for manoeuvre. They are certainly not the kind of issues which are conventionally viewed as 'political' in discussions about party politics, representative democracy and constitutional reform. However, they are the issues and concerns which shape the lives of ordinary people on a personal and everyday basis in ways that may give rise to anger and frustration but also to demoralisation and fear. They are closely related to conditions of power, inequality and structure and are the reasons why more people currently join self-help groups, community groups, voluntary organisations and social movements than political parties (Giddens 1994).

This is especially true in Northern Ireland where political neglect has characterised the relationship between Britain and the province for many years. In the period before the Good Friday Agreement, Direct Rule created an anomalous arrangement in which the six counties were regarded as being neither inside nor fully separate from the mainland. Leadership was exercised through a senior minister with cabinet responsibility, a job that, until the appointment of Mo Mowlam, had acquired the status of a penalty or banishment among British politicians. Day-to-day administration was carried out by non-elected civil servants from the Northern Ireland Office, supplemented by ad hoc quangos. Local government enjoyed fewer powers than in the rest of the UK. Decision-making was neither accountable nor transparent and there was considerable scope for patronage and the abuse of discretion – especially in support of unionist and Protestant self-interests. For many years Sinn Fein and the Social Democratic and Labour Party undertook a boycott of electoral politics – for reasons of partiality, nepotism and discrimination in the system – but the effect was to further diminish the democratic credibility of political structures.

If the working class have been deprived of democracy in Northern Ireland, women have been additionally excluded. In the research carried out by the Women and Citizenship Research Group into political participation in 1995, it was found that all the Northern Irish representatives in the British and European Parliaments were men, and men held 88 per cent of local council seats (Women and Citizenship Research Group 1995). According to Cynthia Cockburn, men in Northern Ireland are firmly in charge of all the major institutions of power – church, state and quango (Cockburn 1998).

In the absence of political structures and a strong feminist movement to reflect women's immediate concerns, working class women in Northern Ireland began to get organised on their own account. The form their movement took was distinctive and was organised around the development of locally based community centres. It is well known that women are more likely to be involved in community groups than men, and more involved in community based activities than in conventionally defined politics (Coote and Patullo 1990). However, the extent of women's participation in Northern Ireland is more noticeable than in many other working class communities in the UK, and has been rising (Evason 1991; McWilliams 1991; Taillon 1992).

In Derry, as elsewhere, local community initiatives and organisations spring into existence like flowers after rain, born out of common needs and collective energy. Developing the resources for a journey of hope (Williams 1989) in circumstances of extreme poverty, violence and political exclusion are monumental, and yet the business of getting on with what needs to be done is also a strong component of everyday existence. In this capacity women play an impressive and frequently unrecognised role, characterised by what Mary Robinson once described as 'shared leadership, and a quiet, radical, continuing dialogue between the individual women and the collective women' (O'Neill 1999).

The significance of women's involvement in community groups has also been recognised by others as central to the well being of their communities (McGivney 1990). The effectiveness of women's community action in challenging women's secondary status is equally well known.

> The values underlying ways of organising emphasise local control and autonomy, local social and cultural activities, relating theory to practice, encouraging procedures and leadership styles which make participants feel confident and involved, and recognising that different views about tactics and strategy may be rooted in real experience and are worth listening to and discussing.
>
> (Murphy 1997)

In difficult times the participation of women confirms the critical significance of receiving support from others; in being the means of helping other women to speak out; in being an expression of pride in self-sufficiency during many years of conflict; and in engendering the solidarity necessary for public campaigning.

The activities which characteristically emerge are concerned with tackling inequality, and about countering prescriptions of deficiency and pathology with an alternative ideology based on empowering the poor. Women who do not readily regard themselves as political – when politics means the Ulster Unionist Party or Sinn Fein, a power sharing Assembly or the Northern Ireland Office – can find in community activities solutions to their problems and a platform for their immediate interests. These usually include making ends meet, tackling the effects of drug dealing in the neighbourhood, the fear and shame of domestic violence and alcohol abuse, the legacy of police and army raids, the loss of loved ones to sectarian violence, the responsibilities involved in caring for elderly relatives, the closure of another factory and the scarcity of decent jobs. In all of these circumstances it is not surprising that women seek out other, similar people, with whom to build community and to become involved in support groups, campaigns, life saving and life enhancing responses.

The Women's Group which meets in the Rosemount Resource Centre in Derry was formed in 1997 and started when a small group of women got together to provide support and social contact for women in the area. The group members are all women from working class, mostly Catholic, backgrounds; the majority are unwaged and many of them are in receipt of state benefits. From small beginnings the number of women attending the group has grown substantially and they now meet three times a week. Initially the emphasis was on issues related to bringing up children and women's isolation but they now organise a number of activities dealing with social, leisure, health and general educational issues. As well as providing a safe and friendly place to meet, the centre is also a place to get welfare advice and to formulate action on personal and local issues including drugs, alcohol abuse, vandalism and domestic violence. It is a place to make contact with other women facing similar issues in an effort to find individual and common solutions. The women's group continues to grow and to develop links on a cross community and cross border basis. A number of its members now sit on the centre's management group, which is currently developing contacts in eastern central Europe and the United States. Increasing enthusiasm and a growing membership has stepped up the demand for education. For women growing up in serious material poverty and in the middle of the troubles, the usual disjunction between gendered, working class existence and the culture of schooling has been even more pronounced. All the women I met in Derry had their schooling seriously disrupted by the war and left at the first possible opportunity. For all the usual reasons, women were initially unconfident about their academic abilities. But they also knew that 'their history' had been largely outside of their control. The solidarity and mutual support being created within the women's group gave the boost they needed —and the determination – to make up for lost time. As many as thirty signed up to take part in an auto/biography and politics project arranged in relation to Ruskin College, Oxford. I include here just a few of the many personal accounts arising from the project, which we used as a basis for recognising and valuing experience, raising issues, formulating questions and working out some strategies for making changes.

WINNIE

I was the fourth born of twelve children. Two boys and one girl older, and six boys and two girls younger. My Dad was one of the few lucky people in Derry because he was always in full time employment – a rarity in those days, especially being Catholic. At the age of fourteen my Dad stowed away on a ship to join the British army. When the war was over he returned to Derry and married my mother.

He worked as a bus driver for eleven years. Those were hard, poverty stricken times. At that point there were seven children in our household. We were all steps and stairs (what I mean is, we were all born one after the other). We had two slices of bread at breakfast, dinner at school, and tea with bread and beans, if we were lucky. Mum used to say, 'Wains – you may be poor but you are decent'. That gave me a very proud feeling and I carry it with me to this day.

By the time all twelve of us were born, we lived in a three-bedroomed prefab. The eight boys were put in the biggest room, the four girls in the medium sized room, and God love my mammy and daddy – they were in the tiniest room you could imagine. Looking back to those years, we were a very loving and supporting family and our house was full of love. We had nothing fancy but we always got what we needed, not what we wanted. Anything we did get, we treasured, for we knew it was very difficult for our mammy and daddy. Mammy used to feed us in relays – four at a time – and we had to draw straws to see who would get the extras. Dad was the 'worker', he did not believe in lifting a cup, but then, no Derry man did anything around the house.

In 1970 our dad did not come home at his usual time. Next morning my dad was still not home. He had taken a heart attack at work and was in hospital. No one let my mum know. Dad was in hospital for two weeks but he was a changed man. He had to take early retirement and that alone nearly killed him. We survived all right because three or four of us had left school, so we were able to go into the factory to work.

I am divorced seventeen years now. I have three children (young adults). One of my girls is married and has just made me a granny. My other girl is still at home and my son is currently unemployed. I love the time I now have to come to the centre. I feel I have got a second chance to further my education. I have built up a lot of friendships doing this which has brightened up my life a lot.

DOLORES

'Well, what it is it like? How did you get on?' The faces of my mother and sisters were grinning expectantly.

'Oh, it was terrible. All I could smell was body odour.'

My mother's face was a picture.

'What did you say Dolores?'

'I said it smelled of body odour.'

I was fifteen years old and had just come back from my first day of work at the Rosemount shirt factory. I will never forget the feeling. I was both excited and nervous and couldn't wait to get started. I was taken to the main office, along with several other girls, and introduced to our supervisor, who took us up two flights of stairs to the main factory floor. The big green doors were pushed open wide, and that's when the smell hit me full in the face. Like a blast of hot air. It was a mixture of noise, body odour, perfume, rubber and a few other smells I couldn't identify. We were taken into another room, which was partitioned off from the main factory floor and was to be my place of work for the next six weeks – the training room.

I was sat down at a machine and given a basic run through the threading and working of the machine. I was given several small pieces of material, with broken parallel lines of different sizes and shapes. I set the cloth under the needle and lowered the foot. I took a deep breath and I was ready to go. What a shock. The needle sped down the cloth like a speeding bullet. I couldn't stop it and the cloth was ripped to pieces. As the morning wore on I got better with a bit of practice and I made some new friends.We got a ten minute break and I was asked if I wanted to go to the parlour. I didn't have a clue what the parlour was, but said yes anyway. It was the ladies toilet, where besides the obvious, the girls gathered to pass around the fags and catch up on all the latest bars and gossip. I decided that being a factory girl wasn't as bad as I thought.

After six weeks of training I was put in the cuff section. There were about a dozen people working there. Some young, and some older women who had been working there for years and knew the ropes. The first couple of weeks all I seemed to do was rip out work that wasn't done right. My job was running cuffs and in time I got quite good at it. A group of us decided we would go to the dance the next Friday night. The days did not pass quick enough. We chatted and laughed on our breaks in the parlour. It was in the parlour that the girls taught me to jive. They sang, 'all my love, all my kissing, you don't know what you've been missing, Oh boy'. Hit of the week. The sense of fun and laughter was great and many a cuff I got back to rip out.

Deciding what to wear was torture, only one thing for it, I had to get something new. May McCartney's in town had all the latest fashion, and best of all, she let you pick whatever you wanted and pay a small sum of money each week. My choice was down to two outfits – a hotpant suit and a red mini dress. The dress was lovely. It had a sweetheart neckline, puffed sleeves, and flared from under the bust to just below the hips. The hotpants were a navy blue pair of shorts, a navy blue top that came just above the waist with front buttoning, short sleeves and a little collar. It was covered in little white stars. I opted for the hot pants.

Friday finally came. Pay packets were passed round and we all made a mad dash to Will Black's wee shop. There was always a queue for cream soda tights, twenty Number Six and a bar of Fry's Cream Chocolate. The fags were for my mother, also the chocolate – to sweeten her up. We met up at a friend's house to get ready. Make-up, combs, shoes, even false nails were swapped that night. A rub of lipstick, a squirt of hair lacquer, a dab of perfume and we were off. Arm in arm, we set off in our platform shoes, and by the grace of God, we never sprained or broke any ankles. At last we rounded Littlewoods corner and there was the Embassy Ballroom, all lit up. We grabbed each other and giggled with nerves.

'Who's going in first?'

'Not me', echoed half a dozen voices.

There was some pushing and jostling but we eventually paid our money and climbed the stairs. What a sight! Four big pillars round the dance floor glittered and a big ball hung from the ceiling, sending out different coloured lights all over the dance floor. It was packed with people. Some dancing, some just chatting. My first dance, and do you know what? It smelled just like the factory.

LORRAINE

I got married in 1977. I had four children, three boys and a girl. It was a lot of fun and a lot of hard work, but you just got on with it because you were young and able. I did not have much bother with them growing up, that was until I found out my son was on drugs – the one thing every mother dreads – he was 15. I did not know the best way to approach this nightmare but I knew I had to get it sorted out for my son and for the rest of the family.

First of all his personality changed. He stopped eating, slept a lot and lost weight. It got so bad at times, we had to sit on top of him nights to keep him in when he was high. I came home from work one day, he had left home. He had moved into a flat with a few others. My husband and I found out where the flat was and went round right away. I could not believe my eyes. It was full of drug users. We brought him home but he was not happy. It was not going to be easy getting him off drugs.

I took my son to the drug clinic twice a week. By this time the strain was affecting the whole family. Everybody knew that our son was on drugs but I did not care because I would not want anybody to go though what we were going through, especially when you could see no end to it. There was a lot of arguments with the other children as they thought he was getting off with too many things. Our son started going out again and it was not long before he was back to drugs. Everywhere he went, we followed him and brought him home.

The year that followed I will never forget. Our son was back at the clinic and had a part time job. I thought this was great and we were finally getting our lives back together – until I was told my father had cancer. Our son was still finding it hard to keep off drugs and my father was in intensive care. I decided to take my son to see his Granda. I knew he would get a shock when he saw him and he went out crying. We sat that night and talked about his Granda. I tried to explain to him that his Granda was fighting so hard to live, and he was ruining his life with drugs. As the months passed my father got out of intensive care but the cancer came back. We looked after him at home, including our son. It was very heart breaking.

My father is one year dead now and our son is off drugs two years, working in America and doing well. I think it was seeing his Granda that helped him a lot and I was not going to let him ruin his life if possible. My mother always said to me the happiest days of your life was when your children were around your feet. I did not understand her at the time. But what happened with my son, I now know what she meant.

BRID

I had a very happy but simple childhood, being the fourth youngest of ten children and always thought we were brought up fair. But looking back now I think the boys got off lightly compared to us girls. We had housework to do after school, and even when we started work, we still had housework to do at weekends.

At 15 I left school with no exams. It was my own fault but I was never pushed at home and if you didn't work at school, you were just left there. I started work in one of Derry's famous shirt factories. Nearly all the workers were girls – only a few men worked in factories and they were either management or cutters. I liked working in the factory. I met my best friend there, called Sally. We both worked in the cutting room which was great. I stamped the collars and she sewed on the stiffeners.

Sally and I would go to dances at weekends and on one of those nights I met a boy called Rusty. He was a lot older than me, not very good looking, with ginger hair. But I liked him and of course, he had a car and plenty of money. He was a Protestant and in those days they had all the good jobs. We went steady for about one and a half years, and in that time he took my virginity and introduced me to alcohol. He always bought me presents. I thought I was the luckiest girl in Derry. Then one night he bought me a beautiful white fur coat. That night I wore it out on a date with him and he asked me to wear this pin he had of the union jack. I didn't want to wear it because I knew anyone that saw it on me would call me a traitor.

Eventually I did wear it for him and that night we went for a drive. He was driving like a mad man. I asked him to slow down but he wouldn't. I knew he was just showing off but I was still scared. He then told me that if we crashed and were killed, we would both be buried as Protestants because I was wearing his pin and he had a big flag of the union jack in the boot of his car.

After that I didn't feel the same about him and broke it off with him. He wasn't very happy about it and started following me everywhere. I got really fed up so I decided to have a talk with him to try to sort it out. I told him how I felt and that I wouldn't go back with him. That's when he raped me. I couldn't tell anyone about what he had done to me because I thought they would blame me. So I put it out of my head and tried to get on with the rest of my life.

Sometime later I met my next boyfriend who was to change my life. He worked in the factory opposite mine and we could see each other through the windows. He would wave to me and I would wave back. He was very good looking. We went steady for about a year when Sally and I decided to go to work in England. He wasn't very happy about it but I really wanted to go. The next week we were off to a place called Brighton to work in an underwear factory.

On St Patrick's Day we wore a shamrock to work. We were sent to see the manager. He told us to take off our shamrocks because the rest of the girls were offended. We couldn't understand why, but we had to take them off. That night we went to a dance in the local parish hall and it was great fun. We wore our shamrocks and green ribbons in our hair.

The next day I was sick and when Sally took me to the doctor's I found out I was pregnant. My boyfriend offered me the money to have an abortion but I wouldn't take it. I didn't want anything to do with him. That was the last I saw of him. I didn't know what to do and I hadn't told my parents. I went back to work in the factory in Derry and Sally eventually came too. I wasn't due until November. There was a man called Tommy who worked in the cutting room who was very good to me, so I told him about myself, and he arranged for me to go to a home in Belfast for unmarried mothers. I told my mother I was going back to England to work and she believed me.

The room in the home were like changing rooms in a swimming pool – well, not much bigger. We all had our share of cleaning. The home was run by nuns and they got you up very early and made you go to mass, then you got your breakfast, and then you got stuck in to cleaning all day. I really hated that home. After a few days I packed my bags and left. I wrote a letter to my mother telling her I was working in a sauce factory in England. It was the nuns who told me to write it. They sent all the letters to England to get posted.

I didn't know my way around Belfast but I found my way eventually to a friend's house on the Ballycreggy Estate. The next day I made my way back to Derry but the troubles had got worse and William Street was on fire. I went to Sally's house up in Creggan. A friend called Bridie phoned her sister in Birmingham to see if I could stay there. She said yes, so I was off again to England.

Bridie's sister lived in a one-bedroomed flat with a husband and a baby boy. I slept on the sofa. I was seven months pregnant. I looked after the baby whilst Bridie's sister went out to work. I was getting about £4 a week benefits then, and as my mother thought I was working, I had to send £3 a week home. I never had any money to buy things for myself. I was a smoker and I couldn't buy cigarettes. At night when everyone was in bed I would raid the ashtrays for the biggest butts and smoke them.

When I went to the adoption office, a very well dressed lady asked me some questions and I had to fill in a form. She asked me my religion. When I told her she said, 'I can't guarantee the baby will be brought up in your religion'. That was it. My mind was made up now. I never really wanted to have the baby adopted in the first place. I walked out of the adoption office a new person and I decided to go home.

That day I wrote a letter to Sally and included a letter for her to take round to my mother. Before she got the letter my mother phoned and so I told her. She told me to come home straight away. I said I had no money. She wired some to me the next day. When I arrived in Belfast my two brothers were there to meet me. When I got home to Derry my mother opened the door and hugged me. She was great. She got the doctor and got me booked into hospital to have the baby. I remember I was put into a room of my own. I knew it was only doctors' wives or people with money who were given a room of their own, so I wondered why. Later I found out it was because I wasn't married. When I went into labour, I was put in another room on my own, with no one to look after me. By the time the nurse came the baby's head was born and I was still on my own. I had a beautiful baby girl that night, 11 November 1969. I loved her so dearly. I was young and inexperienced but I vowed I would do the best I could for her. We clung to each other. Eventually they agreed to let me go in the ward with the other mothers. My brother came to visit every night and everyone thought he was my husband. I never put them past their notion. That's what it was like in the 1960s.

JACQUELINE

The period of my life I have chosen to write about concentrates on my first encounter with Norman until the end of the relationship and subsequent court battles to ensure my child's future safety.

I met him several years ago through work. He seemed to be quite an average person with some troubles like most of us. On getting to know him better, we formed a relationship which subsequently led to me becoming pregnant. We decided to move into his house, which meant me giving up my flat, because we thought a house would be more suitable for bringing up a child. I continued with my work and life seemed normal. Jade was born and shortly afterwards things started to go wrong.

Norman started to show signs of a more sinister side to his nature. Small things which seemed unimportant at the start of the relationship became major issues between us – his drinking, and gambling, which I had assumed was an occasional outlet, was in fact a well established habit of a lifetime. Whilst attempting to hold down two jobs to pay the bills which Norman would not contribute to, and trying to spend quality time with Jade, Norman's irate behaviour was placing an unbearable and emotional burden on Jade and myself. He was secretive about where he was going and unsavoury people were calling at the house.

After a year I moved out to a bed and breakfast to be rehoused. I could never have imagined what would happen next. It started with Norman following my every movement, then two of his friends got involved, then came the threats and unfriendly, late night calls – 'check under your car' – hanging about outside my home in the early morning. Norman and his friends ensured that no matter where I was, someone was there to watch me. They came into my work and degraded my reputation with my boss behind my back. They hurled insults at me in front of my daughter.

I went to a solicitor and the police took out a protection order against him. But it did not stop Norman. He invaded every part of our lives and wrote letters to my parents who are both in their seventies. I think he thought that if he could isolate me from everyone I would allow him to control Jade's and my life.

We went to the high court in Belfast where we came to an agreement about him seeing Jade for two visits a week for two hours and Norman was told to stay away from us on every other occasion. This arrangement lasted for about two weeks and then things got steadily worse – my life was threatened, my child was threatened. I was told she would disappear and I would never see her again. Norman didn't stop. He and his friends kept coming after me, looking to take Jade for overnight stays. I kept refusing. I couldn't understand why this was so important to these men when only one of them had anything to do with her, but I was soon to find out.

I couldn't believe what I was hearing when Jade started talking but with the help of my parents and a close friend I did everything I could to protect Jade. I contacted the right people and believed I was going down the right path. The biggest mistake I made was not letting the police take over. Instead I asked the local social services to help, believing I would not be safe if I involved the police. This did not stop Norman. Again my life and Jade's was made hell. No one wanted to listen or to believe us – only those people who witnessed Norman's behaviour.

A few weeks later we were back in court, only for the case to be adjourned for three months. A lot of hate built up inside me. Against Norman for what he had done and for social services for allowing it to happen. There were two case conferences and by the time we went back to court, he was awarded weekly access, to be reviewed in three months. The access had to be in my home with myself and a social worker present. It was awful. Jade and I were finding it harder and harder to cope with, then the ultimate happened. I was approached by social services who said this had been reported before by a relative of Norman's, and that he had been taking Jade to the house where it happened. I was told not to worry and that he never left Jade alone in the house. I was expected to believe this. I had had enough.

Back in court it was agreed that the visits were to continue for another six months, for one hour in a neutral place. The social worker came to visit Jade at home, Jade asked me to stay in the room with her but the social worker said she preferred to talk to Jade alone, and so I had to leave. Jade was very nervous and distressed. About ten minutes later the social worker said Jade had agreed to go on a visit to see Norman on her own. She gave me a time and date and left. Jade just looked at me. She said I lied, that I had promised to stay with her and I didn't. I decided that I would never let Jade down again.

So far I have stuck to my word – even with the threat of jail and Jade being taken away from me and handed over to Norman. I have stood firm, with monthly visits still taking place – the fight for Jade's future is still ongoing. I really don't know where it is going to end: my own personal view is when Norman is six foot under.

EILISH

In the summer of 1968 my husband and I and our three young children left our hometown and went to England because it was very hard to make a living in Derry. Before we left home we were living with my widowed father and four teenage brothers in a three-bedroomed house in the Creggan Estate. The five of us slept in one bedroom which was 10 feet by 7 feet. My father had a little box room and my brothers had the biggest room, where they slept in two double beds.

In England we watched the television news and heard from our families back home about the civil unrest and the injustices that were being inflicted on our people by the RUC because they were marching for their rights to vote and to have decent jobs and better housing. The RUC is a Unionist force who don't want any changes. We decided to go home because we were worried about our families.

We set sail in August 1969, not realising at the time that I was expecting our fourth child. After a long and tedious journey we arrived home and were shocked to see our town. It was as if we were in the middle of a war zone with the British soldiers on our streets. After the Loyalists, backed up by the RUC and the B Specials (another 100 per cent Unionist government force and totally sectarian) attacked the Bogside, smashing windows and giving people terrible abuse, there was rioting for days. The British government then decided to send their soldiers to keep the peace.

During the rest of 1969 things got particularly scary. My fears were for my unborn child, my children, and particularly my husband, my brothers and my father because I knew they would march for their civil rights and might get caught up in the riots. The Nationalist people were very frustrated by the British government, always giving in to Unionist demands, ignoring and failing to admit the discrimination and injustices that were being inflicted on us – the Nationalist people. It was on 4 May 1970 that our fourth child was born, a little boy. We were all very excited. I remember thinking at the time, by the time the baby grows up, everything will be settled. He and the rest of our children will have their rights, just as our Unionist neighbours have always done.

We were now sleeping six in the tiny bedroom. After several weeks of fighting with the council for a house without success, we went to see some of the organisers of the civil rights movement as we knew they were helping people in the same position as us. At least they listened to what we were saying. It was not falling on deaf ears like it was with the city council. A few weeks later we were allocated temporary accommodation. It consisted of rooms at the top of a four storey house. We had to share the toilet with two other families. There was no bath. It was on the edge of a densely populated Loyalist area – the Fountain Estate. We accepted it because we knew if we didn't we would never get another house.

We didn't stay there any longer than six weeks. It was coming up to the Loyalist marching season and us being Catholics, they didn't want us there. It was after midnight, one night in early August, when a crowd of Loyalists came and threatened to burn us out. There we were at the top of the house, with our four young children, and very much afraid, not knowing how we would get out if they carried out their threat. I don't know to this day how John Hume knew about our plight. The British army arrived and the crowd that was threatening us cleared. The army told us that John Hume was in touch with their commanding officer and they had orders to stay and guard us until the morning. I never was so relieved in my life.

The next day John Hume got in touch with the city council and told them they would have to get us housed that day because we were not safe. They had to open a house that was boarded up and waiting to be demolished. We were glad to know they had found us somewhere to live, even though it was only temporary. When we were packed up, and our furniture and belongings were in the van ready to go, the Loyalists were jeering at us and calling us names. It was so humiliating.

Things were getting worse. The control of the British army was handed over to Stormont which was 100 per cent Unionist. This upset the Nationalists and caused more riots. During the riots the British army shot dead a young boy who they claimed had been carrying a nail bomb. It was untrue. There was no evidence to support their allegation. Everything was getting out of control and the Nationalist people felt very frustrated. Then came internment in 1971. Internment was a way of lifting people and keeping them locked up. Usually their only crime was living in a Nationalist area, being a Catholic or being a suspected Republican. It did not solve the problem, it made it worse. The people felt that here again the State was attacking the Nationalist community which we were not going to take lying down. More people came on to the streets to protest against these injustices.

The worst day of all was 28 January 1972 – now known as Bloody Sunday. Innocent people were shot dead on our streets for marching for their civil rights. The people were numb, they couldn't believe what had happened, the whole town was in chaos. The days that followed saw the whole city in mourning, the atmosphere was so sad, there was real heaviness in the air. Everyone knew someone who was shot. My husband's young cousin, aged 17, was among the dead. The Widgery Tribunal was an affront to the people of Derry and to the memory of those who died. It left the Nationalist population with a tremendous rage.

So like everyone else, my husband and my brothers joined in the defence of the Nationalist people with rioting and whatever was called for. There were many nights when I was at home, worrying for their safety, with my four young children and expecting my fifth, praying that the terrible nightmare would end.

CATHY

I was born in Derry in 1953. In our street there were four public houses, a brewery, a tea factory, an electricity sub-station and two greengrocers. We lived in the middle of it all and there was never a dull moment. I loved all the hustle and bustle. I used to sit on the windowsill and watch the world go by. My mother and father were 18 and 20 when they married and they had ten children, one of whom died soon after he was born. My father drove a hearse and taxied to make ends meet. He was a strong, tall man who took no nonsense. My mother was a sensible, kind person who loved everybody and was, in my eyes, the perfect mother.

Life was happy and normal until April 1969. I'd gone up town to sell tickets for the YMCA when rioting started in the lower town. The rioters were having running battles up and down William Street and it was a nightmare getting home. I arrived back to find my father cooking tea because my mother was sick in bed. There were terrible noises coming from the street below. I looked out of the bedroom window to see what was happening. The police were batoning people outside the door and my father went to see what was happening.

When my father was at the door the police charged and because the rioters were trapped, some of them ran in through our open door. My father, not knowing what was happening, slammed the door. The policemen outside got a battering ram and smashed it down on top of him. They beat him into the sitting room and down into a corner beside where I was sitting. The blood from his head wound splashed all over me. We were all screaming and more policemen started to pile into the sitting room. When there was no more room for any more policemen around my father – they were beating him brutally – they came and started beating the rest of us in the room. I had rolled myself into a ball to protect my stomach. They beat me around the back, head and legs and when they couldn't get at me any more they pulled my legs and dragged me off the settee. They kicked me on my legs and on my tail bone. I must have passed out then because I woke up later with blood dripping down my face. I was lying across the fireplace. I was sixteen years old.

My father was lying in the middle of the floor in a pool of blood. I was sure he was dead. His head was busted open. His glasses were smashed on his face, his false teeth were broken and half hanging out of his mouth, and needless to say, he was unconscious. I couldn't stand up so I crawled over to where my father was lying and the knees of his jeans were soaking with his blood. He never moved and now I was sure he was dead. I tried to take his teeth out in case he swallowed them. I crawled to the hall and our Ann lifted me up and walked me to the sink to wash my face. When we were finished we went into the sitting room. My father was lifted on to the settee and he had a sheet or towel wrapped around his head. He looked awful. His head was bleeding profusely, his nose was broken, he had two black eyes. His hands were double their size because he tried to protect his head with them.

We learned later his breast bone and his ribs were broken and he had bruising all over his body. I think if my father hadn't been so strong, he would have died then. The ambulance came and we had to carry my father out on a stretcher, past the policemen who did this to him. We were really afraid but a lot of the neighbours had come out of their houses, and got around us. I was glad to see them. I went in the ambulance with my father but I don't remember the journey.

The hospital was very busy that night with people hurt in the riots. When we came home the house was packed with strangers and one was trying to brush my father's blood off the carpet. The front door was hanging off and the police were all gone. The street lights were all broken which added to the eerie atmosphere.

My father remained in hospital for four days and the day he was released he took a massive coronary. This was now 23 April. They airlifted him to a hospital in Belfast where he remained for a month. He was discharged on 19 May. Two months later on 17 July he took another massive coronary and died. He was 43 years of age.

The coroner, Dr Marshall said, 'It would be entirely speculative to try to determine whether or not his injuries could have precipitated his thrombosis.' He said my father 'would have been prone to heart attacks and coronary disease'. This is totally untrue. My father was never before treated for any problems with his heart, nor did he suffer from heart problems. He was 43 years old when he died, the father of nine children aged from 2 to 20.

My father's funeral was one of the biggest Derry had ever seen. In the region of 25,000 people attended and we girls weren't allowed to go. My mother feared for our safety, and also girls didn't go to funerals at that time. We stayed at home with our distraught mother whilst the men went to the cemetery. It was the saddest day of my life and I will never forget the intense pain I felt. But far from being the end of our family's tragedy, it was just the beginning.

More trouble was expected on 12 August 1969 – during the Apprentice Boys' march. My mother took us all to Ballybofey – a small town thirty miles into the Republic – because she didn't want us to be exposed to any more violence. Rioting went on for three days and nights continuously. It was so bad they named it the Battle of the Bogside. It was after these riots that the army was brought into Derry and Belfast.

When we were watching the riots on the news we saw our house burned down with all our belongings in it. The Loyalists had come to burn down the cathedral but the men of Derry drove them away from the cathedral, so they burned and destroyed everything in their path, including our house. We arrived home to a burnt out shell. My mother was left on the street with nine children, and nothing left of our lives, one month after she buried my father. But from this my mother rose to become a stronger, more resilient person, and she insisted we got on with things as best we could without looking back.

She took ten driving lessons and passed her test first time. She had no time to mess about, she had to be able to drive to survive. She was 40. She took a job in a shirt factory where she used to work before she was married. She hired a caravan in Buncrana – fifteen miles into the Republic – because we had nowhere else to go. There was no bed for her, so she sat up all night. She said it was her lowest moment, sitting there in the dark while we all slept, with everything going through her mind. Eventually the Housing Executive gave us a small modern house back in Derry. It was supposed to be temporary accommodation but we are still there. Most of us are married now and have our own homes. Sadly, my mother has passed away, so my youngest sister lives there alone, thirty years later.

BERNADETTE

I was 13 when the troubles – as they are euphemistically called – broke out in the six counties. My knowledge of the political situation was nil and at first it was a great adventure for me and the children of our generation to head down to William Street and the Roseville Flats to watch the men and young fellas throwing stones and petrol bombs at the much hated police. We even helped to gather the stones and empty milk bottles to make effective bombs. I remember walking to school every morning and collecting empty CS gas canisters which had been fired at the men who were defending the Bogside from the police. The Bogside had become a no-go area at this time and someone had painted a large slogan on a gable wall saying 'YOU ARE NOW ENTERING FREE DERRY'. The slogan still remains to this day and is now world famous. The rioting and snatch squads remained a daily occurrence. When the British army were sent in to Belfast and Derry the rioting eased off for a few weeks.

My family were strong Nationalists and were very much against the British forces coming into Ireland. My mother warned us to stay away from the soldiers, saying we would soon find out what they were really like. Our home became the place where Civil Rights leaders met from time to time, among them Bernadette

Devlin (now McAlisky). I remember her saying to us the day the army arrived, 'Look which way their guns are pointing – towards the Nationalists!' She was proved right as later events were to reveal.

The riots soon broke out again and I remember seeing two men shot dead. My friend Annette McGaugan was shot as she was running away from a riot. The RUC had been firing rubber bullets but one of them opened up with a live round and shot Annette dead. She was fourteen. This was the incident that brought the Troubles home to me, and when my outlook started to change. I went on my first Civil Rights march with some of my friends but by the end of that day thirteen people lay dead and many more were injured.

My ignorance about politics went. I became well versed about the ways in which Irish Catholic people were being suppressed and about the terrible bigotry emanating from the Stormont government, the RUC and the Orange lodges. From being a 13 year old, naive child I grew, in the intervening years, to become a politically aware, strong nationalist. Whilst not actively participating in any of the IRA operations I found myself more and more on the side of the men and women who took up arms for the cause.

All my school days were overshadowed by army jeeps and army personnel crawling over the whole area where I still live. I remember the way they intimidated even the school children, sitting in their Saracens outside the school gates, taunting them. Stones and bottles would be thrown and another riot would begin. My girlhood was coloured by the actions of the army and the police who regularly raided our home in the early hours of the morning looking for anything subversive, or any of the boys who were on the run, and who could count on a night's shelter in many houses in Creggan and the Bogside – ours being one of them.

When the RUC went on the rampage in the Bogside calling us Fenian Bastards, Roman Catholic Scum – waving their revolvers, running their batons along the fences, smashing windows and kicking in doors – it was amongst the most terrifying experiences of my life. The Civil Rights leaders rounded us all up and marched us to the Creggan – which is situated on a hill above the Bogside – leaving the RUC to do their dirty work. When they found no one left to terrorise they would leave. But we knew they would be back another day.

All through the Troubles I still had a social life. I went to the dance halls in Derry and Muff. Muff is in Donegal and to get there we had to go through an army checkpoint. Everyone was made to get off the bus and be searched, before being allowed back on and off to the dancing. Some of my friends were shot and a lot of them spent many years in jail – all of which has had an everlasting effect on my life. I have done a lot of voluntary work and community work but always I have kept my interest in the politics of the region. I remain convinced that the greatest disaster was the day Michael Collins signed the treaty that divided our country.

These accounts are, of course, immensely revealing about working class women's lives and are described in ways that serve to place on record something of the 'ordinary' existence of Derry women, at a period of time and in a place that will – for other reasons – be viewed as anything but ordinary by historians. These are women who anticipate with pleasure a night out with the girls, go about their business, take care of their families, give meaning to their memories and develop strategies for survival. Their collected words reveal hard lives lived in the spaces between poverty and hard work, family loyalties and family responsibilities, sexual desire and sexual oppression; and between men's considerable capacity for violence, institutionalised by the troubles in the wider society and by the 'compulsory' nature of heterosexuality (Rich 1980) in intimate relationships. These are important voices and subversive spaces – the kinds of contested space in which feminist and alternative explanations can take root. They can be places which Henri Lefebvre (Barr 1999a) refers to as 'spaces of enunciation' and in which Chantelle Mouffe finds, in 'the hegemonic gap', more than a little room for political manoeuvre (Mouffe 1992). They are the spaces within which women still have the opportunity to make their own history and can begin to re-negotiate the terms and conditions of their relationships and their lives; especially when they have spoken 'out loud' about their feelings, their concerns and their priorities in the company of others with whom they share experiences, solidarities and understandings.

In conversation with me, the women talk about what they know as being 'common sense'. They laugh and shrug their shoulders and say, 'but everyone knows about things like this – it's life'. They do not regard their writing as being particularly political. Sinn Fein, the SDLP, the peace process are political – involving decisions made by others, somewhere more important than in the Rosemount Resource Centre.

They do not regard themselves as 'educated' either. Reading some of the accounts of their childhood, it is hard to imagine how school could possibly have been taken seriously. A lot of learning was going on informally about family, poverty, history, imperialism, religion and struggle, but formal education, for the most part, was something that circumstances and schooling persuaded them they were not very good at long ago. This 'having another go' has only come about because they are members of what is now a strong women's group whose enthusiasm is contagious for doing things together that would previously have been thought impossible.

They are probably right not to associate what they know with 'educated knowledge' – a whole his-story of intellectual thought has contributed to the social construction of 'expert' knowledge as something which is masculinist, objective, conceptual, rational and logical. It is something not to be confused with 'common sense' and indeed, there is little danger that anyone 'in the know' would confuse the two.

In more conventional and malestream academic contexts the women's stories would probably be dismissed as 'anecdotal' or 'subjective', from which little 'factual' truth could be generalised about the gendered class relations which are their subject matter. Indeed, the locally based tutor I asked to work with the women's group, corrected their grammar and spelling but would not engage with them in the content of what they had written. She confided in me that she thought their writing lacked analysis and references to theories which would have indicated that they were 'learning something' by doing it. Of course she should have been helping to validate experience, identify issues, make connections and build new knowledge in dialogue with the group. But she did not see why collective discussion of the women's writing was an important recognition of the individual courage it must have taken to write some of the pieces and a way of making connections, developing theories, and enhancing solidarities. Not surprisingly, the women came to this conclusion for themselves.

In more radical academic contexts their words would be regarded as 'subjugated knowledge' which – more than likely – needed the intervention of radical educators and cultural workers to rescue what is being said from oblivion and to reinstate its significance, in the process of encouraging conscientisation. I was, after all, at the end of a telephone, encouraging them to continue, promising a workshop to supply some of the missing links, suggesting they put the stories together into a book for other women to read. This is not to dismiss the intellectual processes which help to connect the 'personal' to the 'political', or which encourages critical thinking in pursuit of personal and social transformation. I have been an advocate and activist in relation to both of these principles for more years than I care to remember, and have drawn considerable inspiration from others in the women's movement and in the radical adult education movement who have shared similar views. But as I get older, I realise that both ideas need to be treated with a measure of humility.

The workshop which was arranged to discuss some of the learning that went on, and to decide what to do next, was attended by all of the women who had taken part in the autobiography project, plus a number of volunteers and centre workers. Jacqueline came on her way to a frightening court appearance concerning allegations of child abuse against her former partner. Bernadette brought her mother in a wheelchair – who is recovering from a stroke – both of whom are half way through writing their autobiographies and did not want to miss the session. Eilish was in the middle of arranging a wedding party. Ann and Frances were on their way to work. Almost all the women inhabit difficult and busy lives but still made space for 'education' when it mattered to them and in a context which seemed relevant.

The workshop was informal, personal, irreverent, thoughtful – and deadly serious. Brid had not talked before about her illegitimate child. Cathy had not talked about her father's death or spoken about how it felt to be kept at home as a girl whilst 25,000 people took part in his funeral. She had not, until this project, attempted any kind of political analysis of what happened to her family in 'the troubles'.

Writing and listening to each other's stories is very powerful and helps women to take another look at where they stand – not only in their own lives but also in each other's battles – to begin to examine what is going on underneath. It is a process that can be painful and can be wonderful. In terms of consciousness and change it is something that has to be gone through, and gone through as collectively as possible. Education will only empower women if it enables them to act collectively on their own reality in order to understand it. Theory cannot be separated from practice and personal experience cannot be related to the wider social context without some reference to theory. This is not an argument for similarity – although I do believe that as women, we have at least as many things in common as things which make us different. In writing about women's identity in situations of conflict – like Northern Ireland – Cynthia Cockburn makes use of the term 'mixity' to denote an intermingling of elements that retain their uniqueness. The democratic space between women must involve bridge building but also allow for difference. The point is to steer a way collectively through the mixity and the difference towards 'a careful and caring struggle in a well lit space' (Cockburn 1998). In the end, women have to make sense of the world together, in order to change it for the better.

Considerable though Freire's contribution has been to the notion of conscientisation, critical pedagogy and dialogical method, as the means by which radical educators should help to empower people to overcome their oppression and acquire what he calls 'greater humanity', they all depend on an extremely rationalist understanding of what constitutes learning, and what is likely to bring about social change. Freirian theory also relies on a fairly singular view of what constitutes 'greater humanity' – which is seen as the antithesis of oppression and the prize for overcoming it.

> As such, the Freirian approach does not consider the possibility that different groups might propose different – even conflicting – definitions of 'humanisation'. In its simple oppressor–oppressed model of power and its implicit assumption that when the oppressed perceive themselves in relation to the world they will act together to change it, it fails to acknowledge the possibility of a contradictory experience of oppression among the oppressed.
>
> (Weiler 1991)

In Derry, for example, some women I talked to made jokes about punishment beatings – which I could not laugh along with myself – in ways that I could only understand as their, not surprising, alienation from 'official' sources of law enforcement, or resignation. It also felt distinctly difficult at times to be defined as British. It made me think about what Barbara Kingsolver says in *The Poisonwood Bible* about walking across Africa with her wrists unshackled, in a white skin, wearing some threads of the prosperity stolen by imperialism: 'Some of us know how we came by our fortune, and some of us don't, but we wear it all the same. There's only one question worth asking now: how do we aim to live with it?' (Kingsolver 1999).

In such circumstances the appeal to 'common humanity' on the basis of only partial understanding and particular definitions of reality seems highly dubious. Like 'sisterhood', 'humanisation' is probably a concept that, although extremely well-intentioned, should now be consigned to history in the recognition that life is altogether more complicated. But at the same time, solidarities and political allegiances that are made between women need to take into account and be able to recognise the ways in which social and cultural differences are sources of both strength and ignorance, which must receive careful attention and more discussion and which require more tolerance than is usual in difficult times.

The capacity to make political sense of the personal, in a way that increases political consciousness, which can then be used as the inspiration and justification for taking political action – although an approach associated with radical feminism – also presupposes some kind of recognisable consensus and overly rational ontology. Whilst this can no doubt be explained by the residual influence of enlightenment thinking on second wave feminism, which also adopted for a while – rather uncritically, in retrospect – the Marxist notion of 'false consciousness' as a characteristic affliction of the oppressed, these are both 'certainties' which now need to be treated with greater caution. The notion of 'false consciousness' is extremely problematic. The exploited and the oppressed are often only too well aware of their exploitation and oppression; what is needed is less the raising of consciousness and more the access to resources and the strengthening of their ability to protest and mobilise for change (Agarwal 1994).

What might be more useful to oppressed groups in the struggle against patriarchy, poverty and social exclusion, for example, might be access to wider networks, assistance with material resources and organisational frameworks that individuals and groups can use to progress their own concerns in their own way. When the locally based tutor turned out to be less than committed or useful, the women got on with organising what they needed themselves. Just as in other areas of their lives they have refused to be defeated or dependent on unreliable others. This is why their group will survive and will go from strength to strength.

The accounts written by the Derry women give no sense of women who regard themselves as victims. They have chosen what to write about quite self-consciously. They might not call it 'political' but they could have chosen instead to write something totally innocuous about a favourite pet or an outing to the seaside. Instead they reveal women who have battled through distressing and appalling circumstances; looking for solutions to their problems; finding friendship, solidarity and some pleasure along the way; who are strong enough and sufficiently eloquent to give meaning and significance to the moments of being that have shaped their lives. And who are still learning from their continuing struggles.

In one way, they are giving voice to what Anthony Giddens calls 'life politics', revealing disputes and struggles about how, as individuals and groups of people, we should live in a world that used to be fixed by nature or tradition but which is now subject to human decisions involving power and, hopefully, dialogue and participation (Giddens 1994). In pursuit of what Giddens calls 'generative politics' and the 'democratising of democracy', it is critical that individuals and groups of individuals are involved in making things happen rather than have things happen to them. It is also vital that this be achieved through dialogue rather than through pre-established and arbitrary forms of power. Finding a voice to do this – and in the Derry women's case, a collective voice – is clearly gathering momentum through the social, mutually supportive, and educational activities of their group. This should be regarded as political activity in which a space has been opened up for public discussion about the issues with which they are concerned. They are forcing into the public domain aspects of social conduct that previously went undiscussed or were settled by traditional practices. And as such, their voices help to contest the official, the patriarchal, the privileged and the academic view of things.

In addition, these are working class women who keep families and communities together, despite the disasters provoked by wider social and political circumstances and by individuals (men, mostly) over whom they have no control. It is a world in which those who are supposed to help – the politicians, the army, the police and social workers, for example – have become part of the problem. It is impossible to read the women's stories without hearing the voices and something of the character and the spirit of the women coming through. These are not the same voices which are heard in the speeches of career politicians and academics talking about working class and women's lives. They tell a different story about poverty, oppression, resistance and resilience that is not statistical, pathological or conventionally political, but which is grounded in the democratic and reflexive authority of lived experience. An experience which is understood as accurately and passionately as any of us ever manage to do when sifting through the realities and contradictions of complicated and shifting uncertainties.

When voices such as these make knowledge, narrow definitions of what is thought to be 'educated knowledge' – and who makes it – are thrown into question. The accounts written by the Derry women reveal 'that people can develop better understandings of their social world through more democratic knowledge-making practices and structures than are current at present; and they can work to transform it' (Barr 1999a). They serve to illustrate and enact part of what Susan Bordo refers to as 'the messy, slippery practical struggle' to 'create institutions and communities that will not permit some groups of people to make determinations about reality for all' (Bordo 1990). They demonstrate, quite vividly, the significance of what Michele Le Doeuff has called one of the 'major contradictions of our times', by which she means the loss of language amongst the learned (brought about by postmodernist understandings), and the urgent need to discuss problems with people other than academics (Le Doeuff 1991). They enable the articulation of what Sandra Harding (Harding 1994) and Jean Barr refer to as 'voices from below', which are not 'truer and more accurate accounts of the world' by virtue of being from below 'but because, in identifying and making available spaces where alternative ways of thinking and being can be worked up, such practices increase the possibilities of knowledge – that is, knowledge which is useful to those who generate it' (Barr 1999a). In this respect, the Derry women and their writing provide some important lessons for us all.

12

ACTIVE IN THE UNION

Throughout the 1980s and early 1990s government and local authority cuts in spending on community based adult education, together with the widespread abolition and downsizing of university extramural departments and the shift in emphasis towards funding for accredited, qualification-led provision at the expense of informal and non-accredited provision, have all contributed to making it much more difficult to sustain grass roots, working class and women's education with a radical edge. Further reorganisation of post-sixteen education is, at the time of writing, the subject of government legislation (Learning and Skills Bill 1999). Community-based learning has been put back on the agenda but it is too soon to predict precisely what this will mean.

At the same time, the absorption of access programmes (for adults returning to education in later life) into accreditation schemes, and Further Education programmes linked to progression routes and franchise deals with universities, may look like a victory for second chance education and partnerships between different kinds of educational institution. But the consequences of 'entering the mainstream' have been considerable in terms of losing the very students – poor, working class, black – which second chance and access programmes were originally created to attract (Taking Liberties Collective 1989).

Meanwhile, the struggle to establish the credibility and relevance of Women's Studies as a legitimate academic discipline in universities throughout the 1980s and 1990s has been 'assisted' by making the most of the research and publications potential of its subject matter and by the widespread shift in emphasis towards gender studies, but also at a price. No one but a dinosaur now expects there to be any connection between grass roots, radical, feminist politics, concerned to change the world for women, and what happens in a university modular degree programme that might or might not include modules relating to gender and identity or women's writing and history (Thompson 1995).

Life on the margins might have made some of us feel marginalised in the past (Taking Liberties Collective 1989) but the space created – often at some physical and certainly philosophical distance from HQ – also provided a fair degree of autonomy with opportunities to be exploited. Before the spread of achievement-driven outcomes and funding, it was much more possible to engage with working class women in educational activities that were life changing but which have now become largely sanitised and centralised. So widespread has the consequence of incorporation become that – with a few rare and individual exceptions – the last place to look for radical and serious learning opportunities, which attract and are relevant to poor and working class women from pauperised communities and in low paid casualised employment, is in mainstream educational provision. The conventional wisdom that 'such women' are not interested in education is not true. What is more true is that in failing to take on board the reality of their lives – including domestic, financial, state benefit, child care and work issues – mainstream educational provision has so far paid only lip service to widening participation and creation of an imaginative agenda for lifelong learning (Thompson 2000).

According to Veronica McGivney,

> those most adversely affected by the loss of informal and low cost re-entry routes are: women who lack the confidence or means to return to formal education; those who left school early with no qualifications; those with little or no post school learning experience; women with very low incomes; single parents; some groups of ethnic minority women and women living in badly served peripheral estates, rural areas and deprived inner cities.
>
> (McGivney 1998)

The potential and actual demand for education by working class women has not gone away, however, but in order for it to re-surface it needs more conducive contexts. The energy unleashed by the women's group in Derry is one example, among many, of the significant part played in community activism by working class women. Another is the glorious and powerful mix of seriousness and irreverence I have come to appreciate in the company of working class women, active in the union, and involved in some recent trade union courses I have helped to develop.

The General Federation of Trade Unions (GFTU), operating as an educational trust, provides a varied programme of courses for its affiliated member unions. The development of a women's studies programme over the last two or three years has begun to change the face of traditional trade union provision, especially in relation to women. Some of the larger unions have made education a priority over the last ten years or so. Unison, for example, has developed an impressive Return to Learn programme in partnership with the Workers Education Association (WEA), and is now involved in workplace learning initiatives – in partnership with education providers and employers – for low paid workers. Some of the smaller unions – typically those which are affiliated to the GFTU trust – have fewer resources and consequently benefit from a more collaborative approach. Women can attend any of the courses on offer – and some do. But for historical and familiar reasons, the general courses remain male dominated, displaying many of the attendant consequences that serve to subdue and minimise the equal participation of women. On the women's courses, however, the significance and effectiveness of women learning together is as powerful and empowering as any other kind of learning I have been involved in. And I include myself as one who has felt inspired and empowered by the experience.

The long march of women into employment has made enormous strides during the last twenty years. Paid work is no longer regarded as something women do for pin money or as a hobby. Between 1984 and 1997 the number of women in full time employment increased by 800,000 whereas the number of men in full time employment fell by 600,000. A report commissioned by Barclays Bank and the Institute of Economic Research at the University of Warwick both agree that this 'scissor type tendency' will continue for at least the next twenty years (Pahl and Scales 1999). But overall, the expansion is likely to be in part time jobs which will not provide the kind of wages that are sufficient to live on.

In 1999, 53 per cent of mothers with children under five were actively employed in work and women in general now make up almost 50 per cent of the labour force. In some areas, especially those which have seen a marked decline in heavy industries and manufacturing (as a consequence of economic restructuring, globalisation, the shift to services and the development of electronically based new technologies) women actually outnumber men in the labour market (Walby 1997; Franks 1999). By the end of 1996, according to the Office for National Statistics, women in paid employment outnumbered men by 12,000 – something that had never happened in peacetime before. One in five women currently earns more than her partner, despite the fact that most women workers are employed part time (Pahl and Scales 1999). Employers on the look out for the 'soft skills' of people management, team working and flexible specialisation are increasingly likely to appoint women in preference to men – especially in the expanding service sectors such as education, health and social work. Looking forward to the year 2020, Ray Pahl predicts that the pay differential between men and women in professional jobs will have disappeared and women will by then make up 50 per cent of the professional workforce (Pahl and Scales 1999).

However, the demands made by second wave feminism for 'the right to work', 'equal pay for equal work' and an end to sex discrimination at work have not yet brought liberation to the majority of women. Women still enter the labour market with prevailing social assumptions about domestic and childcare responsibilities intact. Especially working class women who are least likely to be able to pay other women to help them out on the home front. According to Suzanne Franks, the feminisation of the labour market actually means

> armies of low paid women in service industries. For the vast majority of women, work has not brought liberation; they work in segmented, low paid, part time jobs, because average families need a second wage – a tedious reality far removed from the glossy magazine image of working women.
>
> (Franks 1999)

Marj is part of this army. She has two grown up children, one of whom is still living at home, while the other, a student, still needs her support. She has two jobs – one as a catering assistant in a restaurant, the other as a morning cleaner. She is also doing a college course to improve her own employment prospects and fits the part time jobs around her studies.

> I left school at fifteen with no qualifications at all. I hated it at the time and there were plenty of jobs. My mother made me go to college for a year so I could be a shorthand typist. My mother had it all mapped out for me. Being a shorthand typist was a skill – something to go back to once I'd got married and had my family. My whole life planned out for me at fifteen. So I went to college and I also learned how to sew, how to wash and how to iron a shirt and entertain at the dinner table. I never questioned any of it until about five years ago. Then I got divorced and had to find a way back into the workforce. I have two jobs because I am a part time worker. In the first I can work anything from eight hours a week to thirty eight hours a week. I don't have a limited set of hours. I don't have a contract stating how many hours I am actually supposed to work. I got another job because the hours were so irregular and the pay was so low (£3.12 per hour before the minimum wage was introduced). Because I had to be available between 8.30 and 5.30 for the catering job – it meant something outside of these hours. Because I'm not skilled as a bar worker I got a job as a cleaner. There is no such thing as 'a *wee* cleaning job' by the way! I have two hours to clean the whole restaurant area, mop the kitchen floor, clean toilets, buff the floors – and for that I get £2.60 an hour. It's hard graft. I'm up at 5.30 every morning. The town centre is mobbed with cleaners waiting to get into stores. There are armies of women at half past six in the morning waiting to get in to do hard graft and then having to be out of the way by nine o'clock when the shops open. These are heavy jobs, they're dirty, and they're stressed jobs because you only have a short space of time in which to get them done. I don't even know what my boss looks like because he's a contractor and I'm paid through the bank. I'm not even sure of the company because these contract cleaners change so often. I don't get sick pay and I don't get holiday pay and in the two and a half years I've been working as a cleaner I haven't seen a pay rise. I don't know how to go about negotiating a pay rise – there is no organisation in these places. Now I'm at college and going for a degree. I know the job I want – and I know I could do it without the bit of paper to prove I've got a degree – but you can't have one without the other these days. Fortunately for me I'm enjoying the course and finding it quite easy.

Jenny works five hours a day, five days a week as a cleaner.

> I always wanted to be a nurse from when I was five but my father persuaded me not to go into nursing because it was hard work and poor pay. I tried office jobs but I hated them. I went on a pre-nursing course but when I was waiting to start the real training I got pregnant so I had to kiss the training goodbye. After two years I returned to work as an auxilliary nurse because I had always had my own pay packet and I got frustrated asking my husband for money all the time. After my second child was born I went back to work again because we needed the money. I worked nights when my husband could look after the children but I had to give it up. Problems at home were making me depressed and I was having anxiety attacks and pigging out [eating too much]. My husband didn't realise how bad I felt. I decided I wanted to study – try to get a better job but my husband was threatened. In the end a friend got me a temporary cleaning job. Before I had always stayed clear of domestic work but I thought, well yes, I have been cleaning up human waste, washing up dishes shouldn't be very different. It was supposed to be for two weeks but I have been there ever since. The atmosphere at work depends on the mood of the chef. If he has a hangover he doesn't talk. I have a strong feeling he is prejudiced because I am black but also because of doing a cleaning job. He winds all the women up saying 'a woman's place . . .' and all that. The other women seem to think it is strange to have a black woman on the daytime staff – the boss likes to keep the black workers out of sight. But I have to work around the children. It's the way I've been brought up – to keep the family going. Now they have offered me a full time job with promotion and training. My husband is proud of me but I've stressed things will have to change. He'll have to help with more housework. My only problem is to find someone to look after my children for a few hours a day when they come home from school. I feel pleased with my promotion for myself as a woman and as a black woman.

Like Jenny, most women who enter the labour market are not doing so at the expense of children or partners. It is not because partners have suddenly become keen to re-negotiate the unpaid work on the home front and do more themselves. Or because employers have become generally converted to family friendly employment policies which take account of child-care and other caring responsibilities. Women are more likely than men to spend at least ten hours a week caring for sick or elderly relatives – a responsibility that has increased because of cuts in welfare state provision during the Thatcher years and because of the related emphasis on community care. Women are moving into paid work despite there being little change in social attitudes or related support elsewhere. For the most part, 'the invisible, unpaid economy that makes paid work possible is still a woman's world – and in a bottom line economy, where everything is perceived in terms of financial value, its status is lower than ever' (Franks 1999).

Optimistic forcasts about equal pay for equal work, a quarter of a century after the Equal Pay Act came into effect in 1975, is, for the vast majority of women, still a pipe dream. The average woman working full time still earns only three-quarters as much money as the average man. The Labour Force Survey of 1997 and the Employment Policy Institute estimate that the gender pay gap across all workers is around 74 per cent (Employment Policy Institute 1997). Whether it is in the board room or on the shop floor women earn less than men. In managerial jobs in banks and building societies and in sales women earn around 60 per cent of the average male wage. In manual occupations women's average weekly earnings are 65 per cent those of men. For part time workers, the position is worst of all. The average hourly rate for part time women workers is 61 per cent of the average male rate and has risen only two percentage points during the last twenty years, despite the sizeable increase in women working part time (Employment Policy Institute 1997). All the available research shows a widening gap between highly educated, usually full time women workers who have entered well paid, secure employment, and the majority of women – as many as 90 per cent – who occupy low paid, insecure and low status jobs (Dex *et al.* 1996).

The fact that 45 per cent of women in the labour market work part time compared to 8 per cent of men means that women are six times more likely than men to be in part time employment. This is some recognition of the extent to which women still have to fit jobs and careers around family responsibilities and a great deal to do with the market's increasing interest in casual, short term and part time workers for reasons of maximum flexibility. However, the claim that such jobs are offered to women on the basis of 'fitting in with domestic and family responsibilities' is common but largely spurious. The woman who does two or three part time jobs at the same time – on top of her domestic responsibilities – is trying to earn a living wage. Working part time in deregulated, tightly controlled and low status jobs, for not very much money, is just as much a trap as the poverty trap experienced by those on benefits. The extent to which many women are overqualified for the jobs they do says everything about the deskilling of women's work and about the undervaluing of women's skills when it comes to the so called soft skills associated with being nice to people and in caring related occupations (Franks 1999).

Rajinder is an Asian woman working in a small supermarket for an Asian boss. Here she is speaking about her terms and conditions of employment before the minimum wage was introduced in 1999, when she was earning £2.50 an hour.

> I work from 9.30 to 6 p.m. I get a lunch hour of one hour (unpaid) and a tea break in the afternoon of fifteen minutes that he pays. He's alright but says business is not running well – we do not have the customers we expect. So he says if you want to leave this job, go. He says he cannot afford to pay more.

Before she came to Britain from India Rajinder was working as a teacher.

> I was a teacher in India but here I need 'A'-levels and to do another course. English is my second language – I find it difficult. I can work in any shop because of seven years experience. But I would like a better job, I am trying.

In addition, economic restructuring has increased the proportion of workers on casual, temporary and short-term contracts – many of them women – as opposed to workers on permanent contracts. By 1995 there were one and a half million workers in temporary jobs, a figure that increased by 10 per cent over the previous year and by 50 per cent in the previous ten years (Walby 1997; Dex *et al.* 1996). Temporary jobs and short-term contracts are frequently justified in terms of flexibility but they mean increased insecurity for workers. In such circumstances, the hard won terms and conditions for working life, won by trade union negotiators over generations – to provide fringe benefits, maternity, holiday and sick pay, equal opportunities at work and training opportunities – no longer apply. Flo works in the staff canteen of a well known supermarket chain, where she has seen working conditions for women workers deteriorate in recent years.

> I used to cook for about 90 everyday but now it's very few. They cut all the hours for checkout girls. Now they do three or four hours at a time and they are not entitled to a break. When a full timer leaves they are always replaced with three part timers instead. Then all the full timers were made redundant. At least half the women in the store do eight hour contracts but they work more because of overtime. They've lost out on holiday and sick pay because of it. Now only the managers and team leaders are full time – there are a few on twelve to fifteen hours but the rest are on eight hours. All the managers are men but some of the team leaders are women. You don't really know from one week to the next how many hours you've got. The hours are given out by the team leaders on the checkouts and they tell you on Monday if your hours have changed. The women moan but they say at their interview they can be flexible . . . I don't think they realise how flexible they are meant to be. If they ring you up, you are not supposed to say No. They expect you to come in. Although the girls on the tills have had their hours cut, they have to work faster. It comes up on a computer how many customers you have served and how much money you have taken. Sometimes you get overtime. Sometimes nothing. Sometimes you are forced into it – like when it's stock-taking. You have no choice. You have to do it. In the past you could refuse. Now the new manager says anyone refusing to do it will have disciplinary action taken against them.
>
> It's not a happy place to work anymore. At one time you wore a badge so that the management could recognise you and call you by your name. Now it's just a flick of the fingers and 'hey, I'm talking to you'. People are not happy with the working conditions but still we have a laugh and a

joke. Nine times out of ten it's a joke about how the store is run. It's like a prison camp – what you have to wear, if you want to go to the toilet you have to ask permission. If they won't let you off the till, you have to wait even if you're desperate. When the customers say 'you've never got a smile' I don't think they realise that there isn't that much to smile about. People can't afford to join the union now, they only join when something happens upstairs [i.e. problems with the management].

In the temporary market place, employment agencies now compete to provide a 'just in time workforce' to employers who have become 'lean' through downsizing and outsourcing, but who are still in need of peripheral workers on an occasional basis. In these circumstances the work force becomes simply another commodity, supplied – just in time – like components for cars or computers, by an outside supplier. The 'slack period' becomes the problem of the individual who must adapt to periods of unpaid activity, rather than a cost to the employer. Taken to extremes – but by no means unusual – is the zero hours contract, by which workers are on standby with no guaranteed income – waiting on the promise of work should a class need to be taught, a bed need to be made or a checkout need to be operated. Jean works as a full time organiser in a trade union representing women in the retail industry. She knows from experience what restructuring and temporary contracts have meant to women in the labour market.

The introduction of part time hours over a number of days – instead of part time jobs for two or three days at a time – increases the costs of travel and fitting in family responsibilities. Short shifts can mean unsociable hours – especially as companies introduce twenty-four hour trading. Restructuring generally means reapplying for your job somewhere along the line – and finding either the pay has been cut or extra duties have been added in that weren't there before – or both. Threats of redundancy are a nightmare when people have family responsibilities and living costs to meet. I receive more phonecalls each week from members suffering from stress related illnesses than ever before – people are finding it difficult to cope. One of the main problems is the war going on between companies – in that they are introducing more and more competitive ways of keeping customers happy. In-store creche facilities for customers – which are off limits to the staff who work in the store – is just one example. What might seem like attractive price-cutting deals always means cost cutting somewhere else. It's our members who suffer because they have to take on more and more responsibilities and work longer hours to make a living wage. Some of those hours go unpaid if the tasks aren't completed in the allotted time. Zero hours – where the manager calls you up at home and if you're not sitting by the phone goes on to the next person – is becoming very common. Sunday working for no extra pay, changes to contracts, petty rules and – most of all – the fear factor of

> being unemployed. These all put pressure on our members – many of whom are too afraid and too poor to join the union. When I hear women say 'I'm only a part time worker' I feel distraught. I have to convince them that they have got a worth. They are employees and as such must be treated in a fair and reasonable way. Managers should value their workforce and not treat them like a disposable commodity but as the basis of a successful business. We have to have a strong membership to fight for the rights of all workers but especially women who are particularly vulnerable.

Patterns of casualised, temporary working now cover every kind of job from word processing, cleaning, supermarket sales and nursing to the television industry and education. By 1995–6 over 40 per cent of the teaching, academic and research staff in British universities were on fixed term contracts. The further education sector employed agency workers to fill temporary part time teaching slots. The insecurity affecting workers intensified by the contract culture and the multiplying demands of different workplaces – including the domestic workplace – is clearly much less conducive to health and stress levels than a full time job with regular hours in the same location (Coyle 1995).

The benefits to employers of employing part time and temporary workers are enormous, however, in that they cost less in wages, entitlements and overheads. They are not around long enough to be active in trade unions. And when their energy for doing boring and repetitive jobs begins to wane they can be replaced by the next shift – on and off around the clock. Women doing the week-end or night shift at supermarket checkouts, petrol stations and clothing and textile factories are what gives employers maximum flexibility to open all hours. They are not the terms and conditions that are likely to provide women with the kind of earning potential and career opportunities that will transform their lives – let alone fit in well with personal, family and community commitments.

Women do it, of course, not because they are now liberated compared to an earlier generation, but because they need the money. And because the present government imperative is such that getting people 'off welfare' and 'back to work' is seen as the solution to keeping the lid on public spending, encouraging enterprise and personal motivation, and promoting social cohesion. Rather than welfare dependency, New Labour would prefer labour market dependency – albeit a labour market largely comprised of low paid, casualised and unrewarding jobs. Of course, working class women have always worked to supplement the family income and have usually been remarkably invisible in discussions about the labour market. They still work – and in greater numbers – because they are frequently the sole breadwinners in single parent families; often the only wage earner in two parent families in which their partner is unemployed or redundant; and increasingly the joint wage earner in dual income families in which two sources of income are necessary to live comfortably and well in a country with one of the highest costs of living in the industrialised world.

I have to believe that, in the long run, women will have more independence and more choices in their lives if they have economic independence from men and from the state. Women who take up space in the labour market and in the public sphere are increasingly likely to want a say in how the public sphere operates. The presence of women in the labour market in large numbers does change assumptions about what constitutes masculinity and femininity. Women's issues in relation to paid work may be similar to men's, but they are also very different because women enter paid work on a different basis. Women's issues are more likely to be addressed by women who act collectively to improve the terms and conditions on which they sell their labour.

But equally it is cynical, and bad faith on the part of government, to advocate increased labour market activity as the principal solution to problems of poverty, welfare dependency, social cohesion and long term economic prosperity – so long as so much discrimination remains, and when the kind of labour market on offer to black and white working class and women workers is so de-regulated, precarious and unstable.

The increased polarisation in British society over recent years is played out in relation to the labour market. Those who have reasonably secure jobs and good employment prospects are much better positioned than those who do not. For those without a private income, the labour market is a major, structural determinant of life chances, income levels, health and well being, identity and self-esteem, social relationships and leisure opportunities. Those without reasonable or secure employment are consequently and progressively disadvantaged.

Whilst Margaret Thatcher and Tony Blair have both talked enthusiastically about promoting an enterprise and entrepreuneurial culture, in which, according to Thatcher, wealth will 'trickle down'; and according to Blair, 'a meritocratic society' will emerge, offering rewards and incentives to the many rather than the few; the evidence does not appear to confirm their optimism.

> In 1961 there was a three fold difference between the top decile point and the bottom decile point (in earnings). The differences increased to over fourfold by 1990. In the current decade there was some decrease in those on low incomes during the first half but from 1995/6 to 1996/7 the numbers with 'relative' low income (i.e. half the current year's average income) actually increased.
>
> (Pahl and Scales 1999)

According to a recent United Nations report, the UK is described as one of the most divided western countries, with the third highest proportion of people living in poverty amongst seventeen industrialised nations (Pahl and Scales 1999).

Those who are well placed in the labour market have a better chance of keeping their jobs and getting others. They are more likely to own houses that appreciate in value. They are likely to be healthier and live longer. Their children are likely to go to better schools. They are more likely to enhance their own cultural capital through Further Education or training. They are more likely to be involved in voluntary organisations, to be active in civil society and feel they have a stake worth defending and promoting within the political process.

Those in weak labour market positions will be forced to accept social housing – not always in locations of their choosing. They are likely to work anti-social hours in deregulated workplaces where the turnover of staff is high and contracts are temporary and insecure. These are the kinds of working conditions which make it harder for them to be 'good parents' or to play an active part in their children's education. These are conditions which leave few opportunities to acquire additional cultural capital for themselves by way of further education and training. Long hours and low wages leave little time, energy and resources for consumption of services, voluntary activities, active citizenship or leisure.

For reasons like these, 'really useful' programmes for women trade unionists need to take on board an enormous number of issues and need to begin with a clear recognition of the personal, political and economic realities of women's lives.

The women participating in the GFTU women's courses are union members, reps and shop stewards. Some are fairly new to the union and others have a wealth of experience, built up over a number of years. They work in a variety of industries including, bakeries, retail, textiles and clothing, light assembly work and components factories. Before the introduction of the minimum wage in 1999 most were earning less than £3.60 an hour. Some were able to boost their incomes by piecework and overtime. Some are part time workers; others represent women workers on part time contracts. Persuading part time women workers to join trade unions is a major difficulty. Persuading trade unions to take their concerns as seriously as those of full time (male) workers is still a battle that needs to be fought.

For some, the responsibility of representing other workers in alienating and demoralising workplaces can be a mixed blessing – which the language of solidarity does not always recognise and for which unions do not necessarily offer training and support. Jan, for example, told me how she felt harassed by management and work mates when she first became a shop steward.

> First there was verbal abuse from fellow work mates every time I left the department to do union duties which left them short staffed. Of course management could have replaced me but they knew the men I worked with would make my life hell if they missed their tea breaks and so they did nothing. This turned worker against worker. I made a complaint through my then senior shop steward but he lost the notes he'd made so there was no proof when I later needed it. When this man left I was voted into his position – which was an eight till five job in itself. When the company was informed I was the new senior shop steward they withdrew most of the facilities and time recognition Reg enjoyed when he did the job. I regarded this as sex discrimination – but doing something about it was a difficult matter. I tried to keep on top of my union duties

> before and after my shift – which took my working hours up to seventy hours a week before I even saw my family. This went on for nine months, during which time I was on twenty-four hour call courtesy of a BT bleep from my personnel director because members were complaining they could never get hold of me. They work in terrible conditions – which I really care about and want to change – but I felt very isolated. The men were sexist and the women were scared. It all had a terrible effect on me. I suffered headaches every day. I am ashamed to say I had to buy amphetamines to keep me awake – to even focus. I took the risk of being called for a random drug test which would have meant being sacked on the spot. The general level of abuse from my factory manager didn't help with remarks like 'fuck off, bitch!' 'You bore me with your complaining!' If he didn't want to speak to me, he'd change his clothes – taking his trousers off in front of me – which me feel physically sick.
>
> By the time I had been sacked for the second time in a month, my self esteem was at rock bottom. People would talk to me – I could see their mouths moving – but I couldn't take in a word they said. All my self confidence evaporated and people frightened me. Even now, I find it hard to trust people and my factory manager's insults always come back to haunt me, telling me I'm boring and stupid. One day a section manager asked me to have coffee with him in the canteen and told me he was worried about me. He hadn't seen me laugh for a long time (I was the practical joker – always having fun before). I couldn't tell him I didn't know how to laugh any more.
>
> After I was sacked my union did not want to act on any of this information because I couldn't prove any of it. This did me in as much as the abuse – given all the hours I had tried to put in on their behalf.

Women enter the workplace on different terms to men. There are still men's jobs and women's jobs. Women are still assumed to carry the major responsibility for child-care and domestic labour. Assumptions about sexuality and feminity are not left behind at the factory gate. Although there is perfectly sound historical, sociological and economic evidence to explain why women enter the workforce – and have every right to be there – residual sexism and discrimination operate in abundance. I am sure it is no coincidence that on almost every women's trade union course I have ever been involved in, women raise issues to do with sexual harassment and violence against women as two of their major concerns. Kath puts it like this:

> These old white men who are occupying the leadership seats had better sit up and take notice of us if they want our membership. I was working in an advertising agency, very busy, employed three hundred staff. I used to still try to get in to work on time, even though I'd had a battering the night before and been kept without sleep until four or five a.m. Imagine

> how I felt walking there next morning with a black eye? It wasn't that I would lie like some women do and say I'd fallen down stairs or something because I was ashamed. But I hid it as much as I could because I needed the money from that job to pay my half of the mortgage. One night I'd stayed late to do overtime, missed my train, and his tea wasn't on the table. It was things like that. But it not only affected my work and had me in front of management on a second verbal warning; it affected my chances of promotion and with that, the ability to earn enough to pay my own mortage. The shop steward was useless; I was with MSF at the time. He said it was my personal problem and I'd better sort my life out. Left me to face management on my own.
>
> My women's officer was very supportive when I contacted her; but she was at the other end of the country on the other end of a telephone. I had no confidence in this male shop steward who was old enough to be my father, and quite unsympathetic. At the time I questioned the validity of even belonging to a union. I'd been a member since I was sixteen, paid my subs for five years, and for what? There was nobody capable of putting my case to management, or of giving me advice about how to get out of that violent relationship. Even some older women were saying I should have left work on time and got his tea ready – putting the blame on me. Eventually I went through counselling which made me realise that I couldn't change him; it wasn't up to me to make more concessions, it was better to get out if he wouldn't stop. I did. But what about women with kids who might be doing a night shift at the bakery? How can they just drop everything, go for counselling and leave? They need advice. Right here, in the workplace, from a trained and sympathetic shop steward.

It is women activists, rather than men, in trade unions who have raised the issues about domestic violence in ways that have begun to make a difference. Erika explains why trade unions have to take domestic violence seriously.

> If a woman has been crocked up the night before and she's still got to turn up for work the next day and do her job, but she's physically or mentally suffering, then it becomes a trade union issue. She needs the support of her shop steward before it gets to the stage where her performance at work is affected and she's facing a disciplinary. But, the problems created by putting any absence down to sick leave, when in fact it's recovery from domestic violence, are disadvantageous. For instance, if a woman is aspiring to a career, and her performance over a five year period is examined, she may have far more sick leave on her record than is due to actual sickness, if you see what I mean. Her record might show six weeks sick leave in one year when, in fact five of those weeks are absence due to the effects of domestic violence. That puts her chances on the ladder a few

> rungs down whereas, if it was recorded as, say, compassionate leave, it would stand as a different comparison – as no fault of her own.
>
> Maternity and paternity leave don't have to go down as sick leave; neither should being battered by your husband/partner. In any case it shouldn't be hidden behind other language. What happens to women and children in private is important and should be made public. The personal is political. What we should remember when we're talking about women's issues – and domestic violence is one of those issues which affect our chances of equality – is that we're also talking about the next generation of women; and the next; and the next. We've got to make sure they don't go through the same shit as we did. They've got to be educated too, so they can have better lives, better opportunities. It's not just the lives of men that are important. Women's are too. Wherever the workplace is, wherever women are educated – school or college – there should be awareness raising campaigns, and the trade union movement should be taking an up front role in this. Domestic violence affects our employment and other areas of our lives. Why should any of the aspects of women's suffering at the hands of men be hidden from the rest of the world? Men are getting away with murder.

Women activists in trade unions also have to be vigilant about discrimination and harassment when it comes to challenging the gendered nature of labour market divisions. The fire service, for example, remains deeply misogynist and resistant to women who imagine they can become fire fighters. Jill has joined the Fire Brigades Union but finds

> one of the main things for the blokes is they feel threatened. I mean they don't really give hassle to cooks or to the women up at headquarters – they just feel threatened by women doing their job because it's not such a macho thing any more to be a firefighter. I think the only thing that is ever going to change the culture is getting a lot more women in the job – no amount of equal opps lectures or posters will change it. But really I don't think the men will ever change in the fire service – maybe things will change eventually, but not in my lifetime.

For Yvonne, racism – as well as sexism – has been a constant feature of her working life.

> Everytime they saw a black person they would say 'Look, there's your brother or your sister', they constantly did that. They used to ask me what swear words black people used. I used to say, 'I don't know, my mother never taught me those words.' They used to ask me what the black term for sexual parts of the body were and what did black people call white people. I just used to ignore them or say I didn't know.

> They'd make racist jokes and I told them that I couldn't accept things like that. So they said, 'Why did you join a National Front organisation then?' I said, 'What do you mean?'and they said 'Why join the fire brigade when it's all white males?' I said I didn't know it was a National Front organisation, so far as I was concerned I'd joined the fire brigade.
>
> The station officer used to set me tests during my probationary period. For example, he would get the biggest bloke on the watch to tighten up things and then get me to undo them to prove that I didn't have the strength. On hose tests he would set the hose pressure to seven bars which was enough to knock me off my feet – the usual pressure would be three or four bars.

When the station officer told Jackie to get her hair cut because it was too long, she had

> it cut short at the back and sides and permed on top. When the station officer saw me he had a fit, he went absolutely bonkers. They strapped me to a ladder, put a colander on my head and cut a piece of my hair off. Then they turned me upside down and carried me downstairs. If they'd dropped me I couldn't have supported myself because my arms were tied. I'd have smashed my face on the stairs. Then they left me and he said 'You've got training in two minutes – get out of that'. I was stupid because I didn't tell anybody. I didn't want to make a fuss – I wanted them to think I could take a joke as much as they could. But after that it was just one thing after another.
>
> A couple of them were real perverts – if they weren't in the TV room watching porn movies they were out on the yard watching couples having a bonk at the back of the next door night club. They'd sit by the hedge, just watching them. One night they'd got a pair of knickers from the field that someone had left behind. They were really soiled from someone's period and they came up to the locker room and chucked them at me and said 'here, see to these'. Still being stupid, I never said anything.

Mary feels that it is almost impossible to win the acceptance of men in jobs like fire fighting which have traditionally been done by men and in which women appear to them as intruders.

> It just seems like as soon as you've proved yourself at training school, then you've got to prove yourself as a probationer, then you've got to prove yourself on the fireground. Once you've got all that out of the way and you settle down to a nice routine, the next thing you know, the blokes are saying 'Well, what happens when you're forty?' They run out of excuses once you can do the job and get on with it, so it's like – let's

> stick another obstacle in the way. You find that you're fighting your corner the whole time – for all women.

In circumstances like this the solidarity generated by women-only courses should not be underestimated. For some women it is a matter of gaining additional confidence and exercising assertiveness in positive company, in which the usual sexist put-downs just do not happen. But it is also about the opportunity to have women's workplace issues taken seriously, without the agenda being skewed, or taken over, by the preoccupations of men. Often women are too used to making men feel important – even in circumstances in which their own interests suffer. Frequently the price of being accepted as a shop steward has been to pay attention to men's pronouncements and underplay the significance of women's issues. Those who mention women too often are soon dismissed and trivialised. However enlightened 'new men' in the movement have become in recent years – especially since women's subscriptions are necessary to stem the flow of a declining male membership – trade unions remain masculinist organisations in which sexist attitudes and jobs for the boys are still in evidence. Women who have been persuaded to believe that men know best – or who are browbeaten into acquiescence, even when they know men are talking rubbish – develop different ways of operating when men are out of the way. In women-only courses women are less reticent about speaking out, more supportive of each other and less constrained by heterosexist and patriarchal dynamics which position women in unequal relationship to men.

Women who come on trade union courses are extremely serious about their union and about their responsibilities as reps. The GFTU makes it pleasurable for them to attend weekend schools. Travel and accommodation in comfortable hotels are paid for by the union. Child-care is available for those who need it. Meals are organised and partners are allowed to come along as guests. But the schedule is rigorous – Friday tea time to Sunday lunch time in a variety of teaching sessions, discussion groups and workshops. Written preparation is required before the event and a range of spoken, written and interactive exercises require total attention throughout the duration of the course. For most women this comes on top of a full week's work, numerous negotiations and arrangements on the home front to secure time out, and quite a level of independent travel, back and forwards to the course venue – before being back at work again on Monday morning. Some women speak of travelling by train and aeroplane for the first time ever in their lives, on their own. Checking into 'posh' hotels – with a room of their own – is a novel experience for most working class women. Of course they rise to the occasion and make the most of the opportunity with considerable glee – but the chance to experience things which more privileged social classes take for granted should not be minimised. It all adds to the process of confidence building, and 'taking up space' in public settings, as individuals and groups who are doing something important – which carries recognition and status.

For the most part, working class women who come on trade union courses have little previous experience of post-school education – except in relation to the union. They are frequently irrelevant participants in the formalities of learning. They disguise their anxiety about what education means to them – based on negative experiences in the past or unfulfilled desires – with banter and self-deprecating jokes. The tutor had better not be 'bossy' or 'boring' – like 'a teacher'. If the context and approach are relevant, they take part with considerable commitment.

In general their experience is the basis of enormous insight and political acumen. They know how to challenge works managers, how to 'wind up' pedantic union officials, how to distinguish between serious and scandalous complaints in the workplace. They know what it takes to throw a spanner in the works and how far to go. I am continually impressed by their courage, their humour and their dedication as spokeswomen for other workers.

I am also persuaded that generating a learning environment which allows all this to be put into context; which adds some relevant facts and figures; which practises analytical and practical skills; which tops up experiential knowledge with fresh information and linking arguments; which creates a supportive sense of shared learning and future possibilities for enacting change – is something which makes a big difference and links education to real life issues and struggles in really useful ways. It leads to women like Brenda commenting that her

> self confidence has been magnified beyond recognition . . . I think coming on this course has been good for me but I fully intend to take my knowledge out to other women. I shall use it to help others and to show them how we can change things – not just in their lives but for future generations.

The link between theory and practice is also valued by Mary:

> my political and social consciousness has been raised by becoming more aware of the fact that more needs to be done for the rights of women politically. My general knowledge has increased because while searching for information for the subjects covered on the courses I have learned a lot along the way. It has made me look forward to learning more. My skills have developed – especially in being able to handle awkward problems in my workplace and helping to solve them.

For Janet, much of what she learned helped to validate what she already knew and consolidated her resolve to speak out about issues that are important to her.

> the best thing these courses have given me is to value what I know. I have the ability to inform others about what it is like to be disabled, make them more aware of disability issues without pushing it down their throats. I always seem to have been fighting on two fronts in my life –

> one as a disabled person and one as a woman. These courses have made it clearer to me why I was fighting, what other women are doing and what I can do to help. I wouldn't have been able to get to this point in my life without these weekends, the wonderful people I have met, the tutors, and the GFTU for making it all available. I am going to start on a City and Guilds course at the local college. Suddenly the future has more meaning and purpose.

I always come away from women's trade union courses feeling energised myself, inspired and confirmed in my belief that women working and learning together are pretty spectacular. Also, in the course of a series of linked weekends throughout the year, the evidence of change in women is obvious. Quiet women become more vocal. Personal qualities are recognised. Skills are developed. Aspirations are expanded. Knowledge gained is taken back to the front line to address workplace issues in a more effective way. At the end of the series of meetings it is possible to see real progress. Women are more articulate and well informed. They have evidence and arguments to back up their recognition of issues. They have consolidated new friendships and built a network of contacts with other women in workplaces across the country. They are ready to take on those at work who would prefer them to be ignorant or compliant with fresh vigour. They sign up for other courses. Some change jobs. Some reassess their lives, their relationships and their responsibilities. Once the scales fall away – a familiar outcome of women's education with a radical edge – there is no going back. It is hard to believe that once women have moved collectively out from under – in circumstances in which 'doing it together' is an important impetus – things will never be quite the same again.

I include in this assessment, the personal interaction and mutual support that also derive from the social side of learning. As likely as not, a 'brother' course is taking place at the same time. Some women bring partners, who appear in the evenings once academic work is over for the day. Dinner on Saturday night is the usual occasion to get dressed up and to let your hair down. In come the men – looking for a good time. 'Been shopping girls? Swapping recipes?' In come the women – also looking for a good time: but not necessarily in ways the men can recognise. I am intrigued by the outfits and the dynamics. There is always much more make-up, more glamour, more flesh and more attention to constructing femininity than I can believe is possible. Especially after a few sessions bunched round a flip chart, an overhead projector, a role-play exercise – wearing sweatshirts and jeans. But then, 'a night out with the girls' is also a big part of the occasion. Beverley Skeggs discusses working class women's relationship to femininity in terms of ambivalence.

> Women distinguish between being looked at in 'admiration' and being looked at as a 'sexual object' . . . these distinctions inform the ambivalences about themselves and their relationship to femininity. Feeling

> good, through looking good, offers momentary respite, provides valuing and offsets any potential positionings by degradation . . . Women learn to pass as feminine together. The final product . . . may look like femininity but, in the production of it, raucousness, rudeness, outrageousness and challenge to femininity occur. They may create the physical appearance of femininity by their performance, but their conduct is definitely not feminine. When they spill into [the hotel bar] . . . a lasting pleasure can ensue, based on secret jokes and camaraderie . . . For many men . . . there is nothing more intimidating than this loud, laughing, together group of women. They appear as *terrifying*. They are claiming their right to their pleasure and their social space.
>
> (Skeggs 1997)

I have seen women together create 'having a laugh' that goes on for hours, in which culture and meanings are consolidated, and which is very difficult for men to sabotage or overrun. The other major ingredient is glamour.

> For working class women glamour is a way of holding together sexuality and respectability . . . Glamour offers the ability to appear as something different from the mundane. It is an escape route . . . It is the attitude that makes the difference. It gives agency, strength and worth back to women and is not restricted to youth. They do glamour with style. Glamour is about the performance of femininity *with* strength.
>
> (Skeggs 1997)

On Saturday nights in the hotel bar there is always a lot of glamour, a lot of laughing, a lot of singing, a lot of drinking, a lot of smoking, a lot of innuendo. The men are kept at arm's length and are largely irrelevant to the performance, except as the butt of irreverent jokes. Women 'have a laugh' in each other's company, gain strength from numbers, negotiate the posh hotel space with style, go to bed happy and wake up bright eyed and full of energy for the day ahead.

Mags Nicolson has been a participant in GFTU women's courses and a student on the women's studies programme at Ruskin. She is now involved in some of the teaching on the GFTU weekends. In her study of women's activism in trade union structures, she interviewed fellow participants on trade union courses and full time officers from four different unions. She found that as members of trade unions women talked most frequently about 'lack of respect and recognition within the workplace, especially from male representatives', 'inequality and misogyny', not being recognised as 'full members', and union structures which felt 'inaccessible to women'. The women's responses centred around fundamental issues of discrimination, not only in the workplace, but from within their own union. Mags felt that all the unions she looked at still needed to address residual 'patriarchal attitudes' as well as develop policies and structures to make it more possible for women to actively participate. Trade union structures remain predominantly male structures. 'Let's not fool ourselves that the reason for women's [continuing absence] from union structures is because "women don't want to become involved" or because they don't want "to move to Wimbledon to work". There are plenty of women trade unionists out there who want the responsibility and can do the work – but have never been asked. It becomes all too easy for those at the top to determine what women want or need' (Nicolson 1999).

The reasons for women's under-representation in union structures are also more complicated than this. But the women's courses do reveal insight, commitment, capacity and energy which should leave no one in any doubt about the political and educational potential of working class women to play both an active role in the trade union movement, and to make use of really useful knowledge to advance the interests of themselves and their workmates. In addition, women's education programmes like this keep alive the spirit of subversion, irreverence and a radical passion for learning that confounds stereotypes and challenges technicist versions of workplace training programmes.

13

RUSKIN – THE WORKMEN'S UNIVERSITY (*SIC*)

On 20 February 1999 Ruskin College, Oxford celebrated its hundredth birthday. It was a glorious and emotional day caught on camera in a mood of celebration, commitment and validation of Ruskin's presence in the world, and of its spirited affection in the hearts and minds of the former students and well wishers who attended the centenary gala in the town hall. A hundred years earlier, photographs from the college archive show the same venue, packed from floor to ceiling with representatives of educational, co-operative, Christian socialist, labour and working class movements – dressed in their Sunday best – together with liberal academics from Oxford University, all keen to be associated with this new 'college of the people' (Pollins 1984: 9).

In 1899 the balconies were hung with British and American flags to signify the nationality of the college founders, Charles Beard, Walter Vrooman and Amne L. Graflin. A hundred years later the seats were also full, the walls and balconies draped with the reminders of numerous socialist and feminist concerns, spanning a century of struggle by trade unions, women's peace campaigns, environmental groups, anti-racist and pro-democracy coalitions and the Labour party.

Former students from as far back as the 1920s and 1930s mingled with those of the 1990s. MPs and trade unionists, Ruskin tutors and students contributed to the speeches. The Shirebrook Colliery Band played rousing and emotional music. Bad Habits, the women's choir, sang songs of protest from labour strikes and feminist campaigns. Students old and new queued up for tee shirts, mugs and mouse mats bearing the Ruskin logo, and to order copies of the centenary video and music tape. Inside the main hall, the voice of John Prescott, the Deputy Prime Minister and Ruskin's most famous 'old boy', recounted memories of his first essay, 'Power Corrupts, Absolute Power Corrupts Absolutely: Discuss', and of being chased down the street by his tutor and mentor, Raphael Samuel, trying to persuade him to come back and finish the examination he had just stormed out of. Outside the hall, the lobby and exhibition area were crowded with conversation and reunions, as the sometimes famous and sometimes infamous reminded each other about where it all began.

At shortly after 6 p.m., the Shirebrook Colliery Band led the assembled gathering, carrying banners and flaming torches, through the streets of Oxford and back to the steps of Ruskin, for one more chorus of the 'Red Flag', before the evening celebrations continued in party atmosphere, lasting until the early hours of the next morning.

Caught up in the exuberance of the occasion, with much evidence of energy, social purpose and credentials, it is hard to imagine that this was not a united and welcome event, or that the Ruskin being celebrated – so warmly and with such passion – might be the figment of individual memories: memories involving selection, interpretation and invention; memories constructed in the present, in the complex interplay between individuals – to provide a collective account of the past. And the past that was being created deriving from a mix of personal histories, different political pre-occupations, shifting expressions of identity, cultural meanings and emotional understanding, as well as structural and material circumstances linked to social class, gender and ethnicity – some of which have a lot to do with Ruskin and some of which have nothing to do with Ruskin. Together they produce ideas and assumptions about 'common interests and understandings' which attribute to 'the Ruskin experience' a kind of recognised consensus and solidarity. In practice this is likely to be more diverse and contradictory than collective 'moments of being', such as the centenary celebrations, appear to suggest, but the centenary provides a way of thinking about historical connections, interrogating present contradictions and imagining future possibilities.

If Ruskin College is not exactly a household name, people involved in politics and education are likely to know more about Ruskin than about any of the other adult residential colleges in Britain, or almost any other further education college or new university outside their local area. It might be, as Hilda Kean suggests, that some, if not most, of this knowledge is coloured by a variety of myths created and perpetuated in the process of Ruskin inventing its own history of itself – from slippery, selected and contradictory accounts of numerous and various realities (Kean 1996). Nonetheless the college has acquired the connections and the kind of reputation which other much bigger but less famous educational institutions would be happy to replicate (Andrews *et al.* 1999).

Over the years, trade unionists, left wing political activists of various kinds, pacifists, human rights activists, members of freedom struggles from the third world, and more recently ecologists, homelessness and anti-poverty campaigners, members of minority ethnic groups, community and user groups, have all come to Ruskin as students seeking the 'really useful knowledge' that might help to advance the interests of progressive social and political movements.

By the time women's studies came to Ruskin in 1993, the more radical, grass roots links between the Women's Liberation Movement and the Adult Education Movement elsewhere had been – and almost gone (Taking Liberties Collective 1989).

It is true to say that Ruskin was the venue for the first ever National Women's Liberation Movement conference in 1970, but the college did not own this important historical moment in any recognised way. Accounts of the event do not appear in the official history of the college (Pollins 1984). No photographs or details of the proceedings and copies of the papers which were distributed at the time are kept in the college archives. Accounts of the ways in which male students and college authorities were antagonistic to 'their' college being taken over by 'all these women' has only appeared in print more recently, and only because alternative voices have sought to set the record straight (Alexander 1990).

In the same way, the small detail to do with the money that was needed to found Ruskin in the first place in 1899, and to contribute significantly to its upkeep during its early, precarious years, has been largely overlooked or attributed to the 'good fortune' that one of the 'founding fathers', Walter Vrooman, was married to a wealthy woman. Amne L. Grafflin continued to fund the college after divorcing her disreputable husband and is only now being credited with having helped to establish Ruskin in the first place (Kean 1996). It is extremely unlikely that her recovery would have taken place without the intervention of feminists who are currently active in the college.

In 1993 Ruskin was still caught up in its own history about the ways in which it had come to be defined as 'a workmen's university' (Pollins 1984). At the same time, because Ruskin is a small college, and one of only eight residential adult education colleges, costing collectively less than half of one per cent of government spending on education, its small and ambiguous status – lodged somewhere in the grey area between adult, further and higher education – had meant that, by good fortune rather than political acumen, it had managed to slip through a variety of nets. The consequences of economic rationalism – requiring greater efficiency, transparency, value for money and competition for educational markets – associated with monetarist and New Right policies in the 1980s and early 1990s, did not begin to have a serious impact on residential adult education colleges until long after the sea change in the language, the preoccupations and their implications had taken hold elsewhere.

This respite might have persuaded a more radical institution to profit from its anomalous position by creating a resistant, well-articulated and alternative model for working class adult education, based on its historic connections with progressive social movements. It could have sought to preserve and liberate the spirit of emancipatory learning, critical thinking and praxis-related education in times of technicised, managerial and corporate obsessions with making education into another kind of business enterprise. But it did not (Thompson 1999a).

It is possible that, by failing to be drawn into the kinds of debate that were prevalent at the time, history will describe the college's stance as one of active resistance. It did sack a politics tutor for writing for the right wing press during the Wapping dispute, for example, incurring a huge bill for compensation in the process of securing an out-of-court settlement when he sued the college for unfair dismissal (Andrews 1999). It welcomed and accommodated flying pickets en route between the Kent and Yorkshire coalfields during the year long miners' strike of 1984 (Samuel *et al.* 1986). It continued to teach ANC activists in exile during the period of apartheid in South Africa when the ANC was a banned organisation. Personally, however, I think the college's failure to move beyond emotive and idiosyncratic acts of individualised solidarity to engage with the educational and political arguments of the day – in order to challenge them and demonstrate a conscious alternative – should be read partly as a feature of the wider crisis of the Left during the 1980s, which was unable at the time to mount an effective, coherent, concerted or united alternative to the relentless and ruthless spread of New Right policies in practice.

But also, both tutors and students led a relatively charmed life at Ruskin throughout the 1980s. Although the college has never enjoyed a fraction of the wealth, ambience or privileges associated with Oxford University, its historical connections with the university helped to sustain a rare commitment to small seminar and tutorial teaching, weekly essays and personal supervision, as the basis of teaching and learning. Throughout the 1980s, working class men – and occasionally working class women – spent two years at Ruskin, on bursaries paid for by the state, frequently topped up by trade union scholarships. This gave them access to individual tuition, university lectures, libraries and student facilities; and an entrée into Oxford University colleges and the labour movement via a long history of 'old boys' networking' in masculinist organisations.

In practice this meant that students were able to 'sit at the feet' of great – and not so great – minds, spend a lot of time soaking up the atmosphere and alchohol of Oxford, and make best use of the somewhat individualised 'ladder of opportunity' model of educational connections and advancement that Ruskin offered. College tutors – despite their role as adult educators – benefited from the same conditions of employment as their colleagues in Oxford University, with short academic terms, long holidays, regular sabbaticals, space to do research, light teaching loads and highly motivated – if not highly privileged – students to teach. And this at a time when – elsewhere – funding was being cut, contracts were being rewritten, numbers were expanding and performance was being increasingly measured, scrutinised and inspected. Sadly, for all its radical pretensions, those at Ruskin who were allegedly on the side of the workers in the class struggle – a struggle which was largely being lost elsewhere in education as effectively as in the wider Thatcherite society – did not emerge from their bunkers (or the Bodleian library, or High Table at Worcester College) to draw attention to themselves or to reinvent their world in order to galvanise resistance and build a principled alternative.

However, I did not know any of this when I took up my appointment in 1993. Unlike my previous experience at Southampton University during the late 1970s and most of the 1980s, it felt easier – in one way – to declare myself a socialist, a feminist and a lesbian at Ruskin. The staff common room was full of idiosyncratic and left wing sympathisers, left over from the 1960s and 1970s, sheltering from the worst effects of Thatcherism in a place which, on the whole, had not seen much disturbance to its academic privileges and traditional practices. The main 'attack' on the college's previous provision had been to reduce the two year Ruskin Diploma programme to one year, thereby requiring a yearly, rather than a biannual, intake of around 140 students, so that the number of working class adults able to benefit from what Ruskin had to offer was effectively doubled. This was an opportunity that was not welcomed by the majority of college tutors, however.

When I arrived at Ruskin, it appeared as a kind of retreat – rather than a hotbed – for those whose political views had been shaped in more auspicious times but who had not been able to re-vision themselves in relation to changing circumstances. Some had learnt their politics from the New Left in various – and frequently opposed – splinter groups with Trotskyist, Marxist and Maoist tendencies. Some were more recognisably communist or Old Labour in sympathy. Some had developed their academic stance from universities teaching critical social science and philosophy in the late 1960s – a somewhat masculinist, rationalist and adversarial tradition which has contributed enormously to critical thinking and the development of critical intelligence, but which can be overly negative and arrogant in many ways (Barr 1999a). Some took their reference points from the old alliance between Ruskin and Oxford University which, in practice, has led to liberal rather than radical assumptions about working class education, and to academic elitism (Thompson 1999a).

Raphael Samuel was still a force to be reckoned with in the college. As a Ruskin tutor for thirty years, founder of the History Workshop Movement and intellectual guru to many on the Left – not simply John Prescott – he habitually addressed students, and those colleagues with whom he was on speaking terms, as 'Comrade', but beyond that, there was not a lot of evidence of community or solidarity deriving from shared values and beliefs in socialism. In practice it was possible to call yourself whatever you liked within the broad church of Centre Left and progressive political movements, but it was a mistake to imagine that the apparent tolerance of left wing affiliations equalled much thought or understanding when it came to feminism. Raphael Samuel referred to himself as 're-constructed' in my presence but until the appointment of a woman to teach in 1994 there was not much evidence of feminist – or even women's history – in the curriculum for which he was responsible.

Those women already teaching in the college were, for the most part, concentrated in social work training, which did not enjoy parity of status or academic respectability among staff and college governors in comparison to 'more important' academic subjects like politics, labour studies, economics, history and English studies – all of which, until my appointment to teach politics, were taught by men. A woman had recently been appointed to teach sociology, which had also acquired the reputation of being a 'soft option', and another woman co-ordinated the outreach and access programme in which little interest was expressed by the majority of her colleagues and which was generally regarded as remedial. Like the history curriculum before 1994, most of what was taught in the more prestigious subject areas made no reference to women whatsoever, and was at least twenty years out of date in terms of its content, its pedagogy and its politics. Debates about the social construction of knowledge, interactive teaching methods and the negative and damaging consequences of, for example, sexism and racism in the curriculum, and in the wider college culture, had completely escaped the attention of most tutors. Ruskin had no anti-discrimination or equal opportunities policy, no harassment policy and no codes of practice attempting to promote high standards in professional relationships and college life. Raising some of these issues at Ruskin felt as difficult as it has ever done in patriarchal institutions I have known, despite the ostensible commitment to progressive and enlightened ideas about politics and education.

In these circumstances students were the saving grace, students who, for the most part, were very positive, at least in retrospect, about the time they spent at Ruskin. Across the years the college has attracted large numbers of activists from trade union, labour movement, community and progressive social movements. It has also attracted working class people living 'secret lives' as autodidacts, voracious readers and creative writers – men and women looking for the kinds of formal educational recognition which had previously been denied to them or rejected by them (Kean 1995). Over the last twenty years, the numbers of students who are unwaged on entry, or who are the survivors of economic restructuring in workplaces and communities, homelessness, drug and alcohol abuse, mental ill health, domestic violence and family breakdown, have significantly increased. From circumstances like these 'almost anything' Ruskin might contribute in the way of education would be 'better than nothing', and is usually considerably more significant than this implies, but there are contentious and contested issues to do with working class education – especially in relation to women, black and ethnic minority students, and those whom Veronica McGivney (1999a) calls excluded men – that Ruskin does not begin to respond to as well as it should, given the college's history and pretensions. But that is another story (Thompson 1999a).

During the 1980s I had spent most of my time in the company of women and in teaching working class women at the Women's Education Centre in Southampton which some of us sustained throughout the Thatcher years (Taking Liberties Collective 1989). Although the consequences of patriarchal relationships and patriarchal power figured significantly in some aspects of my life and in my analysis as a radical feminist, it had been some time since I had worked with (socialist) men as colleagues or worried about their educational needs as students. At Ruskin I found some men actively engaged in re-negotiating the settlement with women in more democratic and re-creative ways, and some men prepared to challenge traditional constructions of masculinity in themselves and in others, that continue to make me hopeful for the future. I have also become more tentative about complexity in relation to the formation of gender identities than I used to be, and as a consequence, more tolerant, I hope. However, I can still recognise patriarchal power in operation when I see it.

For women, life at Ruskin has never been easy. Before feminism was reclaimed in the late 1960s and 1970s, there was not much in the way of language to talk about men dominating the discourse, men's concerns framing the content of the curriculum, men's assumptions about women leading to sexist and sexually harassing behaviour – but anecdotal evidence suggests that all of these practices were endemic. Enough is known about educational institutions at the time, and about the culture of the male dominated labour movement, to expect that Ruskin did not escape the institutionalised and habitual sexism with which both of these were associated (Campbell 1984). The minority status of women students and the general absence of women from positions of academic or institutional influence between the 1970s and early 1990s meant that the feminist debates happening elsewhere – about gender equality in the workplace and in academia, for example – were largely still born. Ruskin, it seems, continued in a time warp.

Women choosing to work in the classrooms or the kitchens at Ruskin did so in a masculinist organisation. The college's early beginnings linked to the early labour and trade union movements; its founding ceremony in Oxford town hall in 1899, in the presence of hundreds upon hundreds of working class and philanthropic men; its connections across the years with liberal academics from Oxford university, Labour party politicians and trade union leaders; its famous 'old boys' elevated into prominent positions in the House of Lords and academia; a hundred years of predominantly working class and mostly male students – all contributed to a legacy and a culture in which certain kinds of masculinity were created, expressed and consolidated. Whether it is in 'smoke filled rooms', the working men's club, the football terrace, the regional offices of the Transport and General Workers' Union, the Members' Bar in the House of Commons or High Table at an Oxford college – masculinities are made in relation to other men, rarely in relation to women, and in ways that can be separatist, exclusionary, dysfunctional, adversarial, misogynist and self-perpetuating. In this sense, Ruskin has provided just another context in which boys could become men, and men could be lads; and in which male bonding has been allowed to flourish in ways that frequently diminish women.

So long as women academics were concentrated in 'non-traditional' teaching areas, with little status and in which women were a minority of students – learning men's knowledge in the context of a historic pact between white male academics and white male activists from the Labour party and craft unions – it is not surprising that, as Sally Alexander found on the occasion of the first Women's Liberation conference held at Ruskin in 1970, women's presence could only be tolerated so long as it was not 'disruptive' or 'threatening' (Alexander 1990).

When I began teaching at Ruskin in 1993, even the general ambience of the rooms – the famous male names above their doors, the portraits of men on the walls, the manifest disregard for creating welcoming and conducive spaces – could only have been achieved by those who were seriously un-practised in making the places in which learning is negotiated either hospitable, inclusive or purposeful. One of the best things about the incorporation of colleges (in relation to further education funding and inspection requirements), so far as I was concerned, was the necessity to spend money on a major face lift and spring clean, and the requirement to put other images on the walls apart from those of dead white men and their fellow travellers.

The introduction of women's studies into the college curriculum in 1993 as a Certificate in Higher Education programme, and in 1994 as a part time MA, gave a focus to feminist knowledge and feminist debate within the college. With a few exceptions the women studying at certificate level over the years have come from working class, minority ethnic, recent immigrant and generally poor economic backgrounds. Many are single parents, many are survivors of domestic and sexual abuse, some are lesbian, some have disabilities including previously undiagnosed learning difficulties. About half choose to come to Ruskin because they have some experience of trade union or community activism; others are looking for second chance education in an educational environment that welcomes working class and other disadvantaged students, and which makes a point of discriminating positively in favour of those who have the fewest previous educational qualifications. Students are taught in smallish seminar groups of between twelve and twenty students and in weekly, two student tutorials – as is the Oxbridge tradition. One of the main reasons why women with few or no previous educational qualifications, and any number of social difficulties in their lives, are able to achieve academic work of first year undergraduate level standard by the end of their year of study is as a result of small group teaching, collective and mutually supportive learning methods and lots of contact with tutors.

Students on the two year, part time, MA programme – about twelve each year – are, with a few exceptions, women from the kinds of constituency which Ruskin has always attracted. Some are Ruskin certificate students whose ability and commitment is such that they can move straight on to a master's qualification. About half each year have first degrees gained elsewhere, and who want to pursue further, politically engaged, post-graduate study. The rest are mature students with political, socially relevant and personal life experiences for whom theoretical and practice-related women's studies can provide the kinds of 'really useful knowledge' that support their political and social concerns.

It has always seemed obvious to me that in women's studies teaching the best place to start is with the evidence of women's own experience and the realities of their lives. Gloria, for example, says this:

> My own prospects were severely limited by a teenage marriage, two children by the age of eighteen and a divorce ten years later. Lack of academic qualifications or recognised job skills meant supplementing family benefits with fragmented employment. A few hours occasional work, cleaning, driving or seasonal farm work – for cash in hand. Continuous financial hardship meant that when my children were old enough I moved into the only available work on offer – factory work, four nights a week, ten hours a night. The reality of this was constant exhaustion with a body clock always out of sync. Illness was a luxury I could not afford as company sick pay was only half my normal night's pay. Over the fifteen years I remained in the company I witnessed other women struggling and battle fatigued, then going home from the work place to start again . . . The other women I worked with talked with a certain camaraderie about their lives. Almost all were unhappy with their lot but did

> not recognise any alternative within their grasp. The treadmill effect was of hard work with few resources – the common avenues of escape being seen as marriage, childbirth, retirement, other low paid work. My own solution to the monotony of production work was to educate myself and to become involved in the trade union movement. Being an activist made me a target for disgruntled workers and difficult managers but the work justified itself by winning some improvements for the women I represented and providing me with opportunities for education and possible advancement which would not have been available on the factory floor. My appointment on to the regional and national women's committees was swift as women showing interest and involvement were seized upon with enthusiasm. This opened up a new world for me and gave me access to the women's movement. Feminism ratified my previously unconscious belief that as a woman I had been exploited by men both publicly and privately . . . Trade union activist? Well I suppose if it wasn't for the trade union I would never have been involved in the women's movement and would never have had access to Ruskin. I found that by interrelating my life experience, the information gained from the trade union movement and my course work on women's studies I now have valuable knowledge that gives me an active source of ideas for both my political and my academic work.

Jan also came into education to escape from poverty:

> I was married to a man whose favourite saying was 'he didn't get a dog to bark himself'. The marriage lasted for twelve years during which time I suffered domestic violence at its worst.
>
> Finally I left and found out the hard way what being a lone parent in the benefit trap actually amounted to. With two children to support, there was hardly enough money to live on and certainly not enough to pay bills. Having a job wasn't an option because of lack of child-care, especially in school holidays. These were bad times and my children never had a holiday or any luxuries. Our clothes came from second hand shops which the kids didn't like at all. Poverty brought problems when they were in their teens. They started to shoplift so they could have some of the things their friends had. By now I had a cleaning job on the side, dodging social security. After a while I became an odd job person earning around £30 a week on top of the £57 social I received at the time. It wasn't a lot but the people I worked for let me take the children with me in their school holidays. They also encouraged me to get an education in the hopes of getting a job with some prospects and to get me out of the poverty trap. When my sons left school I did a City and Guilds in horticulture but by then I was in so much debt I had to take a job in a chicken factory. It took me three years working double shifts to repay

> my water rates and poll tax which were impossible to pay whilst I was on benefit. It was quite clear to me that my new employers exploited their workers. The women workers especially were badly paid and badly treated and had no idea about their employment rights. The City and Guilds qualification at least gave me some confidence so I became a shop steward and went on quite a few trade union courses to do with Health and Safety at Work and employment legislation. Unlike my school days, learning took on a different perspective and it was a pleasure not to be ridiculed in the way I was at school. Often I was the only woman on the course – and being treated as an equal by other trade unionists felt good too. Not until I came to Ruskin did I find out that I was dyslexic – which of course explains a lot about my poor spelling and grammar . . . I also learned about what causes the feminisation of poverty and some political explanations of men's violence towards women.

Tsuneyo lived with the constant threat of deportation. She had come to Britain to escape domestic violence in Japan but was running out of 'legal' reasons to be allowed to stay. Her early life in Japan had not given her much sense of self-worth.

> I hated being a woman from when I was a child. I was taught to believe that women were not intelligent, had no ability to be independent, were not able to think logically, were not able to understand abstract concepts and so on. I watched other women who seemed to go along with these prejudices. I did not want to be like that. So I hated women and myself for being a woman . . .
>
> When I came to this country I thought there would be more choice but I realised that I had hardly any choice because of my language problems. Wherever I was, I found myself alongside other immigrants – Africans, Asians, Turkish, Irish. Many of them did not have language problems, but they had no choice either. We were treated as second class citizens, not only by people's attitudes but in relation to the kinds of accommodation and work we could get . . .
>
> The most important lessons I learned in women's studies were self confidence and the importance of self respect. I came to understand how women are restricted in many ways – historically, economically, socially, culturally, politically and sexually. When I was isolated and ignorant I was in a state of darkness and had much fear of what was going to happen to me. As my study went along, it became clearer to me that my belief that what had happened to me in my life was 'all my fault' was not so. I found others who had experienced similar things in different ways. It was not only me. It made it possible for me to stand. Now I am very calm and not intimidated any more.

Beginning from the issues that individual women identify as being important in their lives soon establishes the awareness of common and recurring conditions about which lots of women have some immediate experience. This leads easily into the ideas and explanations worth considering from political, sociological, labour market and economic theories. Frequently references to law and social policy are relevant. The stories told by black and minority ethnic women in the group, by lesbians and women with disabilities, raise issues to do with social and cultural differences, sexuality and discrimination. Historical perspectives introduce notions of 'roots' and 'change' and 'what counts as history'. The words of women writers and poets – especially working class, black and third world writers – contribute cultural, emotional and political insight about the connections between women's personal and political lives. The discussion moves constantly between the personal, the academic and the practical. The purpose is not simply to understand the world but also to change it.

This kind of approach, based on dialogue, building critical thinking, releasing emotion, interrogating contradiction, recognising and celebrating difference, and working out political strategies, has important outcomes in my experience. These are not always easily measured by standard qualifications but they are just as important.

They can help to deal with some, at least, of the issues women carry with them through their lives and which they have been used to accounting for as 'their fault'. Developing a political analysis of male sexual abuse, or familial exploitation, or low paid, boring work, for example, does not neutralise the experience, but it generates new insights and understanding and enables women to stop blaming themselves. Being 'a survivor' and getting back some 'self-esteem' is a powerful recovery of the self and a place from which to move forward. It can also release the kind of anger that can be used creatively, to determine not to keep turning the blame inwards, or dumping it as disappointment on to others inappropriately. It can encourage women to speak out in circumstances in which they once were silent, define themselves as political, and get involved with others to work for changes.

Maureen, for example, stopped leading a secret life and describes the process of becoming more politically and personally courageous:

> In my working life I have become more assertive and more willing to challenge instances of either blatant or unconscious sexism. This is happening more frequently because I have moved into an even more male working environment than before. Previously I may have let sexist comments go unchallenged, now I seldom do. I have also recently come out [as a lesbian] to my boss and some colleagues, something which I would never have even considered a few years ago. In my personal life I have become more willing to face up to difficulties in relationships. Being able to discuss personal problems with women who appreciate the complexities of lesbian relationships has been immensely supportive and helpful.

Anji began the long journey out from under in a marriage that was based on abuse. She talks about 'the knowledge' which gave her the power to make changes:

> Being working class, education is about the only way that I can find to challenge the things that I disagree with or feel passionate about. I accept that knowledge is power – and since I'm never going to have any money – I have to hope that knowledge will give me at least some control over my life.
>
> As a survivor of sexual abuse and violence, knowledge is important to me for two reasons. Firstly I needed to discover my identity and find out who I am. Surviving sexual abuse is one thing but channelling the negative experiences into something more positive becomes an essential part of the survival mechanism. Surviving sexual abuse is an education in itself, but in order to deal with it, and for it not to consume you in a torrent of guilt, fear and self-hatred, you need – more than anything – to politicise your experience. Secondly, knowledge has been the means of rebuilding the self esteem I never had – the lack of which might well have contributed to the cycle of sexual abuse which had become such a massive part of my life . . .
>
> Discussing things with other women in a relatively informal way taught me more about life than any book I might have read – although the talking also spurred me on to become an avid reader about the issues we were discussing. I was very moved by the depth of feeling and emotion I felt listening to women's stories about their lives. Life had not previously prepared me to listen to others, especially women from different cultures and women of different ages. Nothing to do with previous education prepared me for this – the most transforming period of my life . . .
>
> I have learned that if I set my mind and heart to it – I have more ability than I have ever given myself credit for. I have learned to look at issues from all angles. I find that a lot of what I read in books, I already know something about from my own experience, but the books help me to make better sense of it all. I have learned that women are very supportive of each other. There was no competition amongst the women in our group – only a real sense of wanting the best for each other.
>
> When I was doing my project about marital rape I had to hide my computer disc in case my husband found it . . . I could only work at home when my husband was out and the kids were in bed. Time was a great problem . . . travelling to and from College on the bus, keeping house and kids together, finding time to read. I got that I read on the bus, in the loo, in my friend's car – anywhere I was sitting still for ten minutes. Some of the books I was reading caused problems at home – books about male violence and sexual abuse just made him more determined to put

> me in my place! He was threatened by my capacity for learning and he tried to control me in the only way he knew how. I faced criticism from my parents and friends for neglecting my husband and kids for the sake of 'a whim'. Nobody took my studying seriously except me. Luckily I had a supportive girl friend and study group at College.

Four years later, Anji also has a divorce, her own council tenancy, her children with her and a decent job. She still reads avidly and keeps in close contact with the women she met at Ruskin. In a slightly different context, Gaynor found affirmation for the spirited sense of outrage she had developed long before she came to Ruskin – and more idea about what to do with it:

> The position of women within society, I would be glib to say is kack. Token women I believe are never beneficial or helpful to us as realistic role models. Women en masse are used to maintain a service-based economy in the 1990s; few of us have access to positions of power or leadership. This is a class struggle not an individual struggle. We are interminably the butt of policy jokes – a decent minimum wage would be fought for more enthusiastically by politicians if it were men who brought it home and had to live on it. Being unable to accept the complete idiocy of many of the policies that are shovelled at us at present, takes great determination and courage. I shall support the women who have that courage wholeheartedly. Yes, we need to concentrate on educating ordinary women – women from my class who can fight their own battles – but a bit of solidarity wouldn't go amiss. Having the educated middle class coming out to 'help us with our problems' annoys me to the quick of my temper. Domestication? – no thank you. We demand equality, education and a voice. It is as much our right to speak as it is for others – the middle class missionaries – to do so on our behalf. Sisterhood demands equality, freedom of speech, education, respect for difference – building solidarity and connection among those of us with a common purpose to fight.

The sense of being part of something bigger than individual angst or ambitious self-improvement does not invalidate the concern of education to help women change their lives. Of course women want to gain qualifications, put themselves in a better position to get a decent job, and fulfil their intellectual potential in ways that are creative, personally satisfying and exciting. But individualistic and competitive models of education have not served the working class or women well in the past and will not contribute to changing the general conditions of working class or women's lives. Frequently mature students speak of the support they receive from others in their group. In the Ruskin women's studies programme it is common to articulate and make a point of the benefits, friendship, mutual support and collective solidarity to be gained from working together purposefully with others. This involves ways of negotiating difference and disagreements as well as building solidarities to put new knowledge into practice in places that are useful. Women not only learn from each other, they frequently determine to use what they have learnt to advance the causes which they care about, and to do this in alliance with others.

It is clear that education, on its own, cannot change societies in which there are massive inequalities in wealth and access to resources, including access to real jobs, information and democratic participation. But education can play a part in assisting women in their various struggles against poverty, patriarchy, discrimination, exploitation and social injustices. It is likely that education will be useful when it is linked to the ordinary details of everyday life as it not seen as something which 'other people' do or which is irrelevant. It might be most engaging when it captures the imagination and involves the satisfaction of unfulfilled desires and secret passions. There is plenty of evidence to suggest that on an individual basis education can help people to change their lives. But changing the lives of whole groups and communities of people requires a different kind of educational imagination and a different quality of commitment. The biggest contribution education can make to overcoming inequalities in society is to find ways of relating learning to collective engagement in common struggles and common concerns in sustainable ways, which help repair damaged solidarities and collaborate in the building of new ones.

Julie had been homeless before she came to Ruskin and lived a fairly isolated life with a boisterous three year old:

> What held me back in the past from making the best of my education was the lack of help and understanding of my learning difficulties. I didn't get on with my parents and left home after I left school. I have been homeless and I am now on my own with a small child. On this course I met a group of women who have been fighting for themselves and for other women for a great deal of their lives and I learned a lot from them. As a group we all faced our own battles, we all shed tears about subjects and discussions that brought back pain we had suffered or battles we had not yet won . . . the group gave a lot of support to those who needed it – which made the group strong. It was always possible to speak freely in discussions so we could learn so much more from each other and understand things better.

Zarine was involved in a religious cult in India for fourteen years, during which time she was not allowed to read books other than the tracts provided by the cult:

> I was pretty fucked up and cynical about getting into any more group things, but through Women's Studies I feel as though I have liberated my intellect, reinvented my mind, discovered common ground and shared experience – things that cut across class and race. I identify a lot more easily and the differences between us matter less.

Mary also discovered a new kind of solidarity with women:

> Relationships with other women are special. These are loving and caring feelings that I have for my sisters. Sharing my life experiences with them, and they with me, has given me a lot to think about. I count myself very fortunate that I met and have been loved by Ruskin women. And what has made it most unique is that we are all so different: different ages, different cultures, different life experiences. I have learned the working class includes a lot of women, with lots of things in common, despite our differences.

Trisha's previous experiences as a trade union and political activist before she came to Ruskin had left her somewhat cynical about what Beatrix Campbell calls 'the men's movement' (Campbell 1984) when it comes to recognising or representing the concerns of working class women.

> Being a student is quite enlightening when you are an activist like me. For one thing it's hard to take time out for yourself from what you can see needs attending to all around you. On reflection I can see how naive and inexperienced I was in the past, especially in the heartland of that particular shop floor mentality, where I expended so much of my young energy. Now it has become crystal clear to me that if women as a class are ever to break free from patriarchy – whether under capitalism, socialism or beyond – we must organise separately again. Only women have our best interests at heart and we don't need any male trade union officials pimping us and holding us down for the fucking bosses to screw us with part time, low paid work, whilst at the same time the state takes the piss completely by affording us insufficient means to support ourselves and our children when we can't find jobs or we return to study.
>
> Women need economic equity and we need to command it for ourselves. In our own organisations, we could fight for recognition of our paid and our unpaid labours, which contribute massively to the economy. We need recognition for our labour of reproduction, which is crucial to the continuation of society – ultimately I agree with Firestone's views, but it's a long way off for most of us and we need to protect ourselves in the meantime. It's usually said that now is not the time for us to organise separately. I don't know. All I know is that women as a class have never, at any other point in history, been as widely educated, politicised and potentially organised as we are now, at the end of the twentieth century. It provides a great opportunity . . . if we let this moment pass.
>
> Six years ago I would have said, 'life's shit innit?', without knowing why. Since getting into education I can at least understand why life is shit for women like me. Of all the feminist theories available, I think

> black feminists have said it most accurately because of their international perspective: it's the interwoven systems of patriarchy, capitalism, imperialism and racism that hold it all together for dominant groups. But you exploit one woman, you exploit us all. And where does the knowledge leave us if we don't then overcome our differences, unite and be activists? Still in the shit. The sad thing is that a lot of the younger women coming along now take so much for granted. I'm glad they have more choices in their lives than I've had. But they should know about the struggle for education, legal abortions, contraception, Women's Aid, lone parent benefits. I don't think the majority give much thought to building on those gains in any kind of conscious, political way. We need to pass the knowledge on to younger women, open their eyes.

When she left Ruskin, Trisha continued to be active in women's groups concerned with violence against women and sexual abuse. She completed her degree in social policy at Manchester University. For women like Trisha, the intellectual achievements of women on the women's studies programme should not be underestimated. Like most Ruskin students, she started with no previous educational qualifications. The Certificate in Higher Education is the equivalent to the first year of a degree. It requires weekly essay assignments and three major pieces of formally assessed work, including a 5,000 word assessment essay, an examination and a 12,000 word research project. This combination of intellectual challenge, linked to political and social consciousness raising and practical relevance, which is characteristic of the Ruskin women's studies programme, is not always replicated in more mainstream academic environments, however, particularly at universities. Niki chose carefully when she decided to continue with her studies at Leeds University:

> At Ruskin I learned to understand how being a woman, lesbian, working class and all the other bits of my identity had shaped my experience of education. I learned that the way society is structured has got nothing to do with 'nature' and everything to do with maintaining and challenging the existing power structures that perpetuate oppression. It made me feel better equipped and more determined to take nothing for granted. At university I had no problem doing the academic work that was required of me but it was not a good experience.
>
> Women's studies was a new course at Leeds and looked good on paper. Also, it was based in the department of sociology and social policy which bode well because so many women's studies degrees seem to be based in cultural studies. Another reason I chose Leeds was because the women's studies co-ordinator was an out lesbian and that was important to me. After the first semester she stopped teaching and ever since then there has been no permanent women's studies co-ordinator (there have been four occasional co-ordinators to date and I am only in my second year).

> I am really critical of the course because it is taught as a purely academic exercise. We are not encouraged to bring in our own experience (too individual) or make links between theory and the reality of our lives. Also the students are not involved in the planning or the decision making of the course – there is a women's studies staff–student committee which meets infrequently to exchange information, but it is mainly top down, and any challenges or proposals from the students are frequently blocked or ignored. It was also a bit of a shock to be treated as if I was back at school again. The attitude of some of the lecturers leaves a lot to be desired (although there are some nice exceptions) . . . To top it all, last year it was decided that the course should be changed from women's studies to gender studies – with no consultation beforehand with the students. In fact the second year students (of which a few of us are singled out as trouble makers) were not even informed of the decision. The first and third years were invited to a meeting by the co-ordinator to inform them, a case of divide and rule. So on the whole I regret coming to Leeds and wish I'd taken up another offer.

Niki left Leeds with a good degree and has since been working for Women's Aid and in community development with women's groups for a city council. At Manchester University, Trisha came across constructions of knowledge that did not take account of women's lives.

> Women's studies at Ruskin opened my eyes wide – but I found at university they didn't like me opening my mouth about what I had found out, especially about (male) economic theories, which take no account of women's contribution to the economy through our unpaid labours. At university I came into conflict immediately with one (male) lecturer when I said I could find no mention anywhere in the literature of an account of the labour I had expended shagging my bloke, to get the money to travel to the supermarket, to select items that were both nutritious for my family and the least drain on the family budget which I have to manage and be accountable for, before placing them in the proverbial 'basket of goods', returning home on the bus with my arms aching – much as my mother did before me, although she did not have to travel quite so far to find a shop – stashing the food in the cupboard, cooking the meal, clearing it away, keeping the peace. Getting up next morning in time to make sure that my eldest son goes to the job centre and the other one does his community service order . . . The tutor was livid.
>
> Can the university help? I can see that as a malestream institution it does not deserve my loyalty any more than any other male dominated organisation. In my experience, the expansion of higher education to include more women and working class people like me, rather than just a privileged elite, has meant a backlash, and within the backlash is the

> backlash against feminism. Of course they need our bums on their seats to get their funding, but they don't want to teach us over much, because they also have to do research to get more funding. You are lucky if you see any of the tutors from one teaching session to another. And then only at a distance. At my university, lectures attract 200 students and seminars are three times the size they were at Ruskin. It's the same everywhere. I have a friend doing sociology and anthropology somewhere else. Four hours contact a week. It's hardly worth getting on the bus for – let alone changing your life. They say it's lack of resources but the university system as it is now (again in my own experience) is little more than a factory where students are processed, packaged and put out on shelves for employers to make their selections. Degrees are ten a penny and as such, devalued. I don't suppose they dish out this kind of deal to 'proper' students at 'real' universities.

Gaynor went on to Lancaster University to complete a degree in women's studies. She speaks well of some of the tutors but frequently felt as though the recognition of her entitlement to university education was provisional:

> Because of my background I have had to work very hard to overcome some of the academic difficulties I have had to face. I am still extremely poor at maths. When a PhD student I was talking to discovered I could not automatically use a 24 hour clock he announced my inability to a group of people, encouraging them to test me – they were maths and science MSc and PhD students. I had to slap him squarely in the face when he used my ignorance as an argument to support his view that they were letting anyone into university these days.

However, she retained a strong sense of purpose – which got her through:

> For most of my life education has been irrelevant and non-beneficial. Nevertheless as a working class woman I have a strong belief that in order to change society, greater equality in relation to education is a must. Theories act as an index for me. They are like a map, they can help to point you the right direction. The knowledge I need to represent the women of my class is of a particular nature . . . I cannot and will not stand outside of my class or divorce myself from the women I once represented as a shop steward now that I am getting an education. I regard the education I am getting as another way of giving women a voice . . .
>
> When I took my driving test, I truly expected to fail, but I didn't. I passed . . . Two weeks later I had three points on my licence which tempered my arrogance somewhat as queen of the road . . . Now I can drive and change gear without thinking, just as if I was born behind the wheel. The first member of my family to pass a driving test and own a car, the

> first to be 'officially' married – and divorced, the first to call my Dad a bastard, the first to get a place at university, the first to have their own house, hold down a job. A lot of firsts – who says a woman can't achieve great things? All these achievements are maybe small in the great span of history – but a growing sense of determination makes me more aware of what it means to go against the odds to challenge what society had planned for me . . . Why I tell you this is because I never thought I'd be able to change gear academically and use the knowledge with a degree of confidence. However, here I am on a bloody big motorway, shifting gear, anticipating, manoeuvring with confidence, within a system that was never set up for people – or should I say women – like me. No doubt there will be a few points on my licence along the way – but setbacks teach you valuable lessons as well, don't they?

Having personally persuaded Gaynor not to leave Ruskin on at least three occasions and having received weekly updates about her exploits during the first few months at university, I know that her determination did not always protect her very well from the alien and difficult culture of academia. But her capacity for survival and her enormous resilience always resurfaced in the end.

> Well it's Monday again and I have been itching to run out of the women's studies lecture I have just been attending for the past hour. Tutors asked for reactions from the floor about women's experiences of sexism and oppression . . . Now I am the last one to invalidate another woman's experience but the replies in the main made me want to vomit. Various replies came forward ranging from the oppressive regime of having to wear skirts at school to being given a pink paper clip when we registered at the beginning of term to signify gender. Kick me if I am wrong (cynical is becoming my middle name) but the whole reason for women's studies existing as a valid course of study has grown out of historical, economic, social, sexual and political oppressions has it not? I'm not asking you to suck an egg here, Jane, but that is what you taught me wasn't it? I stood up in that vast lecture theatre and said as much – adding that, as a working class woman, oppression based on gender added to the oppressions I experienced as a consequence of my class. I said that because of low expectations and other reasons, women of my class rarely had the chance to succeed, and now that I was here I didn't want to waste my time on trivia. I have fought long and hard to get here and it wasn't about being given a pink paper clip . . .
>
> Law is my other subject. The tutor asked me for my views on law. I talked about the politics of law being patriarchal and gave examples of judges' crap sentencing and comments when it comes to rape. I talked about employment law and part time women workers and the pros and cons of the new health and safety legislation coming in from Europe. She

> let me on the course but she seemed a bit stung that I didn't let her get a word in edgeways. However I was stopped dead in my tracks when she asked me to consider 'rhetoric'. I asked her to be more precise in her question whilst I stabbed around in the bowels of my memory, trying to see if I knew anything about this word . . . Tell me honestly, Jane, do you think she has a point?

In *Learning the Hard Way* the Taking Liberties Collective describe returning to education as mature, working class women as an obstacle race, in which they feel culturally – and in gender terms – out of place (Taking Liberties Collective 1989). The financial and personal costs are high. The knowledge gained is not always liberating. Ten years after that book was published, the language of 'widening participation' to include mature, working class and other non-traditional students is much more fashionable – although the reality still leaves a lot to be desired. In her introduction to *Learning Works: Widening Participation in Further Education*, Helena Kennedy says:

> Even with the exciting expansion of further and higher education . . . the working class have not been the real beneficiaries . . . Sixty two percent of university students still come from social classes 1 and 2. One percent come from social class 5.
>
> (Kennedy 1997)

The first published breakdown of social class backgrounds of students admitted to individual universities compiled by the Higher Education Management Statistics Group (*Guardian*, 12 January 1999) reveals that the students entering old universities are twice as likely to come from middle or upper class families as those starting at the former polytechnics. Not surprisingly Oxbridge remains the most elitist in student intake with four fifths of new students originating from families with higher professional and managerial jobs. Although new universities like East London, Thames Valley and South Bank have the most students from working class backgrounds, three out of five still come from higher socio-economic groups. Once the effects of tuition fees, student debt, high drop out rates due to poverty and alienation are available to be quantified, my guess is that without significant shifts in the culture and funding of higher education, strategies intended to widen participation will be largely cosmetic.

So far as Ruskin is concerned, the focus given to the active and articulated presence of working class women and feminist politics since the introduction of the women's studies programme has contributed enormously to re-constituting the overly masculinist atmosphere of the college. Some of the battles have been 'bloody' – around allegations of 'dumbing down' and 'not real knowledge', 'excluding men' and 'promoting lesbianism'. Seven years on, the development of women's studies teaching has influenced curriculum developments in other subject areas. Procedures have been introduced to tackle issues of equal opportunities, sexual harassment and discriminatory practices in relation to other minorities, as well as women. Women have increasingly been promoted to positions of academic and institutional influence in ways that have reordered the balance of patriarchal power. One hundred years after Ruskin's foundation, the powerful presence of working class women on the stage at Oxford town hall during the centenary celebrations, beneath banners reflecting black and white women's activism in trade unions, the peace movement and feminist campaigns against male violence was highly symbolic of the subversive spaces which women occupy in Ruskin today. Occupy, but do not own, so long as masculinist legacies continue to reserve institutionalised power for men. Given the opportunity in 1998 to appoint a strong woman principal – with good academic, feminist, socialist and relevant experience of leading 'struggling institutions' in times of rapid social and educational change – the male dominated and 'Old Ruskin' governing body – despite their professed allegiances to 'the workers' rather than 'the bosses' and to 'scholarship' rather than 'training' – chose to appoint in preference, a self-confessed pragmatist and self-employed management consultant, without the same credentials, rather than contemplate 'another bloody woman' in a position of power. It was one of those moments in history when patriarchal priorities triumph over principles yet again – just when things appeared to be changing for the better – and which found 'the brothers' in the staff common room greatly relieved, 'despite' – as one of them wryly observed – 'the iceberg surfacing on the not-too-distant horizon'.

14

OUT FROM UNDER

Although it took me a while to get going, in the end this book was written very quickly – something to do with making the most of snatched and discontinuous gobbets of time, in between changing jobs and the usual emotional and material complexities of life. Nothing new about the process I suspect, especially in the production of women's writing, squeezed in between more pressing duties and responsibilities, and often the passion that gets jettisoned in the tension of competing claims. Add to this the structural exclusions operating in terms of class, 'race', sexuality and disability and it's not surprising that the balance is still considerably distorted in favour of white, middle class, able-bodied men when it comes to who gets published, who gets heard, and what is said.

In this sense I have been more fortunate than the vast majority of my sex and almost all my class – which makes the responsibility to 'use the moment' well, and to make room for others to share the space created, all the more urgent.

The book was quickly written but took a long time in gestation: the best part of a lifetime in a way. It was at least forty years ago – as I made the daily journey from one side of town to another – that I began to have a conscious sense of inequalities and difference. Difference – in postmodern terminology, diversity – is always about inequalities. My mother's stories when I was a child, about living as a family of six in a room and kitchen; about my grandmother pulling scabs off the bus in the General Strike; about my grandfather's early death from pneumonia brought on by poverty; and her accounts of romantic heroes who brandished broad swords and lived 'outside the law' to defend a cause – all pre-disposed me to a passion for social justice. But I did not know that we too were poor. I did not know that those we lived beside were working class. Not until the grammar school revealed a very different kind of cultural capital, providing altogether more ambitious possibilities than anyone else in my (biological) family – then or since – has experienced. No one else apart from me – in fifty odd years – 'out from under' as my mother used to put it.

As the light faded across well tended tennis courts and immaculate, secluded shrubberies in 1965, I can still hear the fragments of a song, and girls' voices singing, in a place I have never revisited except in my memory – and now in this book.

> Forty years on, when afar and asunder,
> Parted are those who are singing today.
> When you look back and forgetfully wonder
> What you were like in your work and your play,
> Then, it may be, there will often come o'er you
> Glimpses of notes like the catch of a song.
> Visions of girlhood shall float then before you,
> Echoes of dreamland shall bear them along.
> Follow up, follow up, follow up, follow up, follow up
> 'Til the field ring again and again
> With the tramp of the twenty two men [*sic*].

Or something like that. Forty years on, I have tried to write something not about echoes of dreamland, floating visions or the dying of the light across summer sportsfields – but more about my participation in the long march of working class women out from under, through life politics, activism and education.

If this book has been a long time in gestation and not long in the writing, it did, however, take me quite a while to make a start. I was still under the illusion that being, most probably, the last 'academic' book I would ever write, it ought to be a definitive account of women, class and education. Definitive in ways that would make it more difficult for the 'infinite condescension of posterity' (Thompson 1968) to dismiss as unscholarly, irrelevant, unimportant – or quite simply, wrong. Not for reasons to do with 'academic ego' but because the argument addresses the unfulfilled desires of women's lives, in ways that are not simply an academic or research exercise – but which might be judged as such. Of course, the judgement attaching to scholarship, the discipline attaching to 'the definitive account', the concern to 'map the field' (Johnson 1999), to fix 'the big picture' in its entirety before risking an analysis, has very little to do with caring about working class women. It has everything to do with the modernist/enlightenment tradition which has shaped western intellectual thought for longer than seems credible. A tradition which, although important, has dealt very inadequately with the lives of women.

I needed to start writing to remind myself that, despite my lived experience, in which most of the really useful knowledge I have discovered has come through a mixture of experience and struggle, I was still caught up in reasons to be rational rather than personal or emotional or partisan. What now appears in this book are reflexive and contingent accounts about a process of personal involvement with others in questions of inequality, class, life politics and the radical potential of education to make a difference – to women in particular. I hope the energy of other women's participation in the project comes through. Re-visiting their influence on my life and intermingling their stories with my own has confirmed how much I have learned – am still learning – from this continuing engagement, in ways that make me doubt, in the event, that what appears here will be my/our final word on the matter.

For women (and men) of my generation, with roots in working class beginnings, getting out from under was about ladders of educational opportunity. Scaling them successfully provided for the occasional transfusion of working class intelligence, imagination and determination into the middle class bloodstream. It meant that – rather than the bakery or the factory – a few of us entered professional occupations, especially in education and the public service. Working for the government, the state or the economy in a professional capacity is, of course, a rich and complex site of struggle, in which the part played by education and active knowledge-making is a fiercely contested terrain. These are settings in which the sense of being both 'within and against' has real meaning, and real possibilities. The problem with the ladder and the transfusion approaches to advancement and influence, however, lies in their individualistic assumptions about meritocracy and legitimacy. Meritocracy, after all, is a better basis for a reasonable society than an aristocracy or a plutocracy. But none is as desirable as participatory democracy, in which the commitment to inclusion reaches across difference, and in which principles of equity and social justice are the measure of achievement. One member of my family into higher education in fifty years – generalised to the class as a whole – seems like a pretty limited advance in the interests of equality of opportunity.

In the city where I grew up, 30 per cent of children in 11–16 schools still require free school meals, and 85 per cent of them live in families in which no one has post 18 qualifications (*Update* 1999). The house in which my childhood was spent now has a derelict garden, a broken-down fence, curtains closed throughout the day and a satellite dish strapped to the wall to deliver round the clock TV to its current inhabitants. Mabel's old house up the road – in the catchment area of the school where, as a young teacher, I once believed the comprehensive solution would change the face of class society – is now in one of the seventeen worst estates identified by New Labour's Social Exclusion Unit (1998). I am not saying 'nothing has changed'. It is possible that the respectable working class, like Mabel and my parents, have also moved out from under in different ways, but all of us have left behind conditions for the poorest in society which have not been improved by the survival, economic and social progress of the fittest in the process.

The movement to the right in both Conservative and Labour party politics in recent years – captured and captivated by the 'logic' of economic changes on a global scale – has lost interest in any kind of revised class analysis to explain all this. In the process it has acted to both incorporate and decimate older, class based allegiances, associated with traditional working class communities, the trade union and the labour movement. The emergence of new social movements to promote the various concerns of women, black and ethnic minorities, lesbians and gays, people with disabilities, user groups, community activists, pensioners, environmentalists, anti-road protesters, peace campaigners, the homeless and land rights campaigners, for example, has kept the radical political agenda alive with issues about inequalities and popular democracy. Although identity politics may appear to corroborate the postmodern conviction that grand narratives of class, 'race' and gender no longer have any relevance in contemporary society, it is hard to ignore the way class stills cuts a swathe (Steele 1999) through ongoing conditions of poverty, access to knowledge, the electronic information revolution and active participation in civil society and the political process.

In such circumstances it is crucial that radicals in education, concerned with social justice and progressive social change, continue to name the significance of class and to work in organic and democratic relationship with social movements at the conjunction between social inequalities, difference and common purpose.

So far as women are concerned, the contribution made by the Women's Movement to redefining the space between personal troubles and political conditions, in ways that create new understandings about difference, and about politics, has been widely contested but immensely influential. It includes the continuing and formidable activism of women in working class communities, in peace campaigns, against racism, in the workplace and against men's violence to women and children. It includes popular education initiatives that create the space in which to imagine alternatives and to create the knowledge and the changes necessary to achieve them. None of this is anything which can be properly understood without joined up recognition that persistent racism, ongoing patriarchy, a disabling society and class based inequalities complicate and intensify the struggles to be waged. But the recognition also indicates which differences we still need to reach across in order to develop combined action in pursuit of more equality and transformation.

Within the recent but (sometimes) forgotten memory of grass roots feminism, some of us also talked about getting out from under in another way. We meant from under the thumb, under the hand (e-mancipation) and, as radical feminists in the United States had it, 'off our backs'. The twinned institutions of compulsory heterosexuality and patriarchy seemed to many of us to account for a culture of violence against women. Violence against women and children takes different cultural forms in different places and in different historical periods, but generally serves to maintain men's power within regimes of fear, and attempts to keep women in their place. Dominant prescriptions about (hetero)sexual practices, and the control of women's sexuality – by individual men in private relationships, and within social, cultural, ideological and economic systems in the public sphere – also produce racialised, hierarchical and repressive definitions and controls from which women need to escape, to be – in any real sense – free to make their own choices about their identity and sexuality.

In this sense, getting out from under has meant moving into a different space – a subversive, hegemonic gap, with enough 'elbow room' to interrogate experience, create new knowledge and organise for change. The purpose of social movements – like the Women's Movement – is to move people from where they are to where they want to be, and to create the momentum to fight for something better. It is a process in which theory cannot be separated from practice. In the end it is necessary to make sense of the world in order to change it. The journey is most likely to be successful when it involves moving others in the process. Others with whom we share common interests and have similar problems to overcome. Others whose condition or experience reveals 'the other' in ourselves and acts to remind us that none of us is free until we all are free.

Education can only hope to empower people if it assists them to act collectively on their reality in order to change it. Radicals in education, concerned with progressive social change, must continue to reach beyond the diversity of women's different experiences and circumstances in order to empower us all. It is also necessary to reach beyond the academy – in which theoretical discussions about diversity and power are in danger of becoming ossified – to women whose lives reflect the kinds of struggle which widespread poverty and inequalities sustain. Not simply in this country, but beyond. Just as capital and international patriarchy know how to profit from women in the global economy, including the profit and power to be gained from the commodification of women's sexuality, so too must women learn how capitalism and patriarchy operate internationally to keep women the poorest of the poor, the least educated of the least educated and the least powerful of the least powerful. Women linking across borders, and across externally imposed boundaries in pursuit of change, creates another kind of globalism – a globalism from below. Repairing damaged solidarities between women, and building new ones must increasingly inform the agenda of women's education for social change in the twenty first century.

When Margaret Thatcher refused to mention social class in case it put ideas into people's heads – ideas that might keep alive loyalties and resistance, structures of feelings, unfulfilled desires, resources for a journey of hope – she thought she could overturn the postwar settlement made between government and people. Although it was built on class differences, it was a settlement that recognised some kind of structural connection between rich and poor which had to be continuously negotiated and reconstituted within the political process and the framework of the state. Thatcherism forced the message home by disempowering the trade unions and local government, replacing democratic institutions with quangos and turning citizens' rights into consumers' charters. It sought to balance sufficient carrots (selling council houses and cheap shares in privatised utilities) with a lot of stick (repressive legislation, the fear of redundancy) to catch the Left off guard – and then in disarray. It aimed to replace loyalty to community and collectivism by a culture based on enterprise, self-interest and competitive individualism. In celebration of this ideological shift in emphasis, and its widespread repercussions in the public consciousness, Margaret Thacher felt able to say with total conviction 'there is no such thing as society . . .'. And the rest, of course, is history.

Her successor, John Major, followed with the promise of a 'classless society' based on individual merit and initiative. By this time the poorest in society were being called an underclass in ways that were unlikely to rekindle damaged solidarities, and which depended on stigmatising the poor, attempting to control and modify their behaviour and encouraging them to police each other – especially in relation to claiming benefits. The social identification of an 'underclass' was also used as a warning to others about what would befall them if they didn't 'get on their bikes' and keep out of trouble. The term 'underclass' was not used to describe the structural consequences of explicit social, economic and political preferences made in favour of more affluent and powerful sections of society. Members of the underclass were portrayed as inherently, even genetically, almost certainly culturally responsible for their own deficiencies. The picture was so well painted by the government, so energetically endorsed by the right wing press, and so frequently legitimised by right wing academics, as to reproduce an ideological climate in which blaming the victim and pathologising the poor made the naming of the underclass seem like a social disease rather than a social disgrace.

It is not surprising, in these circumstances, that a sense of working class pride and working class identity was difficult to sustain. A combination of economic restructuring which destroyed the economy and infrastructure of traditional working class communities, the cultivation of individualism as an ideology, the promotion of market driven versions of reality and managerialism as a new professional orthodoxy, the academic and commercial commodification of identity politics, and the stigma attaching to poverty and pauperised communities – have all made it very difficult for working class culture to 'come out' in any kind of confident way. Once working class culture had ceased to be heroic it stopped being viewed as interesting. Although Will Hutton (1995) estimated that almost 30 per cent of the population were being described in this way, the aspirations and fear of those who were not, sought refuge in dis-association. Being offered the illusion of a classless society seemed, consequently, quite appealing.

Catching the significance of the drift, and in pursuit of votes belonging to self-styled new professionals and the upwardly mobile, New Labour built on the language of denial about class, to obscure its persistence in the New Britain they wanted to create. But they also knew enough about the changing climate to drop some of the Tories' terminology. The success of New Labour in 1997 depended to a great extent on the demise of a widely discredited government, which had appeared increasingly corrupt and increasingly disdainful of various sections of the population – not just the poor.

New Labour's alternative euphemism became social exclusion. It is a term which catches the character of 'civilised' society being beyond the grasp of those who are beyond the pale. The range of opportunities, access to resources, choice of priorities and issues which might be expected to shape the aspirations and achievements of those who have real jobs, decent houses, reasonable education and money in the bank, all provide a stake in political decision making, the economy and the activities of the state. Recognising a 'stake' has less meaning, however, to those whose conditions and circumstances are such that their day-to-day existence is largely outside their own control. Why take an interest? Why vote? Why seek qualifications? Why struggle to develop employment skills? The answers usually imply that individuals can make a difference to their circumstances by adopting the aspirations and values of more privileged groups. Undoubtedly some can, on an individual basis. They are the very useful exceptions which prove the rule. But in order to change the circumstances of entire groups and communities of poor people, a different quality of commitment is required, including the commitment to a bigger redistribution of economic and other resources. The growing polarisation between those with a stake in society which is worth defending and promoting, and those who feel they have lost hope in getting out from under, all contributes to the process of alienation from the values and aspirations of 'mainstream' society. Disengagement from education, the work culture, the knowledge revolution and the political process are all perfectly understandable when looked at from the standpoint of those structurally consigned to poverty in order that others may flourish.

These are essentially the same people whom the Conservatives called the underclass. They are the residents of run down, inner city neighbourhoods and pauperised, peripheral estates, living in substandard housing and dangerous environments. They include the long term unemployed, young men without qualifications or recognised employment skills and teenage mothers. They also include women of all ages taking care of children and teenagers on their own, some minority ethnic groups, the elderly – especially elderly women – without savings or independent means. Almost all of them are dependent on state benefits at a time when the 'logic' of the market requires reskilling of the workforce, further cuts in public spending and 'modernisation' of the welfare state to 'ease the burden' on the tax payer in order to keep taxes low.

However, the notion of social exclusion is also a misnomer. Poverty would be more accurate, as would the terminology of class. The language of powerlessness, oppression, 'race' and sex discrimination, alienation and economic polarisation all retains a better sense of the structural conditions which underpin the capacity of people to change their lives by their own, individual efforts. People opt out, or are put out, when they have not been included, when the odds stacked against them sap the will to live. The fact that life goes on – within and against the very real constraints of structure – is a testimony to the kinds of 'skill' and 'commitment' and 'sense of responsibility' that people in the worst of circumstances conventionally employ in order to survive. Skills which often go unrecognised by those who want to save them from themselves or knock them into shape.

Just as it was inaccurate to refer to 30 per cent of the population as 'under' society, so too is it inaccurate to refer to them as 'outside' society. They are as much a part of society as anyone else. But they are amongst the poorest and least powerful, in a society which is still structurally divided in economic, racialised, gendered and hierarchical ways. Deciding what kind of society we want to live in, and what order of inequalities are the 'price worth paying', in order to service the global economy and satisfy the aspirations of middle income and more privileged groups, remains a site of struggle in which the cards are stacked against the poor. It is a struggle in which managing the poor, tolerating their poverty, keeping them in check, treating their symptoms or tackling the root causes of their condition are a fiercely contested terrain. Arguing for fundamental changes – as distinct from cosmetic changes – necessarily involves the redistribution of power and resources in society, including the resources of income, education, access to knowledge and information, quality of life and participation in decision making.

Although the present Labour government seems more committed to doing something serious – if not fundamental – about combating 'social exclusion' than the Conservatives were inclined to do, it is troubling how punitive the language of New Labour still sounds, especially in relation to alleged fraud, welfare dependency, teenage pregnancy and criminal behaviour (Cohen 1999). Considerable faith is still being placed in individual 'solutions', although the rhetoric includes 'tackling the causes of social exclusion' rather then attending to the symptoms (Blunkett 1999). 'Solutions' still place emphasis on individual mentoring and guidance schemes, enlisting role models, appointing celebrity champions, erecting ladders and awarding prizes to those who scramble up them despite enormous odds.

I am glad we have got out from under the designation of an underclass. Let us hope the language of social exclusion is not yet sufficiently vacuous to mean a range of different things to different people, at the same time. Buzz words breed confusion. They also encourage the illusion of shared understanding in ways that distract attention from the persistence of structural divisions based on social class, in a context which has not nearly eliminated racism or prevented discrimination against women and other less valued minorities.

It would be more appropriate to begin from a sense of outrage that – in the midst of relative affluence, enhanced opportunities and increased expectations – the 'price worth paying' still seems to depend on one third of the population being managed or contained on the fringes of the good life, in ways that hold them individually responsible for remedying their own situations. In these circumstances the current crop of good intentions – capacity building, popular education, community regeneration, democratic renewal, active citizenship – all offer the opportunity to 'stretch the discourse' (Martin 1999) in the spirit of common purpose, equity and social justice towards the kind of society we could become.

Leaving things as they are is not an option in the present climate. A managerial 'third way' is likely to perpetuate social polarisation. Banking everything on a precarious, pragmatic and vulnerable labour market as the solution to society's welfare, welfare reform and social cohesion, and as the main way of redistributing financial rewards – is in danger of creating a different kind of dependency culture. Dependency on low paid work, carried out during antisocial hours in deregulated conditions, can only be at the expense of personal, family and community life. If we could be certain the labour market would stay strong and sure for the years ahead and be able to encompass shorter working hours, generous family leave, an end to 'race' and gender segregation, more class convergence, households looking after themselves, work sharing, a sensible distribution of leisure with time to pursue active participation in civil society and lifelong learning – things might be different. But these are options which depend on choices being made by government and economic interests unused to prioritising the common good above the profit motive in an age of cut-and-thrust market competition, globalisation and rapid technological change. They are also choices which would need to be made in partnership with poor people as well as the rich.

People will only activate themselves if they feel they have real choices and they can play a part in making them happen. Education can assist in the process of supporting democratic activity that is well informed, versatile and critically engaged. But building a more inclusive society – in which the class divide really is a thing of the past – will mean 'changing the culture' of the rich as well as the poor. Combating poverty, poor education, demoralisation and discrimination requires not only brave words but also fundamental and serious resources that will turn the rhetoric into reality.

BIBLIOGRAPHY

Abraham, J. (1995) *Divide and School: Gender and Class Dynamics in Comprehensive Education*, London: Falmer Press.

Adonis, A. and Pollard, S. (1997) *A Class Act: The Myth of Britain's Classless Society*, Harmondsworth: Penguin.

Agarwal, B. (1994) 'Positioning the Western Feminist Agenda: A Comment' in *Indian Journal of Gender Studies*, vols. 1 and 2.

Alcoff (1988) 'Cultural Feminism versus Postmodernism: The Identity Crisis in Feminist Theory' in *Signs* 13.

Aldred, N. and Ryle, M. (1999) *Teaching Culture: The Long Revolution in Cultural Studies*, Leicester: NIACE.

Alexander, S. (c. 1971/2) untitled article, Personal Archive.

Alexander, S. (1990) 'Interview' in Wandor, M. (ed.) *Once a Feminist: Stories of a Generation*, London: Virago.

Allman, P. (1999) *Revolutionary Social Transformation: Democratic Hopes, Political Possibilities and Critical Education*, London and Connecticut: Bergin and Garvey.

Andrews, G. (1999) 'Left Apart: Raphael Samuel, David Selbourne and the Crisis of the Left' in Andrews, G., Kean, H. and Thompson, J. (eds) *Ruskin College: Contesting Knowledge, Dissenting Politics*, London: Lawrence and Wishart.

Andrews, G., Kean, H. and Thompson, J. (eds) (1999) *Ruskin College: Contesting Knowledge, Dissenting Politics*, London: Lawrence and Wishart.

Arnot, M., David, M. and Weiner, G. (1996) *Educational Reforms and Gender Equality in Schools*, Manchester: EOC.

Barr, J. (1996) SHEFC Review of Continuing Education, *International Journal of Lifelong Education*, 15 (6), 471–9.

Barr, J. (1999a) *Liberating Knowledge: Research, Feminism and Adult Education*, Leicester: NIACE.

Barr, J. (1999b) 'Women, Adult Education and Really Useful Knowledge' in Crowther, J., Martin, I. and Shaw, M. (eds) *Popular Education and Social Movements in Scotland Today*, Leicester: NIACE.

Barret, M. and Phillips, A. (eds) (1992) *Destabilising Theory: Contemporary Feminist Debates*, Cambridge: Polity.

Bauman, Z. (1998) *Globalization*, Milton Keynes: Open University Press.

Benn, R., Elliott, J. and Whaley, P. (1998) (eds) *Educating Rita and Her Sisters: Women and Continuing Education*, Leicester: NIACE.

Blair, T. (1996) *Sunday Times*, 1 September.

Blunkett, D. (1999) 'Empowering People and Communities for a Better Future', press release, 12 August.
Bordo, S. (1990) 'Feminism, Postmodernism and Gender Scepticism' in Nicholson, L. (ed.) *Feminism and Postmodernism*, New York and London: Routledge.
Bowles, S. and Gintis, H. (1976) *Schooling in Capitalist America*, London: RKP.
Brah, A. (1992) 'Women of South East Asian Origin in Britain: Issues and Concerns' in Braham, P., Rattansi, A. and Skellington, R. (eds) *Racism and Antiracism: Inequalities, Opportunities and Policies*, London: Open University, Sage.
Braham, P., Rattsani, A. and Skellington, R. (eds) (1992) *Racism and Antiracism: Inequalities, Opportunities and Policies*, London: Open University, Sage.
Brodribb, S. (1992) *Nothing Mat(t)ers: A Feminist Critique of Postmodernism*, Melbourne: Spinifex.
Bryan, B., Dadzie, S. and Scafe, S. (1985) *Heart of the Race: Black Women's Lives in Britain*, London: Virago.
Byrne, E. (1978) *Women and Education*, London: Tavistock.
Campbell, B. (1984) *Wigan Pier Revisited: Poverty and Politics in the Eighties*, London: Virago.
Campbell, B. (1993) *Goliath: Britain's Dangerous Places*, London: Methuen.
Campbell, B. (1999) 'Boys will be Boys: Social Insecurity and Crime' in Vail, J., Wheelock, J. and Hill, M. (eds) *Insecure Times: Living with Insecurity in Contemporary Society*, London: Routledge.
Campbell, B. and Coote, A. (1982) *Sweet Freedom*, Oxford: Blackwell.
Cannadine, D. (1998) *Class in Britain*, London: Yale University Press.
Chomsky, N. (1992) *Chronicles of Dissent*, Monroe: Common Courage Press.
Coard, B. (1971) *How the West Indian Child is Made ESN in the British School System*, London: New Beacon Books.
Cockburn, C. (1998) *The Space Between Us: Negotiating Gender and National Identities in Conflict*, London: Zed.
Cockett, R. (1995) *Thinking the Unthinkable: Think Tanks and the Economic Counter-revolution 1931–1983*, London: Fontana.
Cohen, N. (1999) *Cruel Britannia: Reports on the Sinister and the Preposterous*, London: Verso.
Conference Paper (1971a) 'Women's Liberation Movement conference, Birmingham', unsigned: State of The Movement Paper: Personal Archive.
Conference Paper (1971b) 'Women's Liberation Movement conference, Skegness', Comrade Maysel Brar: Personal Archive.
Coote, A. and Pattullo, P. (1990) *Power and Prejudice*, London: Wiedenfeld and Nicolson.
Coyle, A. (1995) *Women and Organisational Change*, Manchester: EOC.
Davie, R., Butler, N. and Goldstein, H. (1972) *From Birth to Seven: A Report of the National Child Development Study*, London: Longman.
Deem, R. (1978) *Women and Schooling*, London: Routledge.
Dennis, N. and Erdos, G. (1992) *Families Without Fatherhood*, London: Institute of Economic Affairs.
Dennis, N., Henriques, F. and Slaughter, C. (1956) *Coal is Our Life*, London: Tavistock.
Dex, S. (1983) 'The Second Generation: West Indian Female School Leavers' in Phizacklea, A. (ed.) *One Way Ticket*, London: Routledge.
Dex, S. and McCulloch, A. (1996) *Flexible Employment in Britain: A Statistical Analysis*: Manchester: EOC.
Dex, S., Joshi, H. and Macran, S. (1996) 'A Widening Gulf Amongst Britain's Mothers', *Oxford Review of Economic Policy*, 20(1).

Douglas, J.W.B. (1964) *The Home and the School*, London: MacGibbon and Kee.
Edgerton, L. (1986) 'Public Protest, Domestic Acquaintance: Women in Northern Ireland' in Ridd, R. and Callaway, H. (eds) *Caught Up in Conflict: Women's Responses to Political Strife*, London: Macmillan.
Employment Policy Institute (1997) *Labour Force Survey*.
EOC Northern Ireland *17th Annual Report*, Belfast: Northern Ireland.
Etzioni, A. (1995) *The Spirit of Community*, London: Fontana.
Evans, M. (1997) *Introducing Contemporary Feminist Thought*, Cambridge: Polity.
Evason, E. (1991) *Against the Grain: The Contemporary Women's Movement in Northern Ireland*, Dublin: Attic Press.
Evason, E. (1993) *The Cost of Caring*, Belfast: EOCNI.
Foley, G. (1999) *Learning in Social Action: A Contribution to Understanding Informal Education*, London: Zed.
Franks, S. (1999) *Having None of It: Women, Men and Future of Work*, London: Granta.
Freidan, B. (1963) *The Feminine Mystique*, Harmondsworth: Penguin.
Freire, P. (1973a) *Education: The Practice of Freedom*, London: Writers and Readers Cooperative.
Freire, P. (1973b) *Education for Critical Consciousness*, New York: Seabury Press.
Fuller, M. (1982) 'Young, Female and Black' in Cashmore, E. and Troyna, B. (eds) *Black Youth in Crisis*, London: George Allen and Unwin.
Gay Liberation Front Women's Group (c. 1971) Personal Archive.
Giddens, A. (1992) *The Transformation of Intimacy*, Cambridge: Polity.
Giddens, A. (1994) *Beyond Left and Right: The Future of Radical Politics*, Cambridge: Polity.
Giddens, A. (1998) *The Third Way: The Renewal of Social Democracy*, Cambridge: Polity.
Giddens, A. (1999) *Runaway World: How Globalization is Shaping our Lives*, London: Profile Books.
Gilligan, C. (1982) *In a Different Voice*, Cambridge, MA, and London: Harvard.
Grimshaw, J. (1986) *Feminist Philosophers: Women's Perspectives on Philosophical Traditions*, Brighton: Wheatsheaf.
Guardian (1998) 'Return to Gender – Success Unknown', 12 December.
Hall, S. and Jacques, M. (1989) *New Times: The Changing Face of Politics in the 1990's*, London: Lawrence and Wishart.
Halmer, J. and Maynard, M. (1987) *Women, Violence and Social Control*, London: Macmillan.
Halsey, A.H. and Young, M. (1995) *Family and Community Socialism*, London: Institute of Public Policy Research.
Harding, S. (1994) 'Subjectivity, Experience and Knowledge: An Epistemology from/for Rainbow Coalition Politics' in Roof, J. and Weigand, R. (eds) *Who Can Speak: Questions of Authority and Cultural Identity*, Urbana: University of Illinois Press.
Hayes, M. (1994) *The New Right in Britain*, London and Colorado: Pluto.
Hearn, J. (1999) 'A Crisis in Masculinity or New Agendas for Men?' in Walby, S. (ed.) *New Agendas for Women*, Basingstoke: Macmillan.
Hester, M., Kelly, L. and Radford, J. (1996) *Women, Violence and Male Power*, Milton Keynes: Open University Press.
Hobbs, M. (c. 1971/2) in *The Cleaner's Voice*, Personal Archive.
Hoggart, R. (1959) *The Uses of Literacy*, London: Penguin.
Hull Daily Mail (1972) 6 May.
Hutton, W. (1995) *The State We're In*, London: Cape.

Johnson, R. (1979) 'Really Useful Knowledge: Radical Education and Working Class Culture' in Clarke, J., Critcher, C. and Johnson, R. (eds) *Working Class Culture*, London: Hutchinson.

Johnson, R. (1999) 'Politics By Other Means? Or, Cultural Studies in the Academy as a Political Practice' in Aldred, N. and Ryle, M. (eds) *Teaching Culture: The Long Revolution in Cultural Studies*, Leicester: NIACE.

Kean, H. (1995) 'Radical Adult Education: The Reader and the Self' in Thompson, J. and Mayo, M. (eds) *Adult Learning, Critical Intelligence and Social Change*, Leicester: NIACE.

Kean, H. (1996) 'Myths of Ruskin College' in *Studies in the Education of Adults*, 20(2), Leicester: NIACE.

Kennedy, H. (1997) *Learning Works: Widening Participation in Further Education*, Coventry: FEFC.

Kenway, J., Willis, S., Blackmore, J. and Rennie, L. (1994) 'Feminist Post Structuralism, Gender Reform and Educational Change' in *British Journal of Sociology of Education*, 15(2).

Kingsolver, B. (1999) *The Poisonwood Bible*, London: Faber and Faber.

Kuhn, A. (1995) *Family Secrets: Acts of Memory and Imagination*, London: Verso.

Le Doeuff, M. (1991) *Hipparchia's Choice: An Essay Concerning Women, Philosophy etc*, Oxford: Blackwell.

Lees, S. (1986) *Losing Out: Sexuality and Adolescent Girls*, London: Hutchinson.

Lefebvre, H. Cited in Barr, J. (1999) *Liberating Knowledge: Research, Feminism and Adult Education*, Leicester: NIACE.

Leonard, D. and Delphy, C. (1992) *Familiar Exploitation: A New Analysis of Marriage in Contemporary Western Societies*, Cambridge: Polity.

Letter (1972) 'To The Organiser, Festival of Light' Personal Archive.

Little, A. (1975) 'The Background of Underachievement in Immigrant Children in London' in Verma, G. and Bagley, C. (eds) *Race and Education Across Cultures*, London: Heinemann.

Lockwood, D. and Goldthorpe, J. H. (1969) *The Affluent Worker in the Class Structure*, Cambridge: Cambridge University Press.

Lorde, A. (1981) 'The Master's Tools Will Never Dismantle the Master's House' in Moraga, C. and Anzaldua, G. (eds) *This Bridge Called My Back: Writings by Radical Women of Color*, Massachusetts: Persephone Press.

Mahony, P. (1985) *Schools for the Boys*, London: Hutchinson.

Mahony, P. and Zmorczek, C. (eds) (1997) *Class Matters: Working Class Women's Perspectives on Social Class*, London: Taylor and Francis.

Major, J. (1996) *The Times*, 25 July.

Mama, A. (1992) 'Black Women and the British State: Race, Class and Gender Analysis in the 1990's' in Braham, P., Rattansi, A. and Skellington, R. (eds) *Racism and Antiracism: Inequalities, Opportunities and Policies*, London: Open University, Sage.

Martin, I. (1987) 'Community Education: Towards a Theoretical Analysis' in Allen, G., Bastiani, J., Martin, L. and Richards, K. (eds) *Community Education: An Agenda for Educational Reform*, Milton Keynes: Open University Press.

Martin, I. (1999) 'Lifelong Learning: Stretching the Discourse' in Oliver, P. (ed.) *Lifelong Learning and Continuing Education: What is a Learning Society?*, London: Ashgate.

Maslow, A. (1968) *Towards a Psychology of Being*, Princeton: Van Nostrand.

Maslow, A. (1970) *Motivation and Personality*, New York: Harper Row.

Massey, D. (1995) 'Masculinity, Dualisms and High Technology' in *Transactions of the Institute of British Geographers*, No. 20.

Mayo, M. (1997) *Imagining Tomorrow*, Leicester: NIACE.
Mayo, M. and Thompson, J. (1995) (eds) *Adult Learning, Critical Intelligence and Social Change*, Leicester: NIACE.
McDowell, L. (1999) *Gender, Identity and Place: Understanding Feminist Geographies*, Cambridge: Polity.
McGivney, V. (1990) *The Women's Education Project – Northern Ireland*, Belfast: WRDA.
McGivney, V. (1998) 'Dancing into the Future: Developments in Adult Education' in Benn, R., Elliott, J. and Whaley, P. (eds) *Educating Rita and Her Sisters: Women and Continuing Education*, Leicester: NIACE.
McGivney, V. (1999a) *Excluded Men: Men Who are Missing from Education and Training*, Leicester: NIACE.
McGivney, V. (1999b) *Informal Learning in the Community*, Leicester: NIACE.
McIllroy, J. (1993) in McIllroy, J. and Westwood, S. (eds) *Border Country: Raymond Williams in Adult Education*, Leicester: NIACE.
McWilliams, M. (1991) 'Women in Northern Ireland: An Overview' in Hughes (ed.) *Culture and Politics in Northern Ireland 1960–90*, Milton Keynes: Open University Press.
Miller, D. (1975) *Children and Race*, Harmondsworth: Penguin.
Mirza, S.H. (1992) *Young, Female and Black*, London: Routledge.
Morris, L. (1994) *Dangerous Classes: The Underclass and Social Citizenship*, London: Routledge.
Mouffe, C. (1992) *Dimensions of Radical Democracy*, London: Verso.
Mullard, C. (1982) 'Multi Racial Education in Britain: From Assimilation to Cultural Pluralism' in Tierney, J. (ed.) *Race, Migration and Schooling*, Eastbourne: Holt, Reinhart and Winston.
Mullholland, M. and Smyth, A. (1999) 'A North South Dialogue' in *Movement, Feminist Magazine* 3, University College Dublin: WERRC.
Murphy, P. (1997) 'Personal, Political and Professional Development for Women' in Walters, S. (ed.) *Globalisation, Adult Education and Training: Impacts and Issues*, London: Zed.
Murray, C. (1989) 'Underclass: A Disaster in the Making' in *Sunday Times Magazine*, 26 November.
Murray, C. (1990) *The Emerging British Underclass*, London: Institute of Economic Affairs.
Newman, M. (1999) *Maelor's Regard: Images of Adult Learning*, Sydney: Stewart Victor Publishing.
Nicholson, L. (ed.) (1990) *Feminism and Postmodernism*, New York and London: Routledge.
Nicholson, M. (1999) 'Women in Trade Unions' in *Federation News*, Spring, London: GFTU.
O'Neill, C. (1999) 'Reclaiming and Transforming the Irish Women's Movement: Notes for a Debate' in *Movement, Feminist Magazine* 3, University College Dublin: WERRC.
Oakley, A. (1981) *Subject Women*, London: Martin Robertson.
Oakley, A. (1983) *The Sociology of Housework*, London: Martin Robertson.
Orwell, G. (1937) *The Road to Wigan Pier*, London: Victor Gollancz.
Pahl, R. and Scales, J. (1999) 'Future Work and Lifestyles' in *Millennium Papers: Debate of the Age*, London: Age Concern.
Pakulski, J. and Waters, M. (1995) *The Death of Class*, London: Sage.
Phillips, M. (1991) *Guardian*, 16 September.
Phizacklea, A. (1982) 'Migrant Women and Wage Labour: The Case of West Indian Women in Britain' in West, J. (ed.) *Work and the Labour Market*, London: RKP.

Pollins, H. (1984) *The History of Ruskin College*, Oxford: Ruskin College Library Occasional Publications No. 3.

Position Paper (1971) Union of Women for Liberation, Personal Archive, 8 April.

Preece, J. (1998) 'Researching Difference' in Mahony, P. and Zmorczek, C. (eds) *Class Matters: Working Class Women's Perspectives on Social Class*, London: Taylor and Francis.

Rampton, J. (1981) *West Indian Children in Our Schools* (the Rampton Report), HMSO.

Reay, D. (1997) 'The Double Bind of the Working Class Feminist Academic: The Success of Failure or the Failure of Success?' in Mahony, P. and Zmorczek, C. (eds) *Class Matters: Working Class Women's Perspectives on Social Class*, London: Taylor and Francis.

Rich, A. (1980) 'Compulsory Heterosexuality and Lesbian Existence' in *Signs: A Journal of Women in Culture and Society*, Summer: 631–57.

Robinson, M. (1999) Cited in O'Neill, C., 'Reclaiming and Transforming the Irish Women's Movement: Notes for a Debate' in *Movement, Feminist Magazine* 3, University College Dublin: WERRC.

Rogers, C. (1961) *On Being a Person*, London: Constable.

Rooney, E. (1997) 'Women in Party Politics and Local Groups: Findings From Belfast' in Bryne, A. and Leonard, M. (eds) *Women in Irish Society*, Belfast: Beyond The Pale Publications.

Rowthorn, B. and Wayne, N. (1998) *Northern Ireland: The Political Economy of Conflict*, Cambridge: Polity.

Russell, L. (1973) *Adult Education: A Plan for Development* (the Russell Report), HMSO.

Samuel, R., Bloomfield, B. and Boanas, G. (eds) (1986) *The Enemy Within: Pit Villages and the Miners Strike of 1984–5*, History Workshop Series, London: Routledge.

Sharpe, S. (1987) *Just Like a Woman: How Girls Learn to be Women*, Harmondsworth: Penguin.

Skeggs, B. (1997) *Formations of Class and Gender*, London: Sage.

Smyth, J. (1995) Forward, Women and Citizenship Research Group, Belfast: EOCNI.

Social Exclusion Unit (1998) *Bringing Britain Back Together: A National Strategy for Neighbour Renewal*, Report: The Social Exclusion Unit, HMSO.

Spender, D. (1982a) *Invisible Women: The Schooling Scandal*, London: Writers' and Readers' Publishing Cooperative.

Spender, D. (1982b) *Women of Ideas and What Men Have Done to Them*, London: Routledge.

Stalker, J. (1999) in *Studies in the Education of Adults* 3(1), April.

Stanworth, M. (1983) *Gender and Schooling: A Study of Sexual Divisions in the Classroom*, London: Routledge.

Steedman, C. (1986) *Landscape for a Good Woman*, London: Virago.

Steele, T. (1999) 'Marginal Occupations: Adult Education, Cultural Studies and Social Renewal' in Aldred, N. and Ryle, M. (eds) *Teaching Culture: The Long Revolution in Cultural Studies*, Leicester: NIACE.

Sturdy, P. (1971) Letter from Pat Sturdy, Women's Industrial Union, Burnley, Personal Archive.

Swann (1985) *Education for All* (the Swann Report), HMSO.

Taillon, E. (1992) *Grant Aided . . . Or Taken for Granted? A Study of Women's Voluntary Organisations in Northern Ireland*, Belfast: Women's Support Network.

Taking Liberties Collective (1989) *Learning the Hard Way: Women's Oppression in Men's Education*, Basingstoke: Macmillan.

The Cleaner's Voice (c.1971/2) Personal Archive.

Thompson, E.P. (1968) *The Making of the English Working Class*, Harmondsworth: Penguin.

Thompson, J. (1980a) (ed.) *Adult Education For a Change*, London: Hutchinson.
Thompson, J. (1980b) 'Adult Education and the Disadvantaged' in Thompson, J. (ed.) *Adult Education For a Change*, London: Hutchinson.
Thompson, J. (1983) *Learning Liberation: Women's Response to Men's Education*, London: Croom Helm.
Thompson, J. (1989) 'With the Taking Liberties Collective' in Taking Liberties Collective, *Learning the Hard Way: Women's Oppression in Men's Education*, Basingstoke: Macmillan.
Thompson, J. (1995) 'Feminism and Women's Education' in Mayo, M. and Thompson, J. (eds) *Adult Learning, Critical Intelligence and Social Change*, Leicester: NIACE.
Thompson, J. (1997) *Words in Edgeways*, Leicester: NIACE.
Thompson, J. (1999a) 'Can Ruskin Survive?' in Andrews, G., Kean, H. and Thompson, J. (eds) *Ruskin College: Contesting Knowledge, Dissenting Politics*, London: Lawrence and Wishart.
Thompson, J. (1999b) 'Rooting Out the Forces of Conservationism' in *Adults Learning*, December, Leicester: NIACE.
Thompson, J. (2000) 'Life Politics and Popular Learning' in Field, J. and Leicester, M. (eds) *Lifelong Learning*: London: Falmer Press.
Tunstall, J. (1962) *The Fishermen*, London: MacGibbon and Key.
Update (1999) 'Changes in Student Funding: The Implications for Low Income Groups' in *Update*: Spring Issue No. 1.
Wainwright, H. (c.1971/2) Letter, Personal Archive.
Walby, S. (1997) *Gender Transformations*, London: Routledge.
Wallis, J. (ed.) (1996) *Liberal Adult Education: The End of an Era*, Nottingham: Continuing Education Press.
Wandor, M. (1990) (ed.) *Once a Feminist: Stories of a Generation*, London: Virago.
Weiler, K. (1991) 'Freire and Feminist Pedagogy of Difference' in *Harvard Educational Review*, 61(4).
Welton, M. (ed.) (1995) *In Defence of the Lifeworld: Critical Perspectives on Adult Learning*, New York: State University of New York Press.
Whitty, G. and Young, M. F. D. (1977) *Society, State and Schooling*, Brighton: Falmer Press.
Williams, R. (1979) *Politics and Letters*, London: NCB/Verso.
Williams, R. (1989) *Resources of Hope*, London: Verso.
Willis, P. (1977) *Learning to Labour: How Working Class Kids Get Working Class Jobs*, Farnborough: Saxon House.
Willmott, P. and Young, M. (1962) *Family and Kinship in East London*, London: Penguin.
Women and Citizenship Research Group (1995) *Power, Participation and Choice*, Belfast: EOCNI.
Woodfield, R. and Saunders, P. (1998) 'Who is the brightest of them all?' *Guardian*, 8 December.

INDEX